Additional Acclaim for Damian Mogavero
and *The Underground Culinary Tour*

"Many years ago, when I worked in a brewery restaurant, it seemed to me that only a few people in the business had what I call "The Sight"—the ability to see, feel, smell, and hear every single thing happening in the dining room at once. The Sight was like a superpower, and the proper use of it could help make a restaurant a success. Not only does Damian have The Sight, but his book can give you this power too."

—Garrett Oliver, brewmaster at The Brooklyn Brewery

"Damian has created one of the most useful software programs there is for the hospitality industry. His passion for wine, food, learning, and supporting the restaurant community has helped our businesses run more profitably."

—Laura Maniec, master sommelier and owner of Corkbuzz Wine Studio

"The majority of tech tends to be more of a distraction than an asset. Well, then there's Avero, a true one-stop shop in restaurant reporting technology that allows operators like myself to dive into data and make educated decisions that affect long- and short-term decision making. Avero is best in class, and Damian, the founder and CEO, lives and breathes the business, both tech and hospitality. If you're looking to stay ahead of the curve in our business, read this informative and compelling book."

—Michael Chernow, restaurateur and TV personality

"On the surface, Damian Mogavero's book is about how data and restaurant trends will change the way we all eat and drink. On a deeper level, it shows us all how innovation, passion, and technology can inject logic and common sense into any business and become a game changer."

—Geoffrey Zakarian, Iron Chef

"I can't imagine running our restaurants without the technology that Damian and his team have created—the access to the data and information allows us to better understand what our guests are looking for, and to better serve them."

—Michael Mina, chef and founder of Mina Group

"Damian's incredible vision and ability to combine his passion for food and analytical intelligence have helped bring an extraordinary tool into existence. The insights and information Avero offers have allowed Lettuce Entertain You and the entire hospitality industry to see a different side of the business."

—Kevin Brown, CEO and president of Lettuce Entertain You Enterprises, Inc.

"Our economy is being reshaped by entrepreneurs who connect content with technology to develop applications and platforms to advance efficiency, productivity, and profit. In the restaurant industry the pioneer leading the charge is Damian Mogavero. And where does Damian learn the trends? As we discover in this remarkable book, from the Underground Culinary Tour!"

—Michael D. Johnson, provost of Babson College; dean emeritus of Cornell School of Hotel Administration

"These days, there are a dizzying number of tech companies sprouting up within the hospitality world—all with the intent of making our lives easier, the guest experience better, and our bottom lines more intact. But Damian has been doing just that for nearly two decades. The vision he showed (and continues to show!) is inspiring. There is a lot to love about Damian, and even more to learn from his book."

—Will Guidara, restauranteur at Eleven Madison Park and The NoMad

"Damian Mogavero has blazed new territory in how to utilize data to improve our restaurants. His passion for food is unparalleled. It shows how loving what you do can be both inspiring and creative."

—G. J. Hart, CEO of California Pizza Kitchen

"In *The Underground Culinary Tour,* Damian Mogavero takes us behind the scenes to see how pioneering restaurants are using data and creativity to serve up a triple win: delighted customers, fulfilled staff, and profitable owners."

—Jan W. Rivkin, professor, Harvard Business School

"Damian has successfully married the art and the science of being a restaurateur. The art comes from his deep passion for food, and the science comes from his natural curiosity of how to genuinely improve the guest and teammate experience. *The Underground Culinary Tour* brilliantly blends both in an informative and entertaining fashion."

—Rick Federico, chairman of P. F. Chang's

"Part history, part map of where to eat, part demystification of what makes a restaurant great—and a great restaurant profitable—Damian's stories are just as appealing as the food and drink he's describing, and just as satiating."

—Katie Carguilo, 2012 National Barista Champion and quality analyst at Counter Culture Coffee

"Damian and Avero have positioned themselves at the convergence of the art and the science that creates a great restaurant experience. . . . Through *The Underground Culinary Tour,* Damian allows you to join him on the exhilarating (and exhausting) tours that he has hosted to highlight great work going on across our industry. Enjoy the ride!"

—David A. Pace, CEO of Jamba Inc.

THE
UNDERGROUND
CULINARY
TOUR

HOW THE NEW METRICS OF
TODAY'S TOP RESTAURANTS
ARE TRANSFORMING
HOW AMERICA EATS

• **DAMIAN MOGAVERO** •
AND JOSEPH D'AGNESE

Foreword by Danny Meyer

CROWN
BUSINESS
New York

Published in the United States by Crown Business, an imprint of the
Crown Publishing Group, a division of Penguin Random House LLC,
New York.
crownpublishing.com

CROWN BUSINESS is a trademark and CROWN and the Rising Sun
colophon are registered trademarks of Penguin Random House LLC.

Crown Business books are available at special discounts for bulk pur-
chases for sales promotions or corporate use. Special editions, including personalized covers, excerpts of existing books, or books with
corporate logos, can be created in large quantities for special needs. For
more information, contact Premium Sales at (212) 572-2232 or e-mail
specialmarkets@penguinrandomhouse.com.

Library of Congress Cataloging-in-Publication Data
Names: Mogavero, Damian, author.
Title: The underground culinary tour / Damian Mogavero.
Description: First edition. | New York: Crown Business, [2017]
Identifiers: LCCN 2016023657 | ISBN 9781101903308 (hardcover)
Subjects: LCSH: Restaurant management—United States—
Leadership—Entrepreneurship—Business—Technology. |
Quantitative research. | Mogavero, Damian—Food and beverage.
Classification: LCC TX911.3.E4 M64 2017 | DDC 647.95068—dc23
LC record available at https://lccn.loc.gov/2016023657

ISBN 978-1-101-90330-8
eBook ISBN 978-1-101-90331-5

Printed in the United States of America

Jacket design by Tal Goretsky
Jacket illustration by Ben Wiseman

10 9 8 7 6 5 4 3 2 1

First Edition

For my parents,
Gloria and Russ

· contents ·

· foreword ·

If you're holding this book, chances are good that you love dining out and are passionate about food. What you may not know is that the restaurant industry has been undergoing a revolutionary shift in thinking that is largely invisible to guests. *The Underground Culinary Tour* reveals the big secret: more than ever, a new generation of restaurant operators are relying upon data and technology to deliver a superb guest experience.

Most of us would agree that anytime we decide to spend our hard-earned money on a meal out, we are entitled to get our money's worth for that experience. But a growing number of restaurateurs want to go well beyond the time-honored transaction of payment in exchange for a fine meal (i.e., "you give us money; we give you food"). Today's restaurant professionals want your experience to be transcendent. Over and beyond what we put in the glass and on the plate, we want to provide you with a level of hospitality so genuine, welcoming, and seamless that you feel as comfortable in our restaurants as you do in your own home. As more and more independent restaurateurs expand to create multiunit restaurant groups, it is going to be increasingly challenging to be able to do that without the benefit of data and technology. If that statement sounds antithetical to genuine hospitality, let me remind you that most of us these days carry a little computer in our pockets that allows us to customize our lives any way we want. Our smartphones connect us with the ones we love, snap our photos, navigate our way, research obscure facts, share our images and music, and find us tables at a restaurant that suits our mood right this very second. And our smartphones allow us to collect and connect dots—all the better for enriching human relationships.

By contrast, when I opened Union Square Café in 1985, my first New York City restaurant, our most advanced operational tool was a clunky, button-laden point-of-sale machine that lurked behind the bar. When we were nimble enough to line up the sprockets correctly and persuade that device to print out reports, we could actually figure out how well we were doing. That information was critical to helping us to improve our efficiency at purchasing ingredients, to optimizing our menu mix, and ultimately to preparing better meals for our guests. We've come a long way since then!

No one likes to plan a romantic night out only to discover that their loved one's favorite dishes or wines are not available. And you can't impress a client if the restaurant you picked for your business luncheon is short-staffed and poorly managed, or if your server doesn't understand every part of the menu.

That all changed in late 1999, when Damian Mogavero appeared on the scene, presciently pleading with the people and the industry he adores to get with the program. To early pioneers who adopted his software, he seemed like a soothsayer or prophet crying out in the wilderness and making a case for innovation and logic. Chief among his promises was the assertion that a great chef or restaurateur didn't have to sacrifice the joy—nor the feel, nor the smell, nor the taste, nor the love—of his or her restaurants in order to become better at operating them.

Damian has since become a good friend. Our offices are only a couple of blocks away from each other, and we'll often see each other as we traverse the neighborhood around Union Square. We are basically in the same business: shaping and delivering the best possible experience in restaurants through people. He is helping to change the way we eat, one white tablecloth bistro, one meatball shop, one restaurant chain at a time. And some of the most recognizable names in the culinary and hospitality world heed his advice.

Today the work of Damian and his entire team infuses all of our restaurants in New York. His technology helps chefs, managers, sommeliers, and our corporate offices to run our businesses more efficiently. Insights from his software empower my colleagues, which ultimately impacts *you,* when you walk into one of our restaurants to enjoy a meal.

True to Damian's prediction, we have found that data and creativity are not mutually exclusive. Both enhance our ability to make you feel welcome when you dine with us.

The human connection will always be critically necessary, because data and technology cannot do it all. We will always need to employ the emotional hospitality skills that can only be found in human beings, but even those skills can be augmented with the benefit of good data.

In restaurants, as in all businesses, it pays occasionally to look beyond the confines of our own silos—or dining rooms—to see how others are innovating. That's the avowed purpose of the real-life Underground Culinary Tour, the "secret" annual tour for senior restaurant executives that Damian pioneered some years ago with the restaurant industry guru Alice Elliot. I'm privileged to have hosted these forward-thinking colleagues at my own restaurants each and every year.

One year I was intrepid enough to attend the tour as a guest. Escorted by Damian and Alice, our group visited fifteen restaurants in twenty-four hours. We came, we saw, we ate and drank. I met fascinating restaurateurs and beverage professionals I'd never known and was exposed to an innovative collection of new culinary discoveries right in my own backyard.

Yet the real Underground Culinary Tour is not for the faint of heart. By the end of day one, I returned home zonked, my mind and body beyond full. When my compatriots and I assembled for day two, we were all somewhat green around the gills. Luckily, Damian had arranged for a great cup of coffee to rouse us.

You are far more fortunate. You have in your hands an excellent guide to our adventure. There are no buses to board, no credentials to proffer, and you don't have to worry about pacing yourself. All the tour's secrets—the cutting-edge trends, the wisdom of employing data and technology, the hidden dining revolution—are yours and may be gleaned with the turn of a page.

Danny Meyer
Union Square Hospitality Group
New York City
August 2016

THE
UNDERGROUND
CULINARY
TOUR

· introduction ·

RESTAURANT METRICS

Thirteen years ago, Jeffrey Frederick, a former chef, took a new job as vice president in charge of every food and beverage outlet in a resort owned by Harrah's Entertainment, one of the big gaming companies in Las Vegas. Jeffrey was young, bright, eager to please, and willing to try anything that would help him succeed at his new job. Unlike the suits who ran the casino, he didn't have a degree from a fancy business or hospitality school; in fact, he had no college degree at all. He had started his career as a teenage dishwasher and had risen through the ranks of the hospitality business, from the "back of the house"—the kitchen—to the echelons of upper management.

I met him shortly after his promotion, hoping to convince him to adopt a software program my team and I had created to bring data and analytics to the restaurant industry. Jeffrey knew that his bosses had teams of analysts and accountants crunching numbers to tease out the most minuscule insights from the casino operations. But the casino's restaurants were run the way eateries the world over have always been and too often still are run—by gut.

Between the staff he had to manage and the daily purchasing decisions he needed to make, the new job, Jeffrey admitted to me, was often overwhelming. Mostly, he was starved for information about how the casino's restaurants were doing. So he took a chance on me and my software. He decided to emulate what the suits upstairs were doing; he would collect data about the casino's restaurants to see what he could learn from it. He used an early version of the software that collected every check punched into the point-of-sale device at his eateries; the number of drinks poured per shift; the number of lunches served; the number of Cokes bought; the tips his servers were earning. And so on. Whenever he had a chance, he proactively studied the software looking for insights.

My team and I created an easy-to-read profile that assembled every statistic on the restaurants' servers, which we called the Server Scorecard. Imagine, if you will, a baseball card complete with performance statistics of every single server who worked in each restaurant. While scanning them one day, Jeffrey discovered a surprising finding about one of his servers, a staff favorite. I'll call her Alana. She arrived punctually each day and worked diligently throughout her shift. But Jeffrey saw something curious when he looked at Alana's numbers: while she took orders for numerous glasses of wine on every shift, she rarely sold a full bottle of wine to any of her tables.

Jeffrey was puzzled. It didn't make sense. Servers who served fewer tables than Alana managed to sell several bottles of wine on each of their shifts. It was practically a no-brainer. What was going on? The data didn't lie.

So he pulled Alana aside one day. After praising her work ethic, her diligence, her success with guests, he asked her: "So . . . this might be a weird question, but your guests hardly ever order wine by the bottle. Do you have any idea why?"

A look of terror washed over the young woman's face. Jeffrey struggled to reassure her: "I just want to understand what's going on with regard to the wine. We love your work. I just want to know if I can help."

As she began to speak, Alana revealed a deep-seated phobia about opening wine bottles. What if she couldn't get the cork out? What if she broke a cork while opening it and pieces of the cork fell inside an expensive bottle of wine? What if the bottle slipped out of her hands as she was extracting the cork? The thought of attempting to open a bottle of wine and looking foolish in front of guests terrified her. Better that the bartenders poured her guests endless glasses of wine than that she should have to open a bottle tableside.

As he listened, it was clear to Jeffrey that Alana was so terrified of this part of her job that she spent her shifts subconsciously steering guests to order only wine by the glass. He marveled at how much mental energy it must have cost her.

And then there was the cost to guests, and to the restaurant. Wines by the bottle are a key part of the overall guest experience. Wine lists are one way restaurants enhance their reputation. There is a far greater selection of wines available by the bottle than by the glass, so Alana's guests weren't availing themselves of the restaurant's vast wine cellar.

Restaurants like selling full bottles because they bring in much-needed additional revenue. But certain bottles actually *save* guests money over buying by the glass. By eliminating an entire category from the menu, Alana was doing the restaurant, her guests, and herself a disservice.

Jeffrey's heart went out to her. If anything, Alana's fear grew out of her intense desire to do a good job. So much of the restaurant business is about performance, about putting on a flawless show before a touchy, critical public. Comparing work in restaurants to acting in the theater is no exaggeration. The moment servers tie on their aprons and begin their shifts, they are onstage, and the tiniest thing can throw them off their marks. The better the restaurant, the higher the expectations of flawless hospitality.

"Has anyone ever showed you how to open wine bottles?" Jeffrey asked Alana.

She shook her head.

"Come in tomorrow early," he told her. "I'll get someone to show you."

Deep down, he was thinking: *Alana is a valuable server. I can fix this.*

The next day, he instructed the restaurant's general manager to do what his predecessor should have done: help train Alana on the protocol of good wine service. Before the evening dinner service began, the sommelier showed Alana how to cut the foils, pull the corks, and pour glasses for guests at the bar. It was the sort of training every restaurant ought to do but often doesn't, assuming that its hires already know how to do all the tasks expected of them.

When Jeffrey reviewed the numbers from Alana's shifts over the next week, he was astonished at her improvement. As a result of this personalized training, Alana's wine sales by the bottle went up dramatically to match the sales of the other servers. And her guests had a chance to enjoy the full range of the restaurant's wine cellar.

Moreover, Alana's confidence improved—all because Jeffrey analyzed the numbers and saw something was wrong. He then did what few restaurateurs at the time ever did: analyzed the data at his fingertips, trusted it, and acted on it.

This book is about how data and technology are shaping the way restaurants, big and small, high-end and more budget-minded, serve you when you dine out. Jeffrey—a restaurant leader that I'll introduce to you more fully later on—and an ever-growing cohort of restaurateurs like him are using data to deconstruct the guest experience with an eye toward ensuring exceptional cuisine and guest service and improving their restaurants' financial health. And they're doing it without compromising on ingredients, culinary artistry, or the expectation that guests have of a spectacular day or evening out. In fact, they're often delivering an experience above and beyond their guests' expectations.

These restaurateurs are part of what I call the New

Guard. At the heart of the New Guard philosophy is making decisions based on insights gained by the systematic collection and analysis of every restaurant's daily home-grown data. It is a philosophy that my team and I helped to invent seventeen years ago. I'm not a chef or a bartender, nor have I ever been the owner of a restaurant. I'm a former restaurant executive with a Harvard MBA. My team and I created the means of collecting the data and transforming it into insights that make it easy to see restaurant metrics. I also happen to be in love with the industry.

I've worked with some of the top restaurants in the world for nearly twenty years. And I can tell you that restaurants cannot succeed on data alone. Rather, data combined with an understanding of the new foodie generation and an insatiable desire to innovate are what create restaurant magic. None of these things is mutually exclusive.

The novel approach to hospitality that my team and I pioneered has been adopted by more than 34,000 restaurant operators in 68 countries. Today our ideas are taught in hospitality schools, and I regularly speak to classes at the Cornell School of Hotel Administration, the top hospitality program in the United States. We count among our clients some of the world's top chefs and their organizations: Tom Colicchio (craft), Wolfgang Puck (Spago), Daniel Boulud (Daniel), Mario Batali (Babbo), Jean-Georges Vongerichten (Jean-Georges), and David Chang (Momofuku). And because the restaurant world is becoming increasingly diverse, you are just as likely to find the New Guard ideas we crafted put to use in fast casual places, the great independent restaurant in the middle of your Main Street suburb, or in eateries on cruise ships, in casinos, and at nightclubs and hotels, airports, and baseball stadiums. The New Guard is everywhere.

Even before data was easy to harvest and analyze, major industries such as the oil business, banking, pharmaceutical companies, shipping companies, and major retail chains employed armies of analysts and accountants to monitor their transactions and records. When they needed to make key decisions, they didn't go with their gut, or use rules of thumb or off-the-cuff hunches. They used hard data to inform their decisions. The ubiquitous presence of computers, and the rise of great software and the Internet, has meant that these handy tools have been stitched into the fabric of our homes and businesses in unprecedented ways. Today businesses are exploiting a powerful new model of delivery—Software as a Service (SaaS)—where the software is hosted by a central server, and businesses pay a subscription to access that computing power. It was only inevitable that such tools would find their way into the restaurant industry.

Today, the restaurant industry in the United States accounts for 4 percent of the nation's gross domestic product and employs about 14 million people in a full- or part-time capacity. Most of us don't realize the scope of the industry. It's vast. We eat out everywhere: In fine dining establishments. Casual restaurants. Fast-food places. Food trucks. We have dinner while seated in the stands at a ball game and stop for lunch between rides at an amusement park. Beyond these obvious locales, we eat at museums and at concerts. We eat at coffee shops, hotels, bookstores, cafeterias in office workplaces, the snack areas of university libraries, and elementary through high schools, not to mention every cruise ship all over the world. We patronize homey mom-and-pop diners, theme chains in far-flung locations, and tiny, romantic hole-in-the-wall favorites that we'll never tell a soul about for fear of ruining them forever. We eat for love, for business, and for the simple reason that we're on the run and are hungry.

And yet, for some reason, the same industry that does more than $783 billion in sales a year has been among the last major industries in the world to adopt data analysis as a critical part of doing business. That's striking when you consider how close to the bone restaurants live. Most guests have no idea that a restaurant is lucky if it sees 7 percent profit after all the trouble it goes to to make and serve food. Most restaurants are solidly in the 4 to 5 percent profit margin.

With such slim margins, you'd think restaurateurs would leap at any tool to help them manage their business, to understand their product, but that's not the case. I've found that turning restaurateurs on to a new thing is about as easy as convincing a meat lover to go vegan. In an industry where survival past the first year is difficult, if you've been around for a long time while your competition is dropping like flies, you naturally assume you have little to learn. So Old Guard chef-owners have typically learned to use their gut, their hard-won experience, and their subjective impressions to determine what dishes guests will like, how many of them they will likely need to serve, and which servers are doing a good job. Dishes on the menu reflect longtime standards, what the chef is able to source from suppliers at a good price, or what the owner *thinks* are the popular dishes.

I have also found that an owner's assessment of a server's performance more often emphasizes and rewards physical appearance and charisma than the server's ability to please guests and help the business meet its bottom line. Moreover, owners and managers base their perceptions of servers on limited interactions with those servers. When I ask chefs, owners, or managers to identify their best- and worst-*selling* servers, they hardly know how to answer the question. Instead they deflect, saying things like:

"Julie is one of our best servers. She's got a great smile, beautiful personality."

"Don't forget Dave. Customers love Dave! He's so funny."

"Kristi is always on time. Very well put together. Such a great role model for the other servers."

Would it surprise you to know that when we actually look at the sales performance of the servers, we find that most managers have incorrectly assessed who their top and bottom performers are?

I can hear your protests already: *But dining out isn't about salesmanship! It's about delicious food and drink. It's about having a memorable or reliable experience that you can return to again and again. Who wants to be upsold when they're out for a night on the town?*

I hear you. And I wholeheartedly agree. At their best, restaurants are places where artistry, service, and hospitality come together beautifully at the end of your fork. But you can be both profitable and magical.

Corporations that rely on salespeople to generate revenue would never make a similar miscalculation about their employees. They know *exactly* who their top earners are, because they have never forgotten that they are in the business of *selling* a product. The principals of real estate agencies routinely sing the praises of their top five or top ten sellers. They broadcast this information because they want potential sellers to believe that if these folks know how to sell *other* people's houses, they'll excel at selling yours.

But for some reason, when I suggest that restaurants are businesses first, some people object. But if you want your favorite restaurants to be around the next time you plan an evening out, they need to be profitable. And that means restaurateurs must know everything about their restaurants, down to the smallest detail. Well-run restaurants are good for guests as well. Every restaurant has culinary gems on the menu that guests may not realize are a "must-have" by the brief menu descriptions alone. The job of a well-trained, experienced server is to amass a deep knowledge of the menu and the daily specials and serve as your guide, pointing out these tasting opportunities as you move from predinner beverages to appetizers, entrées, and desserts. And if that server demonstrates a knack for assisting guests with their meals, wine, and other beverages, and also racks up outsize tips, he or she has clearly done triple duty for the restaurant's guests: educating guests about the menu and delivering great table service that makes guests feel valued and appreciated while making the house more successful at what it does.

Such servers are hard to come by. But every day they are being hired and groomed by New Guard restaurateurs, whose way of thinking about their staff is generous enough to even the playing field for workers who may not be as handsome, beautiful, extroverted, or theatrical as some of their colleagues—but who excel at creating a great dining experience for the restaurant's guests. Every year, too many exceptional people are overlooked and passed over for promotions and better shifts because their employers lack the time and tools to see what these employees have accomplished. Others get a high-five and new opportunities simply because they look attractive or talk a good game. A great many other promising employees lose out on easy ways to bring up their game.

I think it's fair to say that in all professions, new employees often crave feedback, but rarely get what they need. Who doesn't want to learn more and improve their career? All the bottle-shy Alana needed was one coaching session to improve dramatically when it came to presenting the wine list to her guests. She was in luck: working for Jeffrey meant she was on the receiving end of objective feedback, tailored specifically to her performance. What she experienced was actually a beautiful example of how someone's personal and professional growth can be enhanced through the use of data. Her employer noticed a problem that she was displaying. He discreetly called it to her attention. He got her training. And she improved in short order, thus enhancing the experience of the guests she served. Tell me: Isn't that the sort of career trajectory good employers wish for *all* their employees?

Besides meticulously training their staff, in the kitchen and on the dining room floor, New Guard restaurateurs tend to emphasize high-quality, local ingredients that they can purchase and manage meticulously. They understand what the "foodie generation" flocking to their restaurants wants. Their profits improve, because they know how to more closely peg inventory to need. As a result, they lose less to waste or theft. Their trust in their staff increases, and thus they delegate more. And behind all of these decisions? An overarching reliance on data and technology.

Old Guard restaurateurs, on the other hand, tend to go with their gut instead of analyzing the facts and figures that impact their bottom line. They do things the way they've always done them, because they have been successful over the years. Rather than carefully curating a wine list or beverage program that fits their clientele and cuisine, they tell their beverage distributor to simply deliver whatever wines, beer, and spirits are de rigueur in their category of hospitality. They rarely change the menu, preferring to stick with their "house specialties" long after those dishes have ceased to impress. Their point-of-sale device functions merely as a device for computation and running credit cards, rather than a critical collection point for day-to-day data.

They don't take the time or expense to rigorously train their waitstaff and bus people on the fine points of good service and hospitality, assuming that such training is a waste of money, and that employees will pick up pointers over time. They train their staff as if all servers are created equal, but they're not. And when the Old Guard runs out of ingredients, or a particular bottle of wine, their attitude is, if it doesn't occur too often, "Oh well, it happens."

The best of the Old Guard, the ones who've been in business for decades, are savants; it would be impossible to find or train others to be like them. Most of the Old Guard are well-meaning veterans of the restaurant industry in a rapidly shifting culinary landscape, where tastes and expectations change like the seasons. It frustrates me to meet and hear an Old Guarder talk about the challenges they are facing. I know I can help them take their businesses to the next level.

As a guest, how many times have you experienced one or more of the following at a restaurant?

- You ask the hostess for a table, only to be told there's a waiting list. But looking past her shoulder you see that the restaurant has six vacant tables and the back patio is completely empty on a beautiful day.
- You order what sounds like the perfect dish for the evening only to learn that the house is out and you need to make another selection.
- You ask your server for advice on a particular wine or entrée only to discover that he or she hasn't the slightest idea how to respond or offer guidance. Or worse, the server tells you that "everything here is great."
- At every turn, you feel rushed by the staff, from busboys clearing away plates before you are ready to servers dropping off the bill without inquiring about dessert or coffee, or without thanking you for your patronage.
- You have trouble ordering another drink, or getting

the check, because your server has mysteriously disappeared for the last ten minutes.

- One time you go to a restaurant, you get great service. The next time, the service is terrible.

Many guests have grown accustomed to these annoyances, so they don't always expect more. But they're the sorts of things that drive many people crazy about eating out. Which means that when you experience any of the things I've listed above, there is a manager or owner in that restaurant who has not embraced the data that could help provide a better guest experience. I believe that every server should know the menu cold. And I believe that no restaurant should ever run out of a dish or ingredient. No table should sit empty while you and a friend are waiting. My job is to help restaurateurs get back to what they love to do—cook great food, provide great service, build a magical experience, and do it all profitably. I want to liberate them from the back office, safe in the knowledge that technology is helping them make better decisions.

With a good grasp of their data, New Guard restaurateurs can be *extremely* precise. They order supplies appropriately and intelligently, provide personalized training to their staff, enhance their employees' careers, and look for ways to close the gap between an average experience and a transcendent one. Above all, they are forever looking for ways to use the data from their business on a more granular level, to elevate the guest's experience. Like most people, I don't like to pay good money for a sub-par dining experience. I have been known to give new restaurants the benefit of the doubt, returning to them after a period of time to see if they've improved. And if I do give up on a place, I still like to analyze just what's going on beneath the surface. If a restaurant annoys me past a certain point, I won't return. That said, I do make allowances for new restaurants, as I know how hard it is to get everything right when a restaurant first opens, and I will almost always give them a second chance if my first experience isn't stellar. But restaurateurs should know that regular customers may not be so forgiving. It may surprise you to learn that in every case I mentioned above, poor training is not the only issue. Too many restaurateurs have a poor grasp of the numbers underlying their entire operation. They don't understand what service failures cost them in each shift, each week, and each month. As long as they don't have a handle on even these small inefficiencies, they are forever chasing a goal that they cannot possibly attain, like a man bailing a leaky lifeboat with a Dixie cup. Sooner or later, the boat's going to go down.

In *The Underground Culinary Tour,* you'll see efficient, magical restaurants that are living up to my vision of the Brave New World of New Guard restaurateurship. You will meet big and small operators from around the country who are taking on the known challenges of the industry gracefully.

And let's admit this up front: it is a crazy business. Statistically, one out of every four restaurants closes or changes hands in the first year of operation. Overall, 60 percent of new restaurants never see year five—even if they do everything right. It's increasingly costly and more competitive than ever to launch a new restaurant. Guests today are spending record amounts of money eating out, but they're more demanding. Because our dollars don't go as far as they used to, today's guests are increasingly impatient with eateries that don't deliver great experiences. At no time in history have guests worldwide been so sophisticated. Not so long ago, what happened in foodie capitals such as New York, San Francisco, Chicago, Paris, Rome, San Sebastián, and Tokyo took forever to reach Omaha. Today, food trends are beamed into every home via apps like Instagram or countless food and cooking shows aired on Food Network and Bravo every day of the week. Food blogs such as Eater and Serious Eats broadcast up-to-the-minute information on trends, while a legion of apps—from OpenTable to Yelp to countless others—have put powerful mobile tools in every guest's pocket.

Even your twelve-year-old niece can rattle off the names of favorite food shows or celebrity chefs such as Giada De Laurentiis, Wolfgang Puck, Gordon Ramsay, Lidia Bastianich, Guy Fieri—and probably has several of their cookbooks to boot. As a result, this new foodie generation has far higher expectations than generations past. When servers like Jeffrey's bottle-shy server tie on their aprons, they are no longer facing an eager but dining-ignorant audience. Today's guests have heard of all the hot new eateries, dishes, and ingredients, even if they haven't yet tried them. These guests have the ability to make or break a restaurant. If they're unhappy with a meal or a restaurant, they can tweet their displeasure or Yelp their rage before the table has been cleared—rightly or wrongly.

A New Guard restaurateur not only knows what the hot trends are but is also constantly improving, constantly tinkering with his or her brand to anticipate the next big thing. In general, we'll see restaurants innovating in four areas—Ingredients, Beverage, Space, and something I call X-Factor. We'll look at each of these areas in turn, and I'll argue that a New Guard restaurateur is one who not only embraces data and technology but also has a keen appreciation for moving the industry forward—because to rest on one's laurels, or anyone else's, is to stagnate and die.

We'll meet the chefs and owners, hear their stories, and see how the use of restaurant metrics can help consistently ensure a great experience—for restaurants and their guests. Welcome to *The Underground Culinary Tour,* a world where restaurant trends are discovered, the kitchen never runs out, the bar and wine cellar are always stocked, and guests are assured of a special time they will want to relive, again and again.

MAXIMIZING THE MONTAUK SUNSHINE

It's another sun-soaked summer weekend in the Hamptons, and it's clear I'm going to need another glass of rosé. My good fortune is that I've got a beachfront table at Navy Beach, Montauk's fashionable watering hole of the in-crowd, where refills of the colorful, lovely wine are rarely a problem.

As I savor the remains of my salmon tartare, I watch servers gingerly march through the sand carrying seemingly endless bottles of wine and other drinks to guests perched atop crisp blue-and-white daybeds or banquettes, shaded by matching blue umbrellas. The wines hail from France and Long Island, and the bottles range in size from the typical 750 milliliters to magnums, double magnums, jeroboams, and methuselahs, which are typically six-liter bottles of wine that look large enough to sink one of the sailboats bobbing unsuspectingly in the blue waters of Fort Pond Bay ahead of me.

I've come to meet with two of the owners—my clients Martin Cabrera and Franklin Ferguson—to talk about food, wine, ... and data. Waiting for them to finish up with smiling guests gives me a chance to do what I love to do here: watch the Technicolor sunset, an eruption of reds and pinks and oranges dancing among the waves and nuzzling the sand of the restaurant's private beach.

When the sun's just right, Navy Beach feels like the most beautiful spot in the world. When guests post photos of their adventures on Instagram or Facebook, every shot looks like something out of an ad campaign: gorgeous beach images artfully overexposed by a luminous sun shining over the bay.

The town of Montauk sits at the very tip of Long Island's South Fork, about 120 miles from New York City. Getting here takes about three hours by car or train. When you finally disembark at the final stop of the LIRR's Montauk line, you feel as if you've ridden to the end of the world. And, in a sense, you have. The train stops not far from Navy Beach; any farther and you'd hit the wooded tip of the island, home to a pair of state parks and a two-hundred-year-old lighthouse commissioned by George Washington. The parks themselves are studded with massive concrete bunkers erected to protect the island against Nazi invasion during World War II. At one time the US Navy tested torpedoes in the waters just offshore from where I sit today, which is how Franklin and Martin's little slice of heaven got its name.

Despite its history as a working-class fishing village, Montauk and the rest of the Hamptons, the collection of tony towns at this end of the island, today serve as the summer playground for New Yorkers. But come Labor Day, when the sun sinks below the horizon, the summer people flee and Montauk returns to its fishing roots once again. The winter surf pounds the shore and erases those summer memories for good. Suddenly you are reminded that you are at the mercy of nature, weather, and time. As beautiful as the view is, few out-of-towners care to see Montauk in January.

It's a harsh environment, in more ways than one; to understand the setting is to understand why businesses here have always had difficulty surviving from year to year. A few years back, when Franklin, Martin, and their partners signed their lease, they committed to forking over rent for all twelve months of the year, even though the Montauk "season" reliably brings guests in for only three of those months. Montauk's businesses are not alone in this predicament, of course. Visit any seasonal business in the United States, or anywhere in the world, and you'll meet people who cater to the desires of the summer trade. Whether they hawk T-shirts and other souvenirs, frozen custard, fried fish or shrimp baskets, or kayak or boating excursions, nearly all of these entrepreneurs scrape by to survive. And yet Navy Beach has survived profitably for five years and is heading confidently into their sixth season as I write this.

How do Franklin and Martin do it? How do they manage to maximize every single hour of the short, fleeting summer season? How do they exploit nature, weather, and time?

They use math and data.

When Franklin first saw the place, it was a surfer bar called the Sunset Saloon that jumped day and night to reggae music. His wife, Leyla Marchetto, who grew up watching her father run his legendary New York City Italian restaurant, Da Silvano, had been itching to open a place of their own, one that they could run while staying at their getaway spot on the edge of Long Island. A cool, family-friendly restaurant on the beach. A friend of theirs, Frank Davis, called one day to ask Leyla if she was interested in a place Frank had heard about from a friend. The Sunset Saloon's lease was up. So Franklin parked himself at the bar. He watched the bartenders pour shots, watched the servers strut by in their bikinis, carrying trays of Pacifico beer. The interior was a black hole—constructed out of brick and great beams of wood so dark, so unvarnished, and so rough, that they seemed to suck up all the sunlight glancing off the bay outside.

Franklin thought about how they could transform the place. If they could bring in a clientele beyond surfers and other locals, if they could make it a place that attracted young people and families—the summer people—they'd have something.

Franklin has worked in the restaurant business since he was in his teens. He once thought he'd become a doctor, and during those premed years in school he worked his way through a string of unglamorous restaurant jobs—dishwasher, bartender, bouncer—before landing a gig as a general manager of a restaurant and thinking, *This is where I belong.*

His long apprenticeship in restaurants had given him an early view into hospitality mathematics—and how easily an owner could lose the night's or even the week's hard-won margins. At one steak place where he'd worked, Franklin had watched as the owner frequently comped his friends entire meals. *Bad move,* Franklin thought. *Every one of those steaks is a high-cost item. Buddy, you just bought the entire table a Ferrari that everyone drives home but you.*

As it happens, Franklin worked for two of my earliest clients, China Grill and Sushisamba. I'm tempted to say that's why Franklin is such a progressive user of data and technology, but that's only part of the answer. For Franklin, numbers are a balm, a warm blanket that you could throw around yourself and say, *Okay, I got this.*

Though his love of math made him an outlier among traditional restaurant people, it's who he is. Franklin once jokingly told me that the fantasy character he'd most like to be is Tron, the hero of Disney's first computer-generated movie, who dwells inside a computer program and rides a futuristic motorcycle. Franklin thought it might be fun to live inside an Excel spreadsheet.

So it was numbers that convinced Franklin that he, Leyla, and Frank could probably flourish on this beach. At the time he was spending most of his days and nights on the road as the beverage director for Sushisamba, a chain of chic restaurants that blended Asian and South American cuisine in gorgeous nightclub settings. The genius behind these places was taking cuisines everyone thought they knew and combining them with high-fashion décor, music, and wall-to-wall beautiful people. Guests flocked to them because these restaurants were part nightclubs, part food emporia.

Shortly after seeing the Sunset Saloon, Franklin received a phone call from Martin Cabrera, a big-hearted Venezuelan who ran Sushisamba's operations in New York and Chicago, who had heard Franklin was opening a place in Montauk. Martin was intrigued. Every summer, he was accustomed to riding his motorcycle to Montauk to get away from the grind of work. The two men knew each other casually. They were forever crossing paths, but they were rarely in the same place for very long at the same time, one of them flying in from a restaurant location just as the other was hitting the road. Theirs was a fun, exciting life, with six-figure incomes to boot. Franklin was looking to reduce his travel to be closer to the family he and his wife were about to start. Martin was an avowed bachelor, gracious and charming, and the idea of running his own restaurant meant something more, somehow, than just a job, however well paying and fun.

So one day Martin rode his motorcycle out to Montauk to meet Franklin and check the place out. In the dimness of the off-season, all he could see was a main dining room with a low ceiling, surrounded by four dirty brick walls. There were brass portholes behind the bar—like every cheap seafood place he'd ever seen. Outside, the winter wind mercilessly blew sand across the bay. Seagulls cried forlornly overhead.

"This could be a very special place," Martin said, turning to Franklin.

Franklin was an introverted family guy, Martin an

extroverted, passionate host. They could make this work, they realized.

Together with their partners, Frank Davis, and his wife, Kristina, they had just enough money to sign the lease and sit tight until spring. Until the weather warmed, they knew they'd be hemorrhaging money. There would be bills for food and beverage inventory, and labor costs for cooks and waitstaff. If they wanted to get this place decorated, they would have to pinch pennies and do it themselves.

Kristina and Leyla declared the space perfect, even beautiful. Yes, the floors were shot and the brick walls were as dingy and dark as an unfinished basement in the Jersey suburbs, but the place had *character*. Look at those beams! The ceiling of the dining room was built like the hold of a whaling ship.

From there on, there was a beautiful esprit to the way everything came together, all of them busting their butts to whitewash the brick walls and clear out the cobwebs from the rafters. The wood was so old and so rough-hewn that it drank up gallons of paint. They ended up leaving the key timbers untouched. The contrast—weather-beaten wood against textured, white brick—was stunning.

From the start they envisioned a place that projected the feel of a 1950s yacht club. The ladies eBayed like crazy, snapping up vintage women's swimsuits, which they had framed and hung on the wall. They passed up on new lighting fixtures and just wrapped the old chandeliers with nautical rope. They found old seafaring flags and hung them where they would catch the breeze.

Slowly the seasons changed, and the sun poked its face

in the dining room windows. They had counted on sunlight making the restaurant look inviting. And they were thrilled to see they were right. The space *glowed*.

And as the weather warmed, people started coming in.

That was their first year, spring into summer 2010. Franklin and Martin had wanted to splurge on the software we created to help them collect and analyze sales made each day. They had become accustomed to using it at Sushisamba. But Frank wasn't familiar with our product and took some convincing. Franklin decided to pay out of his own pocket to have my team collect their data so they'd have it next year when they activated their subscription. That first spring, they were so low-tech that they took down reservations by writing them by hand in a book. But the calls for reservations and events never stopped.

New York City's original Sushisamba used to be located on the ground floor of the building where I work. I'd sometimes see Martin's mentor, the founder of the Sushisamba fusion concept, Shimon Bokovza, sitting on a bench outside the restaurant. For years he'd been one of my earliest clients, a brilliant and creative developer of numerous restaurant concepts. "Damian," he said to me once, "you went to Harvard Business School. Forget about all these damned reports. Just tell us: what should we do?"

I didn't have an answer for Shimon on the tip of my tongue, but if I could go back in time, having seen what

Shimon's former employees have done with Navy Beach, I'd say, "Study and understand the trends in your restaurants."

In the business world, a *trend* is the pattern that emerges when you analyze your sales. *Metrics* are the way we describe that pattern. At a very basic level, a restaurateur should want to know things like this: How many people (or "covers," in the parlance of the industry) do you serve on a weekday? On a weekend? What are your busiest days? Your busiest nights? How many covers did you have on the last seven Sundays? From there, it gets slightly more complicated. If you are diligent about collecting every scrap of data you can about your business, you can then ask any number of questions, which is not so different from the vast collection of statistics—called sabermetrics—that has developed around the world of professional baseball: batting average, earned run average, slugging percentage, on-base percentage, WHIP (walks plus hits per inning pitched), and more. If you can think of a question, there ought to be a way to capture that data and generate an answer.

The "black box" of the hospitality industry is the point-of-sale (or POS) device that tabulates every check and is a repository of data. If you dine out frequently, you've probably seen countless servers or bartenders use these over the years. Every time a server logs in to a POS to send an order to the kitchen, they're presented with a screen that spells out every single drink or menu item. They can also easily punch in special guest requests: "dressing on the side," "hold the onion," etc. The drink orders are sent to the bar to be fulfilled by the bar staff. The food order goes to the kitchen. Each new item—additional drinks, coffee, dessert—is plugged into the same machine. In restaurants where tips are customary, the tip is plugged in to arrive at the final tab. The POS is the entry point for all the guest checks. If you capture and store it properly, all this data can later be mined for insights on every aspect of the shift or evening. It's all there: who waited on which table, the average check, the average tip, what entrées sold the most, and so on. By tying in what a restaurant is selling at the front of the house (the dining room) with its inventory at the back of the house (the kitchen), managers can see if they are running low on critical ingredients. Of course, extracting the critical data from the point of sale that isn't informative or helpful is often a time-consuming, manual task. It's a job most restaurateurs know they should be doing but rarely do because they have better things to do, or so they think.

That first year, even before they opened their doors, Franklin and Martin could pretty much bet on the trends they were likely to see at Navy Beach. Since the Hamptons are fairly dead during summer weekdays and busy on weekends, they predicted their biggest days would be Friday, Saturday, and Sunday, with Saturday the busiest. And that's exactly what the numbers showed. But this was no big revelation; it's common sense.

Franklin and Martin had so little data to work with that the kitchen was running out of ingredients all the time. But in their second season, they installed our software and got to work analyzing what it showed them. With each passing year, they got better at forecasting their restaurant's trends. Yes, they knew Fridays were strong in terms of revenue, but the data revealed that Saturday's business wasn't just better than Friday, it was the equivalent of *two* Fridays—and then some.

Today their grasp of their trends is remarkably robust. On a recent afternoon, five years after their opening, I overhear Martin and chef Randy Santos discuss their supplier food orders for the coming weekend. "Okay," Martin tells Randy, "on the last five Fridays you did fifty-seven steaks for the night. And we did about ninety-eight burgers in one shift."

This is just the beginning. The longer they talk, the more detailed they get. How many New York strip steaks are they going to need? How many buttermilk fried chickens? How many scallops? The data spelled out the demand for each of the menu items.

They were using what we refer to as a prep calculator, which automatically dictates their menu item trends by the day of the week. It can show, for example, the last five Fridays and tell managers which items they can expect to sell. An Old Guard restaurateur would have no problem telling the chef to expect more orders on Friday; that's child's play.

But he or she would not be able to say, "Over the last seven weeks, we have sold twenty black bass on Thursday and only twelve black bass on Friday. So let's order accordingly." Counterintuitive trends—selling more fish on a Thursday than a Friday—are invisible in the analog world of the Old Guard. Without reliable data, they're prone to missed opportunities (the chance to sell twenty fish entrées on Thursday) or wasted food (fish that must be discarded because it didn't sell).

Because it can gauge its seafood needs down to the scallop, Navy Beach knows how much to order to accommodate its guest needs, but with little waste. This has a powerful impact on the restaurant's margins. It means that even a seasonal business like Navy Beach can splurge on better-quality ingredients for its guests, like fresh, off-the-boat fish from local fishermen. Chef Santos loves that. But not as much as Navy Beach's guests do.

The chef nods and leaves and then Martin turns to fill me in.

"It was hard to get the kitchen guys to use the computer, but they started coming around a few years ago. 'Hey,' they say the morning after, 'how did the special do last night? What's the report say?' Now it's become a matter of pride for them."

What's so different about this way of making purchasing decisions at Navy Beach? At first blush, not much. Listening to Martin and Santos's plan, I can hear echoes of countless Old Guard restaurateurs sniffing haughtily, "I know how many steaks I need like the back of my hand!"

Yes, you probably do. But it becomes more complicated when you start tossing in other factors. For example, what if you want to ask questions such as, "How does the weather impact how many covers we'll have? And how many steak orders will we get on a cloudy day?"

Our software automatically collects and stores weather data by zip code, which allows restaurant operators to make some interesting findings. Remember, weather is critical at Navy Beach. You might guess that Franklin and Martin get the best crowds on beautiful sunny days. But that actually isn't the case. When they compared Saturdays this year with the same Saturdays last year, they could see that the biggest variable was the weather. In fact, the data showed that their covers dropped during gorgeous—cloudless, windless, sunny—days. Their covers actually increased on *overcast* days. Why? To get definitive data on that, we'd have to ply every guest with questions like "Why didn't you come yesterday when the weather was so nice?" No restaurateur would do that.

But we can speculate. My working theory is that on flawless summer days, people park themselves on the beach and don't hit the bars and restaurants until the temperature drops. This would support Navy Beach's sales spike on overcast days. In fact, the best numbers at Navy Beach are the result of days when the weather is cloudy, followed by clear, perfect nights. On days when the sun hardly shows itself, people might spend a good part of the day and well into the night hanging out at the restaurant—and why not?

The fluctuation in temperature and other weather variables should play an important role in restaurant planning, but it rarely does. Typically temperatures between fifty degrees and seventy degrees Fahrenheit will trigger the *may-we-sit-outside?* question. And though it seems obvious that on warm days people will want to be outside, many restaurateurs never think to look at the weather forecast *a week in advance* to plan when they should open and staff their patio or sidewalk cafe.

Think back to one of the problems I mentioned earlier: when the hostess says that she can't seat you in an otherwise empty section, the critical issue isn't whether or not she has open tables. The problem is not having enough *staff* to service those tables. Every restaurant employs its own rule of thumb to figure out how many tables a server can safely work. Any more, and service drags. Conversely, owners are always fretting about bringing in more staff than they need. They don't want to jack up their labor costs paying servers, busboys, cooks, dishwashers, and bartenders to stand around in an empty restaurant. A sufficient number of each of these staff members is imperative in order to turn over tables efficiently, leaving guests smiling on their way out the door.

Owners who leave it up to their staffers to decide how many tables they can take on may not realize it, but they're butting heads with an inherent conflict. Servers and bartenders need to make money. So a server's natural instinct is to take on more or larger tables, hoping to pocket more tips. They don't always realize that too much responsibility slows the guest experiences to a crawl.

Juggling these issues becomes a catch-22. If the restaurant can't seat you, you leave. If they seat you and service stinks, you may not return. Despite this, most Old Guard restaurateurs continue to base their staffing decisions on estimates, hunches, and guesses about what their needs will be, rather than specific numbers based on their longtime trends. As a result, they lose revenue.

Other businesses have been using weather-based data to anticipate customer demand for years, but the restaurant industry has lagged behind in this area. In 2005, after Hurricane Katrina devastated New Orleans, the US Senate and Harvard University's John F. Kennedy School of Government found that the response of the discount retailer Walmart was actually *faster* than that of FEMA (the Federal Emergency Management Agency). Even before the hurricane made landfall, Walmart's trucks were on the ground outside the danger zone, stocked with batteries, flashlights, blankets, and easy-to-prepare, shelf-stable foods. How was that possible? What did Walmart know about weather that the US government didn't?

It turns out that Walmart has, for years, employed the services of an in-house meteorologist and a staff of weather researchers. Their job is to assess the statistical likelihood that a storm or tornado will strike, and to predict it far enough in advance that Walmart trucks can load up and start rolling toward the chain's impacted stores with additional inventory of disaster supplies.

What are some of the other factors that impact restaurant covers? Micro-events such as nearby street festivals, Little League games, fireworks displays, parades, concerts, conventions, and sporting events typically increase a restaurant's numbers. If a manager keeps track of these events on a calendar, he or she is better able to plan for the increase— or *decrease,* if the event will draw people away to the *other* side of town. We developed a digital logbook and calendar that allows GMs to either manually plug in known events, or automatically upload local events and holidays, and then safely forget about them. (These digital programs are an updating of the red logbooks Old Guard restaurateurs manually use to keep track of their operation.) When the time's right, the software reminds the GM that a big event is fast approaching that can impact their covers.

Some New Guard restaurateurs have gotten so good at reading this kind of data that they can predict the subtle differences between what different demographics of people like to eat or drink after attending different kinds of events. In Las Vegas, for instance, the wines that attendees of a Celine Dion concert are likely to order are markedly different than the rounds of beer demanded after the Wrangler National Finals Rodeo. Armed with an event calendar, a New Guard restaurateur can plan for his or her guests' preferences accordingly.

One micro-event Franklin and Martin began planning for concerned not guests but suppliers. Their beverage distributor reps typically vacation during the summer months, so deliveries are apt to be spotty or nonexistent. Though distributors usually warn restaurants to place orders in advance of these interruptions, Old Guard restaurateurs tend to shrug it off for fear of placing too big an order. *Why tie up so much cash in inventory?* goes their thinking. Most traditional restaurants take their chances: *if we run out, we run out.* But if you can predict your patronage with accuracy, you'll have the confidence to place, say, a $60,000 alcohol order, as Navy Beach recently did. They were able to do it because their beverage rep's annual vacation is embedded in their digital calendar, and they have a firm grasp of their "item trends"—just how many bottles of each type of wine, beer, or spirits they are likely to sell during that time.

Macro-events also affect restaurants' revenues. These are the obvious holidays that everyone celebrates. In the United States, they're days such as Valentine's Day, Mother's Day, Thanksgiving, and Christmas. Navy Beach's season is punctuated by three major holidays—Memorial Day, Labor Day, and the Fourth of July. Predicting how many guests you're likely to get on the first two holidays is fairly straightforward because Memorial and Labor Day always fall on a Monday. Fourth of July is a bit of a wild card, since it can fall on any day of the week, so managers and owners need to carefully analyze their logbook and calendar to plan ahead for the Fourth. Easter Sunday—the traditional start of the season for many businesses—also moves annually, so restaurants have to be ready for bigger-than-usual crowds on unusually warm days from Easter on.

So if your business needs to generate as much revenue as possible in the shortest window of time, how can you do it? One way is to work as efficiently as possible and reduce the amount of work your staff has to do. Ten minutes is a long time for a guest to wait in a restaurant setting. While a server retraces his or her steps a half dozen times to place orders or fetch forgotten utensils for one table, the clock is ticking. In addition to guest frustration, there's the equally problematic issue of not turning tables as quickly as possible in the course of a night.

As Franklin analyzed his servers' Server Scorecard, he could see right away that some of his servers needed coaching, while others were so good at their jobs that he was compelled to study what they were doing differently. One woman was remarkably good at serving "deuces"— two-person tables. Her overall lunch tabs weren't as high as some of the other servers—$35 per guest, say, versus their $40—but she turned over her tables three times to their two. Her virtuosity was evident in the mathematical narrative of her shift: $\$35 \times 3 > \$40 \times 2$. Watching her in the course of several shifts, Franklin realized that she had mastered the art of making the fewest number of trips to each table.

Top-selling servers have a knack for sizing up tables at a glance and tailoring their service accordingly. They can tell if guests are there for a leisurely drawn-out meal, a fast dinner before an evening engagement, a quick dessert and coffee, just drinks, or something else. A huge family with kids? Get water for everyone and ask if you can bring bread and appetizers, pronto. The best servers didn't wait for guests to ask what was good; they immediately volunteered the specials, as well as what was popular, and a few of their personal favorites. This accelerated ordering, drawing people's attention to items that they might otherwise have missed. Such servers were so efficient that every time they touched the table, they were taking or delivering another order, or dropping off the check.

How many times have you spied a server bringing an appealing dish to a table and asked, "What're they having? I'll have that!" We've all done it, even those of us in the business. We do it for the same reason homebuyers prefer to see a house filled with furniture to fully grasp its potential. Visual cues are always far more powerful than the printed word. But there's something even more powerful: clear, persuasive *advice* from a person in the know. Personalized advice that conveys the message: *You don't want to miss this.*

Because of everything he was learning, Franklin came

to see dessert menus as antiquated. Too much reading and interpretation. Too many steps. Now he coaches servers to return to each table near the end of the meal and say something like, "The kitchen has four great desserts tonight. The Key lime pie. The bread pudding, *which is my favorite.* The chocolate mousse. And a raspberry sorbet. What kind of coffee can I get you?" Most of the time, someone pipes up for coffee, and once that happens, the rest of the table capitulates to sharing one or more of the desserts. *Great,* says the server, *I'll bring four forks.*

For Franklin and Martin, looking at the numbers was like analyzing a massive operations management study on their own restaurant. They could zero in on servers who were doing something right, and reverse-engineer their tactics to coach others on those best practices. They were *investing* in their staff in a way most owners never do. The restaurant industry is renowned for having a high burnout rate. Most eateries lose 50 percent of their staff over the course of a year, says Martin, and are constantly hanging out the HELP WANTED shingle. Navy Beach enjoys an 80 percent retention rate. "They want to come back every season," Martin tells me. "They know we groomed them properly. They know guests love it here, and they can see it in their tips."

This book is about so much more than data. It's really about *creativity.* I don't care how many statistical insights you lay before entrepreneurs, they will not be able to harness the full worth of these insights unless they push themselves to be creative with the results—unless they obsess and dream up ways to grow their business and impress their guests. Data and technology are only as good as the way they are used.

Earl Nightingale, the late radio personality and motivational speaker, used to tell a story about a man who ran a gas station in Arizona. The man was filling a customer's tank one day when he happened to see his customer pacing around in front of the mechanic shop, bored out of his mind, and jingling change in his pocket. *He has money in his pocket,* the gas station owner thought to himself. *He'd buy something from me right now but I have nothing to sell him but gas.* From that day forward, the gas station owner began stocking everything he could think of: auto supplies, sporting goods, trinkets for kids, soft drinks, a variety of snacks. He transformed his business on the strength of that insight.

Once Martin and Franklin began to absorb the message that their business was critically dependent on time and weather, they began to see opportunities everywhere to grow Navy Beach's business. In every case, the data drove the insight, and their creativity addressed the insight.

For example, when they analyzed their hourly sales over the past five Sundays, the hourly trend data confirmed that Sunday sales dropped precipitously after three p.m. Makes sense, right? Sunday, the day when everyone fled back to Manhattan, is typically one of their slowest days. From morning on, they were treated to the sight of cars, cabs, or people toting rollaboard suitcases past their restaurant on the way to the station. They found themselves thinking: *If we had a place for them to park their luggage, they'd spend more time with us, and leave when it's time to catch their train.* So they started checking their guests' bags, and it worked. Why? Well, because the Montauk train station is just down the block. Franklin and Martin maximized the amount of time those visitors were in their place and made it easy for them to stop by for one more drink, one more Navy Burger with bacon-onion marmalade and Cabot cheddar. And sales on Sunday spiked.

The fact that they sold numerous cases of rosé wine over the course of the summer got them thinking about ways that they could grow that business. Rosé has become the drink of choice for this summer crowd, so much so that the national media has a field day each summer when local bottle shops and importers announce with utter seriousness that they are in danger of running out. *There's only so much wine an importer can fit into a shipping container from France,* they say, *and local Hamptons vineyards such as Wölffer Estate only bottle about twenty thousand cases a year.*

Franklin and Martin's use of data to crack the "Great Rosé Challenge" was masterful. First they analyzed their hourly checks and discovered that during peak hours—six to eight p.m., just before sunset—the number of checks flowing to the bar increased 100 percent. The bar was always slammed during that two-hour period, and the bartenders were struggling to keep up with orders. Next, they analyzed their average party size and discovered that the bigger groups always tended to come on Saturdays. Careful attention to their "item sales trends" revealed that over the past four years, their rosé consumption had doubled.

These three pieces of information suggested that there was a missed opportunity. How could they better handle the Saturday night crush for drinks? They couldn't add more bartenders and servers because there just wasn't enough room for them all behind the bar. The answer was staring them in the face: if you can't make cocktails faster, serve more of the easiest-served drinks. Judging from the sales figures, they decided to replace labor-intensive cocktails with large-format rosé wines.

They began carrying a greater range of rosés and stocking increasingly *larger* bottles beyond the traditional "standard" 750-milliliter wine bottles (which serve four to five glasses), such as magnums (twelve glasses), jeroboams (twenty-four glasses), and methuselahs (forty-eight glasses). Now, granted, these aren't sizes you'd regularly buy for your home, but if you're out with a group of friends and everyone's drinking, it might make sense to order the bigger bottle. Seeing a server marching across the sand with a gargantuan bottle destined for your group seems to give everyone a thrill. After all, presentation is everything.

And if you're a New Guard restaurateur thinking of the numbers, large-format wine makes good sense. As Franklin explains, "Big bottles are more efficient. The bartender pulls out the bottle, the server makes one delivery to the table, pulls the cork, and everyone's done for a while. It's gotten to the point where our guests, without even thinking, will go up to the bar and order a magnum."

Another time, Martin came in one morning and said, "We need to get a boat."

It turns out, he'd been studying the data on how the weather impacted covers. On clear, windless days, you'll recall, their numbers drop because people are out enjoying the beach—and boaters are out enjoying the water. Martin had been thinking about the lone surface road that led to their tucked-out-of-the-way spot on the beach, and about the *entire ocean* in their backyard. Could he attract boaters to the restaurant on those sunny days when they were out on the water? There is no dock on their bay, but already some of the larger yachts were dropping anchor there and lowering a small launch, or inflatable motorboat, to ride to shore. At first, it was a surprise seeing guests showing up on the sand, fresh off the water. But there was a world of other boaters out there in smaller vessels that weren't transporting second boats and whose passengers had no plans to swim to shore. Why should the yachtsmen have all the fun? What if getting guests to shore was as easy as a mobile phone call to the restaurant?

So, in keeping with the theme of the restaurant, they found a refurbished 1967 Boston Whaler dinghy, a sweet little wooden vessel with an attached motor, that they could use to run out and pick up guests on the water. During crunch time when there's no staff to perform the task, Martin himself hops aboard the dinghy, nicknamed Torpedo, and pilots out to ferry guests in. He's delivering first-rate customer service, maximizing the number of people who have access to his restaurant, and single-handedly transforming Navy Beach's weather data. Historically, their numbers have always *dropped* on nice days. Now, covers on those days have increased because sunny days are precisely when boaters hit the water. Franklin and Martin managed to sew up a small gap in their sales record with a stylish, low-cost addition to the Navy Beach story.

Another bit of creativity is their way of handling weddings and other private events. Here, too, the numbers guide them. Say a couple wants to be married on a Saturday, and their budget is $25,000. Franklin, who usually handles such events, asks if they're open to options—like a daytime wedding or a nontraditional date. Then he begins studying his digital calendar and its historical sales data to figure out how much to charge. He asks himself, "According to our historical data, when is the next Saturday where we're likely to earn well *under* $25,000?" In other words, what day in the future will that wedding income actually represent a profit over and above what they're already predicted to earn? He compares, say, the same Tuesday and Saturday date in a particular month over the past four seasons. He then compares the revenue he made on those dates, daytime versus nighttime. That tells him exactly how to price those dates and times.

The average Old Guard wedding booker, without consulting any date, will tell a couple, "It'll be cheaper if you get married on a Saturday in October instead of a Saturday in July." Sure, the ideal thing is to schedule weddings toward the end of the season—September and October. But if you have a good handle on your data, you can squeeze weddings into weekdays during the high season. Franklin's able to quote a specific price for a Tuesday, Wednesday, or

Sunday afternoon in *July* down to the penny. That's a significant difference.

Franklin doesn't like to close their beach for private parties; it irritates regular guests. And he doesn't want to close the entire restaurant for private events; it's rarely in their best interest. Chances are, they'll lose money doing it. But they *will* do it if the price is right. Sometimes a whale materializes—a high roller or a ridiculously big spender. A hedge-fund guy hosting an event for investors. A paterfamilias with deep pockets who cannot bear the thought of his daughter marrying on a Thursday.

"I'll pay you seventy thousand dollars to close the restaurant."

"Well, *okay.*"

Whales are nice to do business with, but they do muck up the data. They're such anomalies that you have to exclude them from your annual averages the following year.

Martin and Franklin have come a long way from the days when they took down reservations by hand. Today, Navy Beach has access to real-time operational data. Our software polls their POS device every couple of minutes, and the raw data is transformed in the cloud, where it becomes instantly available via our mobile application. The software tells them which table has been experiencing slow service, or has had a check open for several hours, or which table hasn't been ordering wine. If you were to come in during one of the busy meal periods, you'd see Martin walking around the restaurant, occasionally glancing at his iPhone as he summons relevant data that will tell him what he ought to be checking on at this very moment.

Since opening the restaurant, all of the Navy Beach partners have moved to the Montauk area. Martin has gotten to know other restaurateurs who own eateries on the beach but don't share his appreciation for data. He tells me about a neighbor who says he doesn't use data.

"How can you run a business like that?" Martin chastised him. "What if you run out of beer?"

"Hey, it happens," the other guy shrugged, like it was a fact of life.

Martin walked away, shaking his head.

That's crazy, Martin thought. *At Navy Beach, we never run out of beer. We never run out of anything.*

That's the beauty of data. And that's why places like Navy Beach will still be in business when their competitors have been lost to the winter wind.

· 2 ·

STARTUP TO VEGAS, BABY

I first got into the hospitality business as a busboy, working for a restaurant with the unlikely name of Ginsberg & Wong. It was an unusual concept: Jewish deli meets Chinese, where matzo ball soup cozied up to shrimp lo mein. The place was housed in a fourteen-story, 409-room Hyatt Hotel in Cherry Hill, New Jersey, not far from Haddonfield, where I grew up. I loved that job, loved watching the spirited choreography of the chefs, kitchen help, and servers. Most of all, I loved the way the guests flowed in as the evening wore on, selected dishes off the menu, and then kicked back to relax and enjoy dinner. I still have fond memories of chowing down on leftover spare ribs and Chinese chicken wings with a soda in the back room where we kept the silverware after breaking down the Wednesday night all-you-can-eat buffet.

I was sixteen the day I observed a portly female guest

gesturing toward her neck. Her husband was trying to get her to speak. But anyone who'd spent any time in restaurants knew she couldn't. Her face was turning beet red.

She was choking.

I dropped my water pitcher and dashed from the kitchen door to her side. It took me three tries to get my arms around her large body, but my fingers finally found each other and tugged—once, twice—and out popped a mouthful of food.

Her relieved husband tipped me five dollars. And later that night, the general manager treated me to a cheeseburger. I felt like a hero.

Something else stayed with me about that job—the wisdom of the hotel's manager. Many times Stephen, who ran the entire Hyatt, would pull me aside and ask, "Do you like the hospitality business, Damian?"

I did. I could see myself spending my life in it.

"If you want to be successful in this business," Stephen went on, "you only need to remember one thing—exceed customer expectations!"

It was the sort of aphorism grown-ups offer up to kids all the time, and the kind kids mentally tuck away without realizing the implications.

I went to college and ended up on Wall Street, learning how to build spreadsheets and underwrite high-yield bonds instead of cleaning up in a kitchen. But my passion for food never left me. Anyone who works in corporate finance is familiar with the closing dinner, when the deal team and client get together to break bread, congratulate themselves, and have a good time. I always made sure I was in charge of picking the restaurant venues, choosing the menu, carefully selecting the right dishes and wine pairings. Years after Ginsberg & Wong, the glory of the restaurant business was still in my blood.

I attended Harvard Business School, where I worked with my professor, Gary Loveman, on a thesis studying themed restaurants, trying to analyze what made places like Rainforest Café so special—and how a smart restaurateur could help a venue like that gain repeat guests long after the novelty wore off. Rainforest Café was an interesting—albeit production-heavy—example of a themed restaurant. Each of its twenty-nine locations worldwide is designed to look as if you are dining in the midst of a tropical rainforest. The dining spaces are decorated with trees, waterfalls, and animatronic animals. Depending on the location, you can expect to be treated to volcanic eruptions, rolling fog, or torrential thunderstorms. It's a good time.

But it wasn't until after I got my MBA that I landed a job, working as the chief financial officer of a restaurant group in New York City. My boss was a chef who had four restaurants and a catering company. But he was a whiz at food, not money management. What little he had, he spent. What I learned the first day on the job scared the hell out of me. I soon became a frustrated CFO. The company reaped millions in revenue a year, serving hundreds of guests daily, but we didn't have any data to govern our purchasing, hiring, or training.

It was crazy.

My boss, his restaurant managers, and chefs couldn't answer basic business questions such as: "Who are your top and bottom performers?" and "What are your most profitable menu items?"

Many times, I sensed that they were concocting an answer to pacify me. On occasions when the general managers and chefs of our restaurants earnestly tried to research responses for me, I'd later learn that they were spending hours in their back offices, printing out tons of paper instead of doing what they were supposed to be doing— spending time in the dining room with the guests or in the kitchen with their staff. They simply did not have the tools to help any of us do our jobs better.

For months I went around wondering if we were the only company who suffered from this kind of institutional blindness. *Is it just us,* I'd think, *or do all restaurants in the industry struggle with this?*

In fact, the longer I worked there, the more I realized the awful truth: this problem plagued the entire restaurant industry. The answers to these key business questions were buried away and deeply inaccessible in our POS systems and a bunch of Excel spreadsheets.

As a result, I didn't see how my boss's restaurants could do anything *but* disappoint his guests and investors. Without proper planning, his kitchens were running out of critical ingredients. We'd under-order food and disappoint guests. We'd over-order and waste ingredients. And we were always under- or over-staffing our restaurants. It was a lethal combination.

So I set out to change it. After all, I thought, *This is 1999! No one runs a business without data, right?* Wrong. The chef-owner thought of himself as an artist. He had little interest in what he probably thought was a minor business detail. Meanwhile, his cash flow was so tight that I was forced to scrape together the money each month to pay our vendors, including the sanitation contractors who hauled away trash from our restaurants. This much the world of restaurant finance had taught me: *Always, always, always pay the garbage guys.*

I was once on the receiving end of a sanitation man's dead-eyed stare in my office after I'd told him we'd have to pay next week. *Holy shit,* I thought, as he made an obscene gesture at me. *These guys could hurt me.* No businessman wants to go through that, believe me. Virtually everyone else will float a restaurant till the money comes in. But if the owner stiffs the Teamsters, he's in a world of pain.

All of these shortcomings forced me to obsess on the ways I could help my boss make an impact on his guests and grow his business.

That's when the words of Stephen, my old boss at the Hyatt, returned: *Exceed expectations!*

It makes perfect sense. You walk into a dumpy-looking joint for a quick bite, not expecting much, and order the blue-plate special at a nominal price. If what shows up is average fare for average money, you eat your meal—it's what you expected—and never come back. But if what lands before you is the most amazing dish—the best Philadelphia cheesesteak you've ever tasted—suddenly you're telling everyone about this hole-in-the-wall. The disparity between low cost and high quality, between low expectations and outsize satisfaction, jumps out at you in a way that is impossible to forget. After all, how often does that happen in life?

By the same token, if you score reservations at a fine dining establishment after months of hearing rave reviews, but the food and service are unremarkable, or only ordinary, what will your response be? *Yeah, I went there,* you'll tell anyone who'll listen. *Cost an arm and a leg, and they kept us waiting for forty-five minutes. The food was meh.* What is the likelihood of you going back?

During this period of my career, I became convinced that there had to be a way to eliminate the risk inherent in managing restaurants. I began to think about software that could help the most stubborn, analytics-averse restaurants, chefs, and owners. If I could make it easy for guys like our chef and managers to crunch data with their busy schedules, I thought, I just might solve the biggest obstacle to exceeding those expectations in the restaurant business.

Eventually I left to start my own company focused on solving this critical problem. I had virtually no money, so I indulged in my own brand of fiscal irresponsibility. I called Harvard Business School and asked them to defer my student loans. Then I bootstrapped the company until my first round of financing came through, by floating my new business for several months on credit cards.

My initial team was made up of two kinds of people who theoretically shouldn't mix: restaurant people (a chef, a sommelier, and a former restaurant manager) and a team of techies.

At least once a week one of the software guys would pull me aside to complain about one of the chefs: "What are *they* doing here? They can't even write code!"

And at least once a week one of the restaurant guys

would pull me aside to bitch about the coders. "They're a bunch of geeks. They've never worked in restaurants!"

Both groups kicked and screamed, but I held firm. "Restaurateurs—please be nice to the techies. Without them. we won't be able to change the industry! Techies—you can't build anything without consulting with the restaurateurs. Otherwise it will never be easy to use. You guys have to huddle up," I told them. "We're not doing anything without everyone in the room agreeing."

A funny thing happened. It took several months, but the food guys eventually became tech savvy. In the morning I'd find them hunched over their laptops, testing what the software guys had created. The former owner of an Upper East Side restaurant brought his old POS machine to work and started tinkering with the data we extracted from it; he eventually became head of product development and today writes software code himself.

The software engineers—guys who had little interest in food culture—were soon talking about the foie gras they had tried at some hip new restaurant the night before. Over time they became devout foodies and wine lovers.

That became the culture of Avero to this day. But my work with them was just beginning. Eventually we had software that we could show to restaurateurs. Among our first customers were Danny Meyer and chef Tom Colicchio, back in the days when they were partners in the legendary New York restaurant Gramercy Tavern. Shortly after, we worked with chefs such as Daniel Boulud, Geoffrey Zakarian, Wolfgang Puck, and Bobby Flay; restaurants such as China Grill and Sushisamba, which I mentioned in Chapter 1; restaurant groups such as BR Guest, Lettuce Entertain You, and the Gerber Group. Avero was off to the races.

To grow my business, I knew I needed to attract even larger clients. Naturally, I thought of my old Harvard Business School mentor, Gary Loveman. Gary was an MIT-trained economist and PhD with a fascination for customer service in the hospitality industry. Now, incredibly, he was commuting regularly from the Boston area to Las Vegas, where he had taken on the position of chief executive officer of Harrah's Entertainment, one of the largest gaming companies in the world.

So I packed a bag and my laptop.

I was heading to Vegas, baby.

Shortly before I arrived in Las Vegas, Jeffrey Frederick, the young executive and former chef that I introduced you to earlier, was nervously pacing the gaming floor of the Brazilian-themed Rio All-Suites Hotel & Casino, one of the casinos owned and operated by his employer, Harrah's Entertainment.

Jeffrey was in his early thirties with jet-black hair and an imposing frame. He'd been working about five years behind the scenes in various Harrah's kitchens. But he was hardly an anonymous presence. His fellow chefs always knew when their executive chef was coming. In the kitchen Jeffrey wore a shirt and tie under his chef's jacket, wooden clogs, and a twelve-inch toque—the hat favored by chefs—that dwarfed everyone else's in the room. Given his size and getup, you could *hear* him coming—*clack, clack, clack*—a mile away.

For a while he'd served as the company's corporate chef, flying out to their far-flung operations around the United States, training the chefs in their riverboat and Native American gaming operations. Back in Vegas, he'd been tapped for a promotion—to be the firm's vice president of food and beverage. At the time, the Rio alone had seventeen restaurants.

As he strolled the casino floor in his new position, Jeffrey knew that his life had been changed forever. His promotion meant that he'd oversee every morsel of food and every drop of liquid refreshment consumed by guests in this resort.

Jeffrey's boss, Tom Jenkin, a friendly Montanan, led his young mentee around the floor of the Rio. Tom, then the Rio's general manager, was legendary and still is after forty years in the business. He had started his career as a fry cook at one of the Harrah's resorts in 1975. No doubt he saw a lot of himself in Jeffrey. The two had a good relationship, with Tom feeling comfortable enough to call Jeffrey by the affectionate nickname "Bubba."

The two men paused at each of the food venues: the classic Vegas buffet; the bars; the flashier sit-down eateries. They stood on the carpet and watched as a parade of cocktail servers in sexy, Brazilian-style outfits made the rounds of the slot machine guests with their trays. Tom paused within sight of the blackjack table, nodded his chin at the action, and said, "What do you see?"

He led Jeffrey to the poker room, where they watched deadly serious players facing off across their hands of cards. "What do you see?" Tom asked again.

Well, shit, Jeffrey thought. *What* do *I see?*

Tom was asking Jeffrey if he was noticing the body language of the casino's guests, the sorts of nonverbal cues every practicing food and beverage (F&B) vice president worth his salt can pick out at a glance. Seasoned F&B guys can tell in a second if the cocktail servers are lingering too long at their stations, leaving parched guests in their wake. They can tell if someone seated in a restaurant is waiting for drinks, food, dessert, or the check—all at a glance. They know that if a guest has a cocktail napkin in front of him but no drink, the server has probably come and taken his order. Their eyes will take in a guest's melted ice, diluted cocktail, and castaway plastic straw, and they will immediately know that person is in desperate need of a fresh beverage. They can tell if guests are enjoying themselves or not. And they know exactly which employees and employee behaviors are wasting the company's money.

But at this stage, Jeffrey didn't really grasp what Tom was driving at. He tossed off a few comments that missed the mark, before Tom gently filled him in.

I'm messing up here, Jeffrey thought, feeling a sense of insecurity creeping into his mind. He was determined to make this job work. At the time he was starting a new chapter of his life with a new girlfriend and thinking about how a blending of their family of five kids would work. His future looked a great deal brighter; he just needed to start seeing the workplace differently, to master a huge learning curve.

Of course, there was no reason Jeffrey should have expected himself to notice the cues Tom asked about. He'd spent his career in the back of the house. If you took him into the kitchen of a restaurant and asked him, "What's wrong with this kitchen line?" he'd rattle off half a dozen problems at a glance. The grill chefs didn't have enough space. The lights where the chefs set their finished plates were too low. The fryer hadn't been changed. He could spot such things cold.

But gazing out at the floor of a busy casino where food and drinks were secondary to the main course, *gambling,* he was a complete neophyte. The evidence of the health of the company's food and beverage programs was right in front of his eyes, but he had never been trained to see it.

"It's okay," Tom assured him. "It takes time."

An incredibly nice guy, Tom is also whip-smart and shrewd. He has the rare ability to cut through the BS inherent in most business meetings and get to the point faster than any other executive I've ever met. "You know, Bubba, as a chef, the job is yours forever if you want it. But out here, running all this? You have to show us that you can make a difference."

Jeffrey had no trouble reading between the lines. *Make the guests happy, make us a lot of money, or you're back in the kitchen.*

Gary Loveman was pleased to see me when I arrived for our meeting. And it was great to see him again. Loveman is a big man with broad shoulders. In the 1990s, he'd landed a consulting gig with Harrah's when he sent an earnest letter to the company's chief executive officer urging him to focus on customer loyalty. He won the business; and his consultancy ended when he took the post of chief operating officer in 1998. During that period he established the firm's first loyalty program for repeat guests, and the data he collected on those guests' habits turned Vegas on its ear.

Until then, it was a given that high rollers were Vegas's bread and butter. But Loveman's data showed something distinctly contrary: it was the slot machine gamblers, the small-time moms and pops who pumped endless coins into the one-armed bandits, who actually generated the most revenue for the casinos.

Loveman had overturned a paradigm. He took over as Harrah's CEO in early 2003. His would be a challenging reign, but during that time he turned Harrah's into Caesars Entertainment, the largest gaming empire in the world. To many, it was strange to think of an economics professor at the helm of one of the largest gaming companies in the business, but on second thought, maybe it wasn't so strange at all. Math—particularly statistics and probability—is at the heart of every gaming operation, and good old-fashioned principles governed the business side.

As I opened my laptop, I was eager to talk about statistics and food. Loveman had always been a great speaker, but he was perhaps an even better listener. He watched my presentation with growing interest. I wasn't quite done when he picked up the phone and summoned two executives—Harrah's head of analytics and the head of the western region—into his office. "Go on," he said, gesturing at my laptop. "Show them what you showed me."

Once again I patiently explained that I was helping restaurants to collect their own point-of-sale data and transforming it to glean insights into everything from identifying server strengths and weaknesses and scheduling staff, to ordering the appropriate amount of ingredients and flagging suspicious employee behavior.

When I was done, Loveman turned to his two senior executives. "Can we do anything remotely like this?"

The two men hemmed and hawed. They finally deflected by talking about how well the company was gleaning insights from their *gaming* operations. It was just as I'd suspected: they were whizzes at understanding gambling operations; but they lacked the proper tools to aggressively analyze their restaurants.

Which was perfectly understandable. Food was an afterthought in Old Guard Vegas. The Strip was legendary for $6.99 all-you-can-eat buffets. Rafts of iceberg lettuce, boatloads of mashed potatoes, stiff as glue. Prime rib so salty that an hour later your lips would feel as cured as the late Joan Rivers's marquee smile. The tourists flocked to the buffets, stuffing themselves silly, and rationalizing that because the food was so cheap, they could afford to drop more at the gaming tables. To quote the late Garry Marshall from the movie *Lost in America,* back then Vegas was still about "gam-buh-ling."

But beginning in the late 1980s, Vegas got a kick in the teeth. Casinos began popping up all over the United States. Las Vegas was no longer special. Today there are about

1,500 casinos in the United States. Anyone who has a jones to crank quarters into a slot machine can take a bus ride to the nearest commercial casino or Native American reservation to get his or her fix. When the Las Vegas bosses realized that they were losing market share, they scrambled to figure out ways to make Vegas special again.

As a result, today Vegas is no longer strictly about gam-buh-ling. It's about nightclubs, dayclubs, hotels, spas, retail, entertainment, world-class spectacle, and *quality* dining. That metamorphosis was still in its adolescence when I appeared in Loveman's office.

Loveman shooed the two executives out, then ordered a car for me. He wanted me to speak with the man they'd recently hired to run their food and beverage operations at the Rio.

"Go," Loveman said. "Talk with him."

The fellow was a chef-turned-executive named Jeffrey Frederick.

Jeffrey's office was drowning in paper and binders. He had taken to printing out reams of spreadsheets culled from Harrah's accounting operations and its restaurant cash registers, studying them at night in search of something, anything, that would help him figure out what was going on in the company's restaurants. Anyone who works in the industry is familiar with those heavy binders filled with P&L reports.

Monthly reports are critical, but their use is limited. You can't use them to identify operational insights on a daily or weekly basis. By the time an owner or GM prints those reports and clips them into a binder, their content is long outdated—a rear-view mirror perspective on a restaurant's past, so to speak. They aren't granular enough to pinpoint what a restaurateur should be doing today.

Jeffrey eyed me nervously as I entered his office, wondering what the hell I was doing there, and what I'd report back to Loveman. I was just as edgy. This meeting was critically important to me. I had maybe twenty minutes to convince him that I came in peace, and that the software on my laptop could help, not add to, his woes.

Almost immediately, we discovered that we were speaking the same language. We bonded over the fact that so many people who reported to him were unable to answer critical questions about their restaurants. In the context of a resort casino, those questions might go something like:

"How many covers are you going to do this weekend at each of our restaurants when that convention comes back to town?"

"How will the average check increase at your fine dining resturant versus your casual restaurant in light of the convention?"

"Why do you have such disparity between top and bottom servers?"

Just as I had found when I had asked similar questions during my restaurant CFO days, everyone seemed to treat Jeffrey as if he were nuts. They rolled their eyes and implied that the answers to such questions were unknowable, forever warped by anecdote and gut-feel estimates.

I promised Jeffrey that if he gave me and my team a shot, he'd have solid data at his fingertips in about a month. I found out later that as soon as I left his office, Jeffrey was on the phone to Loveman, telling him, "I'm going to go with this guy. Data is just what we're looking for."

We launched a pilot of the software at three restaurants in the Rio—the Voodoo Lounge, Buzio's, and the Cafe São Paulo. We analyzed how well servers and bartenders were serving guests at the Voodoo Lounge. We hoped that whatever we learned would help us make employees more accountable, and help Jeffrey's managers train staff accordingly. We noticed that accomplished servers had an effective way of suggesting that drinks could be made with top-shelf or super-premium liquors. When they did, a significant number of guests sprung for the higher-end items. The result? For the same amount of work, these servers brought in a ton more revenue, and higher tips—and their guests left feeling as if they'd drunk something special. With what we learned, Jeffrey's managers could reverse-engineer the best practices and train their other servers to do the same.

At Buzio's, which was popular with local businesspeople by day and tourists at night, we tried to get a handle on its entire beverage program, specifically its wine sales. At the Cafe São Paulo, we focused on what are known in the industry as "server-controlled items." Servers who forget to ring up seemingly inconsequential items such as cups of coffee or orange juice are a huge issue for restaurants. Guests often ask for such things as an afterthought, typically as their food is brought to the table. The harried server rushes to fulfill the beverage request and, in his or her haste, forgets to ring it up.

Coffee and orange juice may seem unsexy, but these "invisible" transactions can add up and bleed a restaurant dry. Our software was able to surmise when such moments had occurred. It all came down to tracking a server's "item per cover" metric, which is typically expressed as a percentage, and is analogous to a baseball player's on-base percentage. For instance, if my coffee item per cover is 50 percent, and yours is 20 percent, it means that for every one hundred customers, I'm typically serving coffee fifty times, and you're serving coffee only twenty times. If your coffee or juice item per cover never changes, and you're routinely lower than all your fellow servers, then your employers are within their rights to talk to you about why you're forgetting to ring up those items, or single you out for focused training. It may seem like a lot of trouble to go to, but when a restaurant is struggling, buttoning up server-controlled items can make a difference. The income derived from coffee and orange juice really is like free money.

So, as the software collected numbers, Jeffrey became a man obsessed, dreaming up new metrics to better understand his employees and the businesses.

As I eventually came to realize, Jeffrey is a natural overachiever. He had learned from his mother that you work hard, then you work hard some more. It was she who had insisted that as a teenager, Jeffrey meet her every day after school at the Doubletree in Aurora, Colorado, where she worked. A Taiwanese immigrant, Jeffrey's mother didn't trust Jeffrey's peers, or the schools that educated them. She made Jeffrey plunk himself down at a table in the empty employee break room to do his homework while she was upstairs cleaning rooms. He was not allowed to leave the premises. Being home alone, in her eyes, invited trouble. And so Jeffrey completed his schoolwork in the silence of an empty restaurant, bored out of his mind. Every day, he would watch the hotel chef and his staff carry in deliveries from the loading dock. One day they asked him, "Hey kid, you wanna give us a hand?" Delighted to have something to do, he did whatever they needed: carried supplies in, ran the dishwasher, cleaned; he worked his butt off. The day the chef handed him a knife to chop some vegetables, he knew he'd found his calling.

Jeffrey's father had worked for decades as a comptroller with the US Air Force, and somehow his son inherited the older man's facility and fascination with numbers.

Jeffrey had become his parents' son: hardworking, indefatigable, someone who thrived on facts and data. Bury him with paperwork at the close of business, and he'd go home that night, eat his dinner with his brood of five kids, then do a deep dive into the digits, color-coding and using Post-its like crazy. The next morning, if one of the bosses asked a question about the previous day's tallies, as Jeffrey's colleagues looked nervously at each other and started reaching for their spreadsheets, Jeffrey usually had the answer.

He began asking his chefs to weigh the food they discarded from the Rio's buffets at the end of each shift to estimate how much guests were actually eating and how much the casino should prep. That directive drastically reduced food waste. He asked chefs to draw maps of their kitchens, pinpointing exactly where their line cooks and sous chefs were standing. That helped him determine if kitchen staffing had become redundant. If he saw that a restaurant was tossing out too many unfinished plates, he'd call in his chefs and deconstruct their entire menus, tweaking entrées, reducing the proteins or appetizers that often went unfinished.

Later, when our software showed that 80 percent of parties served in one of the casino's restaurants consisted of only two people, Jeffrey stomped through the casino to stand in the doorway of the São Paulo, a restaurant under renovation. What he saw made him see red. Most of the tables they were planning to install were four-person tables—known in the business as "four-tops." When two people show up to dine at a restaurant filled with four-tops, "table yield"—the amount of income earned per table—plummets. People end up waiting at the door, and the restaurant is not using its seating to its fullest potential. I suspected that guest satisfaction also dropped on those occasions, because people are waiting too long for tables.

When Jeffrey told the architect to toss out the four-tops and install deuces instead, he encountered resistance. Apparently, four- and six-tops look nicer on blueprints. *Tough—we can't do that,* Jeffrey thought. A server could always push two deuces together to make a four-top. Or push three together to make a six-top.

It just wasn't the way things had always been done. The same casinos that had deconstructed the engineering behind slot machines, roulette tables, and craps tables had never given a thought to the earning potential of their restaurant designs.

The architects were not the only ones irritated at the way this big-shouldered new VP was doing things. One longtime chef who had started his career as a butcher balked when Jeffrey deigned to ask for a report on how much beef, fish, and poultry he was cutting on a daily and weekly basis. If someone in human resources happened to ask why so many of the longtime employees were leaving and the younger chefs were being promoted, those fleeing griped that they had been hired to cook beans—not count them.

Looking back, Jeffrey wonders if he tried to change things a little too quickly. But his measures were saving the company millions of dollars. And that restaurant that was filled with deuces? That space was suddenly turning a decent profit. And when Jeffrey began attending meetings with the bosses and his general managers, they were all throwing around the new lingo that could only have come from the software Jeffrey used. Unbidden, they bragged about their restaurants, using restaurant metrics such as average checks, table turn times, table yields, average daily and weekly covers, item per cover, and so on. What he had started innocently in his office at the Rio had risen all the way to the top. And the young employees Jeffrey was training along the way—chefs and servers and GMs—began to look up to him and speak the same language.

This tension and transformation were being played out against a larger, overarching corporate story. Under Gary Loveman's regime, Harrah's had gone on a buying spree, snapping up more casinos—Bally's, the Flamingo, Paris, and Caesars Palace. During this time, the firm increased its holdings from fourteen to more than fifty-four casino and changed its name from Harrah's to Caesars Entertainment.

Suddenly, Jeffrey found himself running restaurants in three different Caesars casinos—the Paris, Bally's, and Planet Hollywood—and consulting with his superiors and his counterparts on restaurant developments happening at other Caesars resorts in the city. Like a growing brood of children, the restaurants under his purview all needed attention: staffing decisions, menu tweaks, and serious data analysis.

These were pretty exciting years for both of us. Just as we were getting a handle on things, Caesars decided to add *new* restaurants, particularly ones branded by celebrity chefs. That, they decided, was the wave of the future.

· 3 ·

THE UNDERGROUND CULINARY TOUR
(PART 1)

I'm standing in a rooftop restaurant at the NoMad Hotel in New York City, part of the same hot restaurant group run by Will Guidara and Daniel Humm, who also operate Eleven Madison Park, recently ranked the third best restaurant in the annual ranking, The World's 50 Best Restaurants. The views outside the windows of this elegant old Beaux Arts building are stunning. It feels as if I can practically touch the Empire State Building.

But instead of gazing out at the view, I'm staring intently at a pretzel sandwich.

Chef James Kent has outdone himself with these scrumptious single bites, appetizers he's prepared for the kickoff of my annual event. There's tuna tartare so fresh it smells of the sea on crisp toasts with black olives minced so finely that they almost resemble caviar. French breakfast radishes, butter dipped, with salt. Ultra-fresh crudite with chive cream. Fried chicken bits with yogurt, chili, and lime dip. And last, this chubby little sandwich the size of a slider, the bread an almost perfectly round sphere fashioned of pretzel dough, topped with coarse salt and stuffed with ham, cheese, and a pickle. I'm about to devour it in a single, satisfying bite.

But then I remember.

As the co-host of the Underground Culinary Tour, I have to serve as a good example for the fifteen other restaurant leaders from across the country I've invited to New York for the culinary experience of their lives. I have to pace myself. We've lost a few of our guests over the years to food fatgiue. I have to make do with a bite.

The start of our two-day journey into the frontiers of New York cuisine feels a little like a freshman college mixer. As I look around the room, I see awkward glances and shy smiles. This is the first time my guests have been in the same room together. Dressed in their best casual Friday attire and radiating their best corporate behavior, they trade curt handshakes and murmur light, nonthreatening industry gossip.

You can't buy a ticket to this event; you have to be invited, by me or my Culinary Tour partner and cofounder, Alice Elliot, CEO of the hospitality industry's most sought-out and respected executive search firm, The Elliot Group. Alice, a longtime friend and mentor, has served on Avero's advisory board for years, giving me the benefit of her thoughtful insights and advice.

Our host today is Jeffrey Tascarella, who is making sure everyone is feeling at home at NoMad. Our guests are all major decision-makers—CEOs, owners, founders—for large restaurant chains, up-and-coming regional restaurant groups, or even small independent groups. Together, their companies feed millions of people a year. Kat Cole, who runs Cinnabon, is chatting amiably with Randy De-Witt and Jack Gibbons of Front Burner Resturants. In the past, we've had other progressive, forward-thinking casual-dining CEOs on the tour, such as Rick Federico from P.F. Chang's; Sally Smith from Buffalo Wild Wings; G. J. Hart from California Pizza Kitchen; Sandy Beall, the founder of Blackberry Farm and Ruby Tuesday; Ian Baines, the CEO at Cheddar's Scratch Kitchen; and Bill Freeman, the CEO at Michael Mina.

At this point, everyone's being exceedingly polite. But as Chef Kent brings out each new course, I can see their eyes widen. There's a look of consternation and concern on some of my guests' faces. Wow, they're thinking, this is a lot of food. What the heck did I sign up for?

The Avero-Elliot Underground Culinary Tour is a highly secretive trendspotting tour of New York City restaurants that Alice and I created back in 2007. Over the next two days, our shuttle bus will whisk guests to fifteen or more restaurants and culinary and beverage destinations in the restaurant capital of the world. The goal? To eat, drink, listen, learn. Specifically, they're here to drink in ideas and trends that they can embrace or adapt and can put into practice back home.

I think that in order to be a true New Guard restaurateur, you must embrace both data *and* foodie trends. The future of this business lies not just in technology, but creativity and avant-garde thinking as well. The most efficient restaurants on the planet could also serve the most uninspiring food and cater to a dwindling clientele—and many do. On the Underground Culinary Tour I want my guests to draw inspiration from any and *all* elements of restaurateurship. What these executives see in the world's most cutting-edge eateries will ultimately flow to restaurants on Main Street, both in America and around the world.

The tour has taken on the lore of legend for foodies, long whispered about but never penetrated by journalists or other outsiders. Alice and I are very selective about who we invite to our annual event. A lot of the CEOs I meet recognize that the restaurant world is changing, but they're less interested in changing *their* game. Worse, they aren't convinced that their guests in the heartland want them to do so. Frankly, I don't want that kind of Old Guard thinking on the tour. I look for industry executives who are open-minded, people who are willing to think innovatively about what they're seeing and tasting, and willing to entertain the idea that what happens in the Big Apple could very well be the next trend in Dubuque or Fort Worth.

For a year before the first executive flies into town, I sift through a couple hundred New York restaurants, selecting about seventy that I personally visit and dine at in search of those that I think are doing something innovative and groundbreaking. I whittle that list down to about thirty or so, then start approaching them to see if they're game to be one of the fifteen to twenty hosts for the next year's tour. Typically, those negotiations and logistics continue up to the last minute, with Alice, my staff, and me hammering out a grueling schedule and series of customized menus together with our host restaurants and venues. A few restaurants I approach decide not to participate. Chefs and owners can be extremely protective about their ideas, and concerned about sharing the secrets of their success with others. I've had other chefs and owners turn me down because of the demographic of my guests. "Why should I help some restaurant chain?" I've heard more than once.

I don't push or judge. If people don't want to join in the fun of the tour or its mission, I move on to the next cutting-edge establishment. I am gratified that over the years, some of the top and emerging names in food have been willing—even delighted—to share their knowledge with our tour. We've visited restaurants such as Brooklyn Bowl, L'Artusi, Mermaid Oyster Bar, Roberta's, Meatball Shop, Everyman Espresso, and Eataly. We always stay at foodie hotels where food and beverage are integral to the experience. And we've met with people like chef Daniel Boulud, who once hosted us at his French-American brasserie DBGB, brewmaster Garrett Oliver at the Brooklyn Brewery, whose beverages are consumed the world over, chef Tom Colicchio, who elevated simple ingredients to the level of art, and Danny Meyer, the restaurateur who has revolutionized the concept of hospitality.

Sipping or noshing until the wee hours of the morning may sound like a foodie's idea of paradise on paper, but it's exhausting to eat so much food in so little time. That's why, at the opening reception at the NoMad, Alice dutifully warns everyone to pace themselves. It's a marathon, not a sprint. To make it to the end without collapsing from overeating, they must eat the way professional wine critics taste wine. If they like what a chef or server is offering, they ought to try a single bite of everything and stop there. If they *enjoy* what they've tasted, they can take two bites. Or three, if they *love* it. Anything more and they're liable to pass out before we hit our midnight break to catch a few hours of sleep. Over the years, a few of my guests have passed out on the bus from food fatigue.

Is our crusade to educate restaurateurs and transform America's palates working? I think so. I'm proud of the outsize impact our tour has had. Jeffrey Frederick recalls that he'd never really thought about kale as an interesting and healthy ingredient until he tasted it in a salad served on our 2011 tour. When he returned home to Vegas and touted kale to his chefs, they pooh-poohed it at first. Its texture was too fibrous, its taste too strident, its look too, well, weird for American palates. "Let's do it anyway," Frederick urged his chefs, and soon that single ingredient began showing up in entrées and salads all over Sin City, and before long, throughout the country.

That was also the year that I unveiled to executives a small North Carolina–based artisanal coffee roasting company called Counter Culture and its unique way of training baristas. Despite the ubiquity of Starbucks, this higher-quality brand is now making its way into third-wave coffee shops and increasingly onto restaurant menus all over North America.

One year we were privileged to hear the late mixologist Sasha Petraske, the young man who pioneered the modern speakeasy movement, hold forth on the subject of cocktails. Sasha was truly an original. In 1999, Sasha opened a small bar, Milk & Honey, on New York's Lower East Side, taking a deliberately old-fashioned approach to his drink making. He never served a single syrup in his place that he didn't personally hand make, or a single juice that he didn't hand squeeze. His techniques were later embraced by millions of mixologists the world over.

We visited Sasha at one of his bars, Little Branch. I remember him saying that if you run low on lime juice, there is only one legitimate thing a conscientious bartender can do. When there's a break in the action, he or she must squeeze more, even if exhausted and short-staffed. Those who labor behind the bar must never, ever resort to prepackaged juice, or, heaven help them, concentrate.

Different cocktails, he noted, require different sizes of ice cubes, lest their flavors be compromised too quickly by melting ice after they are served. Since restaurant ice machines typically pump out the same uniform size of often-hollow ice cubes, Sasha and the legions of bartenders he'd trained or inspired bought or froze their own giant blocks of ice, which they cut and shaped by hand to craft their artisanal cocktails. This has become a major trend in the world of great cocktails, one that few guests recognize on a daily basis unless they're obsessed with the craft cocktail movement. I could see the assembled executives' eyes pop during Sasha's presentation. *Holy shit,* they thought, *we're doing ice wrong!*

Sasha was so well regarded that he was posthumously given a Lifetime Achievement Award in 2016 from the Spirited Awards.

Now, you might think, who cares about high-end coffee or kale or the size of ice cubes? The answer is: foodies do. Every year the bar is being raised. If you've tasted Counter Culture coffee on vacation and a cup at your favorite restaurant back home tastes, relatively speaking, like swill, that's the last coffee you are likely to order from that place. You'll get your coffee elsewhere or stop ordering it at all. If you're introducing kale into your diet because you've been watching Alton Brown, you'll choose a restaurant serving kale over the eatery that's still slinging the same boring iceberg-romaine mix.

Ten years ago, a casual dining chain in, say, the Midwest could ignore what was happening in Los Angeles, San Francisco, Chicago, or New York. But with social media and the Food Network beaming the latest trends into people's homes and consciousness 24/7, trends that used to take twenty years to go mainstream now take twelve months. Restaurants no longer have the luxury of relying on the same old same old. As the restaurateurs on our tour this year are about to discover, in today's higher-stakes hospitality market, if they don't embrace a coming food trend early on, one or more of their competitors will, and they will quickly appear obsolete and lose guests.

Oh, you've got to excuse me for a moment. The Underground Culinary Tour bus is leaving.

WEDNESDAY, 1:30 P.M.

We snake down Broadway to the heart of Greenwich Village. The driver's got the music tuned to a rock station, but no one seems much interested. Early in the tour, the CEOs are still eager to make a good impression. They're all feeling a bit like a newbie, shy about letting their hair down.

The bus shoots over the Manhattan Bridge to the heart of downtown Brooklyn, Manhattan's edgier neighbor borough. Flatbush Avenue is a mishmash of small mom-and-pop shops and businesses. We travel two miles to the edge of Brooklyn's busiest traffic circle, Grand Army Plaza, marked by a great limestone arch that denotes the entrance to Prospect Park. The arch, dedicated to the memory of Brooklyn's Civil War dead, was erected at a time in the borough's history when Brooklyn expected to morph into a city greater, perhaps, than Manhattan itself.

Considering the choices I've made for our first day of touring, I think it will soon become clear that modern-day Brooklyn has culinary experiences that are different from what you'll find across the river in Manhattan. Our first stop is Franny's, one of my favorite pizza places in the city. It's a far cry from the dough-slinging palaces found throughout the city and the region. Proprietors Andrew Feinberg and Francine "Franny" Stephens are activists who believe that the way we eat can change the world.

Theirs is a simple-looking space. White subway tile, plain wooden chairs and tables. A bar on one side of the room. A divider in the middle to hold stacks of firewood for the wood-burning oven in the back. As our servers bring us some appetizers—crostini topped with spinach and chestnuts, roasted beets with pistachio-slivered salsa verde, and a plate of hard-boiled eggs with spicy pickles and anchovies—I explain to our group why I think Franny's is so special.

Pizza is a beloved menu item in American culture, but so much of the pizza dining experience is highly disposable. Most pizza places buy their dough, sauce, and cheese in large quantities, eliminating any opportunity to create a distinctive pizza based on unique and fresh ingredients. If you ever peeked in the Dumpster behind your neighborhood pie shop, you'd see giant empty cans of premade pizza sauce. When guests come in for a quick slice, they're served off paper plates and given paper napkins and plastic utensils. If guests order pizza for takeout, they've generated even more waste in the form of a large cardboard box.

But okay, you think. That's the way we consume pizza in the twenty-first century.

But it doesn't take much effort to design a more sustainable business model that serves great food *and* inspires guests by example. Andrew and Francine are trying to do in Brooklyn what Chez Panisse, Alice Waters's legendary restaurant, did in Berkeley, California, back in the 1970s. They use produce and ingredients from farms in the New York area, so they only serve vegetables that are in season. (Their partner farms are listed on their menu.) Their meats and dairy products are organic, and none are treated with hormones or antibiotics. The energy that keeps the lights on in their establishment is generated by wind power and by hydroelectric power purchased through a special program provided by Con Edison, New York's main energy provider. Franny's serves only fair-trade, sustainable coffee. Its cleaning supplies are green and "earth-friendly," and its to-go containers are biodegradable. Menus are printed on recycled paper. Even its kitchen grease is recycled and made into biodiesel fuel that will power someone's retrofit-ted Mercedes tomorrow. These best practices all add up to a brand and a taste that foodies appreciate. Sustainability is becoming increasingly important to guests.

Okay, okay, you say, *I get it. Franny's works hard to tread lightly on the earth. But how's the pizza?* Well, it's pretty freaking good. The ten- or twelve-inch pies are Neapolitan-style, thin crust, a little imperfect, a little bubbly, and a little charred around the edges, just the way you'd get them in the birthplace of pizza. The crust is crispy but silky and pliable. And the toppings are amazing, because everything is fresh off a farm.

While most of my group have just met, they quickly find that the food and the atmosphere create a bond that few can resist. Jack Gibbons, president of Front Burner Res-taurants, and Anthony Pigliacampo, one of the CEOs of the Mod Market chain, get busy passing the food. We go around the table, tucking into the steaming hot pies: basil, tomato, and buffalo mozzarella; tomato, homemade sau-sage, and buffalo mozzarella; ricotta, buffalo mozzarella, garlic, and basil. The group's favorite is clams, chile pepper flakes, and parsley. Some people have never tried clams on pizza, but it's one of my favorite toppings—I make it at home on special occasions.

I'm closely monitoring the time as our meal progresses. By the time the desserts arrive, we have to be heading out the door.

I'm able to grab one mouthwatering bite of our creamy cannoli before sprinting for the bus.

WEDNESDAY, 2:40 P.M.

It's so expensive to open a restaurant these days in major cities that many young chefs and restaurateurs go farther afield, where landlords are more reasonable and residents are grateful to have a great new eatery in their neighborhood. Even "name" chefs with numerous restaurant credits have resorted to off-the-beaten-track neighborhoods or smaller cities to test concepts before committing to the higher costs of a major metropolitan area. And as our bus heads north out of Park Slope into the Williamsburg section of Brooklyn, I see this lesson playing out yet again.

Once Manhattanites rarely ventured into Williamsburg unless they had an artist friend throwing a party in a great crumbling loft he or she was renting or squatting in. A few intrepid travelers ventured to the old German section of the neighborhood to grab a porterhouse at the Michelin-ranked Peter Luger's, the neighborhood's legendary 120-year-old steakhouse, but few dared to go farther.

But that has changed dramatically. Gentrification has marched on, as it has in other cities. As our bus pulls down Metropolitan Avenue, I'm reminded that though Williamsburg is still rough on the eyes, it's brimming with a vitality and an avant-garde food culture that is hard to miss. Noodle shops are tucked in between Dunkin' Donuts and Laundromats; abandoned Italian bakeries have been converted into vintage clothing shops and antique stores. Pigeons coo in the verdigrised steeples of an old church in desperate need of a coat of paint. Artists display their work in vacant lots. Traffic rumbles by on highway overpasses, and there's the constant steel scream of the subway trains underfoot.

Food trucks have become the rage in Manhattan, but when we pull up in front of Zona Rosa, my guests are treated to an astonishing reworking of the concept. The kitchen of this extraordinary Mexican eatery is housed inside a 1956 Airstream Spartan trailer, which is stuffed into the front wall of the restaurant. As passersby stroll past the building, they can see kitchen staff toiling away through the propped-open windows of the Airstream. Guests can cozy up to the bar inside, order a shot of tequila or mezcal within inches of the vehicle's license plate, or hit the roof deck overlooking Metropolitan Avenue. The ground floor is imbued with sunlight streaming down from the greenhouse-like space upstairs. Peace lilies and cacti complete the effect, making us feel like we've wandered into a garden of earthly delights.

I dash inside the trailer kitchen to tell chef Ivan Garcia that our party's arrived. A thin, aproned young man with a thick mop of black hair, Ivan is hunched over the counter, spooning avocado coleslaw over the tops of beer-battered mahi-mahi tacos. Ivan grew up in Mexico City, watching his mother and grandmother turn out traditional dishes. His latest restaurant pays homage to their creations, and to the bohemian neighborhood in that city, which flourished from the 1950s to the 1970s.

I picked Zona Rosa because I want my guests to see how something as simple as Mexican street food can be elevated to high art if you're willing to be picky about ingredients, and bold in terms of ambience. Ivan's choices

are mostly farm-to-table. Grass-fed skirt steak is incorporated into the tacos. Organic chicken hides in the enchiladas drizzled with the Garcia family's secret mole sauce.
When I head upstairs to the enclosed greenhouse, the others on the tour are already launching into the octopus and
shrimp ceviche. Someone hands me a bright-red margar-
ita festooned with a slice of watermelon. Another tempting drink is being passed around topped with a wedge of
pineapple.

So many Mexican restaurants overdo it with the tortillas. You're bloated by the end of the meal because you've
eaten more corn flour than anything else. Ivan inverts that
ratio. His tortillas are intentionally petite, but packed with
meat and flavor. Typically they're brought to the table in
groups of three, artfully arranged on wood-and-steel racks.
Steaming tacos sit on the lower board, and three ramekins
of salsas—red, green, and spicy—are on top.

"Pace yourself, people!" I call out to everyone across
the table.

I'm saying it to John and Randy and Kat, but I'm really
saying it to myself. So far I've only sampled three kinds of
Franny's pizza, so I'm doing well.

The crunchy mahi-mahi tacos are gone in millisec-
onds. Next, we are served grass-fed beef cheek tacos with
onions and cilantro. Finally, out come the veggie tacos
stuffed with earthy sautéed swiss chard, zucchini, tomato,
avocado, and cheese. After a pairing of mini enchiladas,
Ivan sends up a classic Mexican showpiece dish, chiles en
nogada—roasted poblano peppers stuffed with shredded
pork, organic chicken, peaches, pears, apples, and almonds,

covered in a captivating white walnut sauce studded with pomegranate seeds. The legendary dish is said to approximate the colors of the Mexican flag: green poblanos, white sauce, and red pomegranates. Ivan actually serves this dish at Zona Rosa's sister restaurant, Mesa Coyoacan, but because he knows I love it so much, he's tossed it onto the menu today.

The stuffed poblano in its warm bath of walnut sauce looks almost too perfect to eat. But one of my guests bravely gathers up a little of the sauce on a spoon and lifts it to his lips.

"How is it?" asks Jay Jerrier, who runs a high-end pizza chain called Cane Rosso in Dallas/Fort Worth.

We don't wait for the answer. We fall on the dish and sweep it clean. A wise person would walk to the next stop on our tour. It's less than a mile away, and the walk would give us some much-needed exercise and help our digestion. But we're already late. So we tear off bites of Chef Ivan's sugar-dusted chocolate churros and dash down to the bus.

WEDNESDAY, 3:50 P.M.

We streak down Metropolitan Avenue and hang a left. A senior housing center glides past our windows to the right. A hookah shop. An organic grocery. Another vacant lot wrapped in trash-strewn cyclone fencing. And a guy selling used, mismatched clothing off the exterior wall of a Chinese takeout place.

Across the street is the entrance to Maison Premiere, which won the 2016 James Beard Award for Outstanding

Bar Program two years after our most recent visit. When we walk through the double doors, I feel instantly transported to another period in American history. A broken antique clock hangs on the wall to our left as we come in. It is stopped just before five p.m., but it might as well be frozen in time a few minutes after midnight, January 17, 1920, the day Prohibition first went into effect in the United States. We are greeted by Ben Crispin and Cat Mallone.

I see shabby plaster walls, ornate radiators, brass lamps, green copper window panes. The space feels like a jazz club in the French Quarter of New Orleans; bluesy music emanates from the speakers. The staff's attire evokes the era of 1920s speakeasies. Some of the gentleman servers wear well-groomed mustaches that twirl at the ends, and stiff shirts accented by smart vests and debonair bow ties. The female staff wear lacy black vintage dresses and bright-red lipstick, and their hair is coiffed in the blunt bobs and bangs of the 1920s.

A server is setting out huge platters of Rocky Nook and Kaipara oysters on the horseshoe-shaped marble bar where we're about to take our seats. A bartender in suspenders and a bow tie spins wooden dowels between his palms to mix our Pimm's cups, four at a time.

The staff at Maison Premiere take their cocktails seriously. The centerpiece of the bar is an absinthe fountain modeled after the one in Jean Lafitte's Old Absinthe House in New Orleans. Absinthe, one of the world's legendary spirits, is a bright-green anise-flavored drink once cherished by bohemian poets and artists for its perceived psychoactive properties. Maligned throughout history, the drink was banned in some countries, including the United States, in the early twentieth century. But today it is making a comeback, after science demonstrated that absinthe's alleged psychedelic properties were much ado about nothing. Countless small indie distilleries around the world now produce the drink; Maison Premiere features almost thirty different brands on its "absinthe drip" menu.

As the bar's cocktail maven, Maxwell Britten, can attest, mixology is steeped in ritual. New Guard restaurateurs recognize that ritual is endlessly fascinating to guests, particularly foodies. Today the proprietors have invited us to sample New World absinthe produced by a small distillery in the Chicago area called Letherbee. Their absinthe isn't the typical bright green, but instead caramel-colored, a trait acquired after being aged for six months in oak casks. Straight out of the bottle, Letherbee absinthe is 128 proof—64 percent alcohol—too insanely high to drink. Which is why absinthe is diluted with water.

I watch as one of our bartenders, Will Elliot, sets up beautiful etched goblets on the bar. He carefully measures out a jigger of absinthe. The traditional absinthe glass is equipped with a little bulge or reservoir at its bottom. The brown spirits fill the reservoir, and then some. Next, they set our glasses under the spouts of the water fountain. A flat slotted spoon goes on top of the glass rim. A sugar cube is placed on top of the spoon. Our bartender gently turns on the fountain's spouts to a slow drip. Drip, drip, drip, the cold water slowly trickles down, pecking the sugar to pieces, washing it into the absinthe, sweetening the drink as it flows.

There's another miraculous side effect to the ritual that bartenders call *la louche*. Traditionally, as water mixes with absinthe, the neon-green color turns an opalescent, milky-green color. In Paris, the old absinthe drinker's version of the happy hour was *l'heure verte*—"the emerald hour." As I watch our drinks being made, I'm delighted to see that even the Letherbee's brown spirit acquires the cloudy look of the *louche*.

This is not a quick drink to make, mind you. Maison Premiere's absinthe fountain sports only four spigots. Watching our drinks being crafted, four at a time, as we inhale our oysters, is a lesson in self-restraint and patience. Everyone's eyes are on the ice-cold water melting the sugar. Drip, drip, drip. When the finished drink is set down in front of each of us, the first thing we're compelled to do is swirl the pretty spoon around the liquid, as if trying to prove to ourselves that yes, the sugar has indeed melted, swimming in suspension inside the glass. And in fact not a crystal remains.

I watch as the gaggle of CEOs lift their glasses to their lips. For most of them, it's the first time they've ever tasted absinthe. One sip of the anise-kissed drink, and the radiant smiles that appear on their faces tell me everything I need to know. A well-made absinthe drip refreshes, delights, and excites. In an instant, these restaurant executives understand why Europeans can linger for hours under umbrellas in outdoor cafés sipping their drinks. Suddenly, the previously undiscovered and misunderstood world of aperitifs and digestifs seems not only civilized but mandatory.

Turning away briefly from the spectacle, I return to my oysters, glistening on the plate before me.

In the nineteenth century, New York was famous for oysters. Customers bought them off street carts and slurped them down on the sidewalk. Further back, in the days of the old Dutch patroons, the city's waterfront was paved with oyster shells. That's how Pearl Street in the financial district got its name.

But closer to the present, oysters seemingly vanished from restaurant menus. Concerns about pollution, about freshness, about bacteria, jettisoned the oyster from the diets of otherwise intrepid guests. Today, however, thanks to the growth of state-regulated oyster farms and sustainable aquaculture on both coasts, the United States is seeing a resurgence of oysters' popularity and availability. When guests take their seats at Maison Premiere, they're presented with a tiny pencil and a checklist that spells out all the seafood on the menu today. It varies, of course, depending on the catch. This afternoon, scanning the list, I see twenty-three types of oysters, two types of clams, and an assortment of shrimp, lobster, sea urchin, and beautiful local Montauk pearl oysters. There's a massive scallop that's served in its shell. It's so striking that an image of it has made the front cover of our annual culinary tour gift book—the one we send to each guest a few months after their visit—two years in a row. The fact that the scallop is locally sourced blows my guests' minds.

The visit to Maison allows us to teach a powerful lesson about a fascinating trend in seafood procurement. Some of the oysters hail from Long Island, just beyond the outskirts of the city. Others are flown in from far-flung locales—Washington state, Virginia, Rhode Island, Massachusetts, Maine, British Columbia, New Brunswick, and Nova Scotia. Rather than rely on third-party distributors to deliver their oysters to their door, Joshua Boissy and Krystof Zizka, the dapper hosts of Maison Premiere, take turns driving out to JFK, New York City's major international airport, every morning to pick up their latest shipment, to be sure that the oysters are as fresh as possible.

They have found an interesting way to capitalize on the current oyster bonanza. They sell them for a dollar each—virtually at cost—during every weekday happy hour. The price is so low that Maison actually loses money selling them. But as anyone who has eaten a half dozen or a dozen oysters will attest, they're not exactly filling. So Joshua and Krystof make up the loss in drinks and other meals on their menu. The allure of cheap, plentiful oysters draws such a crowd that Maison Premiere has been known to shuck fourteen thousand oysters in a single weekend during the summer.

Our empty oyster shells are whisked away; chef Lisa Giffen's razor clams are up next. Such an unusual bivalve, I think, as I sip my second drink. The meat is dressed with mint and chopped radish, resting on a striking rectangular shell.

One bite is all I need to bring back vivid memories and the smell of sea brine.

WEDNESDAY, 5:00 P.M.

We have to backtrack to get to our next stop, Fette Sau, which is sandwiched between a Spanish bodega and Tony's Auto Repair in the same neighborhood. As we wind our way down the alley that leads to Fette Sau, housed inside an old industrial garage, we're greeted by a delicious melding of wood, smoke, and meat.

Despite its name, Fette Sau—"fat pig" in German—is a classic, down-home, American BBQ joint. It's the brainchild of Joe Carroll, a former music industry executive who turned to food when the record business tanked in 2001. When I walk into the old rehabbed garage, there's a giant glass case on my right filled with hot meat. Brisket. Pulled pork. Pork ribs. Short ribs. We tell the server behind the counter what we want; he or she weighs it and serves it to us on a giant aluminum baking tin covered with a sheet of brown waxed paper. Of course, while we're making our decisions, the incredible smell of smoking meat tempts us to eat well beyond our intentions.

The staff at Fette Sau sell by the pound. The smallest portion they'll sell is a quarter pound of whatever's in the case. Most people order a quarter of this, a half pound of that, and come away happier for the experience. The bar is set off to the side, where repurposed John Deere tractor seats serve as barstools, and the beer taps are fitted with old cleavers and chef's knives.

The old cinderblock walls are painted with images of various cuts of meat. Our tour group heads toward the mural and sits down at a long picnic table. The servers bring us giant platters of BBQ, along with three kinds of sauce. They bring along gallon jugs of Fette Sau Brau, the house's signature beer, copious amounts of German potato salad, baked beans ladled into giant paper cups, kosher pickles, and huge rolls of paper towels.

The moment feels like a backyard barbeque party in the American South that just happens to be in the heart of urban Brooklyn. The meal is a perfect example of a trend I've noticed—simple foods amped up. BBQ is a traditional American standard, but everything we're eating is a triumph of organic, local, and small. The meat hails from family-run meat purveyors or farmer's co-ops, the beer from a brewery twenty miles away. They're also obsessed with whiskeys at Fette Sau, and the whiskey we sample at the end of the meal comes from a distillery five miles away, a block from the Gowanus Canal, Brooklyn's famed cargo waterway.

Most of us know what good BBQ should taste like: moist, smoky, flavorful. Fette Sau's is so glorious and redolent with flavor that even my Texas guests give it a thumbs up. In a second, our palates know: *This is the real thing!* But when you sample something prepared by a highly regarded chef at the top of his game, surprises emerge. Dig into a cup of Fette Sau's baked beans, and you're blown away by the burnt-end bits of briskets. In one mouthful, your preconception of baked beans is changed forever.

As I look around the table, I'm pleased to see that my tour guests are starting to loosen up. Everyone's talking shop, telling stories of restaurants they've loved, chefs they've known, meals they've consumed, cities where they've had unforgettable meals.

"Everyone," I say. "We're gonna have to go soon."

It's the fifth stop of our tour. Some of the fainthearted mention that they are getting, oh, a tiny bit ... *full.* But they're professionals, determined to tough it out.

"Before we go, pass me the pickles," someone asks.

After all, vegetables are important.

WEDNESDAY, 6:15 P.M.

The brick walls of chef Marco Canora's restaurant Hearth in the East Village are painted with a gorgeous celebration of vegetables, declaring his intention of only serving the freshest local ingredients. I look around in anticipation of what Marco has in store for us. I can't help but think how great restaurants and great chefs are sometimes linked by a grand family tree. When Marco first came to New York, he worked as a line cook under Tom Colicchio at Gramercy Tavern. From there, he helped Tom open the first craft restaurant. And today he runs the show in a cozy, home-style restaurant devoted to the Italian aesthetic and cuisine. In response to his own health concerns, he recently retooled Hearth's menu to eliminate highly processed oils, sugars, and flours and commit to procuring the most unadulterated ingredients possible.

As soon as we sit, the staffers surround us with housemade charcuterie—rabbit ballotine, pastrami duck breast, country version pâté, pig's head terrine, pork rillette—and a sprightly fava bean salad. The board of meats in front of us looks gorgeous and enticing enough to be on the cover of *Bon Appétit*. We wash it all down with sips of a crisp white from the Veneto.

It is all spectacularly good, but I'm already bragging to my guests about Marco's meatballs. You know how there are certain foods that you just crave? Meatballs have become a national trend that way. You'll see small hole-in-the-wall eateries devoted to just meatballs. They're enormously popular, of course, because a) who doesn't love meatballs? and b) they manage to elevate something we all remember from our childhoods to the level of a gastronomical luxury.

Marco's secret? Ricotta. For every batch he cooks up, he uses a one-to-one ratio of ricotta to meat, whether beef or veal. And despite what every sweet Italian American nonna would instruct you to do, Marco doesn't fry his meatballs on his stove top. Instead, he browns them carefully, then bakes them in the oven, submerged in his incredibly rich pasta sauce. The result is a perfectly tender, cheese-rich meatball infused with tomato and spices.

The meatballs come to our table with a large platter of pasta twists—gemelli topped with spring vegetables, basil, and mint. I let the others swarm the pasta, and impale one of the meatballs with an accuracy that would make a spear fisher proud.

My mouth explodes with flavor. So good.

I love what Marco does and frequently use his story as an example of how a chef can also make his mark with a single amazing dish. One of his other offerings is a business called Brodo—Italian for "broth"—devoted to variations on that single delicious meal. He has innovated this business since our tour. To keep things simple, he sells only three types of bone broth soup on any given day. You can add extra ingredients, mix and match, buy a big carton for dinner, or just have a cup to drink as you would coffee. To reach customers, Marco built a window in Hearth's kitchen that overlooks the sidewalk. Customers walk right up, place their orders, pay, and leave with their broth.

This is the message I want to drive home: you don't have to create a huge menu to create a successful restaurant and satisfy today's foodies. You just have to give your guests something that they crave and want to come back to. They eat it once, and the next time they think of that one food—whether it is soup, meatballs, a unique sandwich or entrée—they will think of *your* restaurant.

But of course, while I'm explaining this to the executives on the tour, the forks are flying. By the time I look up, the meatballs have vanished and I've missed my chance at seconds.

WEDNESDAY, 7:30 P.M.

Our bus heads south from Marco's place in the East Village before it hits the Bowery. We have the music cranked, and my guests are hobnobbing about the business, job hunting, and deal making. One restaurant president I know landed his current job on one of our culinary tours, right there on the bus. Magic happens when you ply like-minded restaurant professionals with food and drink and let them talk.

A busy downtown metropolis rolls past our windows. There are restaurant supply shops and trendy bistros and hordes of lighting supply shops, Asian groceries, Chinese food emporia, banks, hair and nail salons, and statues of Confucius and Lin Zexu tossed in for good measure. And then, after we've traversed what feels like an entire Chinese province, we dip under the Brooklyn Bridge and arrive in Ireland.

Our destination is a charming old two-story tenement on Water Street, two blocks from the southern tip of

Manhattan island. This is the Dead Rabbit Grocery and Grog—one of the most famous drinking establishments in Manhattan, the United States, and the world.

That may sound fatuous, considering that this Irish American bar only opened in 2012. But in that short a time the Dead Rabbit has racked up more than a dozen industry awards for its incredible cocktail program. In 2016, *Drinks International* magazine ranked it as the best bar in the world. As recently as 2013, co-owner Jack McGarry won the coveted International Bartender of the Year Award, only the second time an American has won the prize awarded by the Tales of the Cocktail festival. Dead Rabbit also won an award for Best New Cocktail & Bartending Book. McGarry and co-owner Sean Muldoon, both from Belfast, had long wanted to open a bar that paid homage to New York's great Irish American heritage. If you've ever seen Martin Scorsese's *Gangs of New York,* you'll realize that the bar's moniker refers to the name of the Irish Catholic gang.

Muldoon and McGarry wanted their cocktails to be historically accurate. So they pored through old texts on mixology, researching cocktails dating back as far as the seventeenth century, before testing and adapting them until they were perfect for the modern palate. Today their cocktail list boasts seventy-two drinks, most of which you've never seen or tasted anywhere in your life. Groups of eight or more people can order giant bowls of communal punch. Spiked punch, sometimes flavored with various juices, was a common sight back in the nineteenth century. People would sit around the bar, ladling punch into their glasses or mugs. If you taste something at the Dead Rabbit that you absolutely can't live without, you can buy one of the bar's gorgeously bound, privately printed drink manuals to re-create your drink at home.

The bus gets us there early, so we have time to scope out the ground-floor tavern, which is the perfect place to grab a pint and a burger. The old exposed joists are decorated with hundreds of black-and-white photos of Ireland. The shelves behind the bar boast dozens of different brands of Irish whiskey. Our feet kick up sawdust from the tavern floor. In the back, there's a small grocery carrying UK foodstuffs. The walls are covered with images of Irish-born pugilists and war heroes, John F. Kennedy, and Jesus.

Upstairs, in the parlor lounge, a bronze eagle graces the bar in front of a portrait of George Washington; Irish actors, poets, and athletes gaze down at us from the walls. General manager Chris Szablinski tucks us behind one of the tables, and staffers offer us small bites and cocktails.

One of my guests shakes his head as he looks at the food that appears before us. Thank goodness the portions are small. Fried oyster sliders. Deviled eggs topped with shimmering caviar. Foie gras mousse with toast points.

Perfect cocktail food, I might add.

The first drink up is called the Immigrant: Jameson Black Barrel whiskey infused with nettle tea, Pernod absinthe, cucumber, and elderflower. It tastes like licorice made in heaven, served in a classic absinthe glass. Brett Schulman, the CEO of Cava Mezze Grill, and Sabato Sagaria, the chief restaurant officer of Union Square Hospitality Group, are seated next to each other, and raise their glasses in unison, huge grins on their faces.

Next we taste the Suit of Spades—Absolut Craft Smokey Tea Vodka, mezcal, white chocolate, and salt. Followed by the Thunderbolt—Powers Gold Label Irish whiskey, banana, ginger, and pimento dram, a classic liqueur infused with allspice berries.

Many of the drinks and nibbles in the upstairs parlor at the Dead Rabbit are served on bone china, in keeping with the 1880s period the bar evokes. When the Suit of Spades arrives at the table, it's served in exquisite teacups of various patterns. As we raise our cups to our lips, someone in our party yells: "Pinkies extended!"

Everyone laughs. But every one of us follows suit, pinkie out, to partake in what is for many of us the first cocktail we've ever sipped from genuine Irish china.

WEDNESDAY, 8:50 P.M.

On the way uptown, people are seat dancing to U2 cranked loud. The group has loosened up in a way that would have been hard to anticipate earlier today. As I start to talk about our next destination, I hear groans from several of the CEOs.

Please, no more food!

I sympathize, but we must press on. We're about to pay a visit to culinary royalty.

Tom Colicchio—now in his fourteenth season of the TV show *Top Chef*—is waiting for us in the private dining room of one of his restaurants. This is the first year he's been a host on our tour, but my company would not exist if it weren't for Tom.

Back in 2000, I was talking about our software development with Robert Bohr, who was an early employee of ours and who would go on to become one of New York's great sommeliers, importers, and restaurateurs. Robert had helped us nail down some of the user interface issues—how the software would actually look to our clients. But I was interested in finding early restaurant clients who we could learn from as we went about collecting their data. "I know just who you should talk to," Robert said. "I'll set up a meeting."

Which is how I ended up walking into Sushisamba to have lunch with Tom Colicchio. We were both younger men then, eager to make our mark in the business. At the time, Tom was the executive chef at Gramercy Tavern. He had not yet opened his restaurant, craft, and was even further away from becoming the star of TV's *Top Chef*. First and foremost, though, he was an Italian American Jersey boy, like me, and before we had conducted a lick of business over our lunch, we bonded over our love of the Jersey Shore. He told me he'd grown up crabbing in Barnegat Bay, and how his family would cook an amazing "gravy"—tomato-based pasta sauce—from the crabs they caught. By bizarre coincidence, I had *virtually the same memory* from childhood. In a matter of minutes, we were comparing recipes for this versatile crab pasta dish.

It turned out that Tom was fascinated with technology; he told me he'd love to have us collect data from his kitchen. There was just one thing: I needed to talk to his partner at Gramercy Tavern, Danny Meyer. He promised to set up a meeting. Tom went on to become a member of my company's board and introduced me to many people in the business who he thought might benefit from our software. Many of our board meetings over the years have taken place in his flagship restaurant, craft, with his chefs preparing our meals. He's become a dear friend, and I've benefited greatly from his culinary and business counsel over the years.

Long story short, it was not a surprise, then, to have one of his restaurants as a stop on this year's culinary tour. Of course, by the time we arrive late in the day, every one of our tour guests insists that they can't eat another bite. But Tom's staff has prepared a simple menu with appetizer-size portions that fit the moment perfectly. Four courses. Four beautiful pours of wine. We sample three quick canapés with an Italian Oltrepo Pavese sparkling rosé from Baruf-faldi, before moving on to a smoked black cod with leeks and caviar. With that, we sample a 1995 French Muscadet Sévre et Maine Sur Lie from Domaine de Fiefs aux Dames. The centerpiece of the meal is a juicy, perfectly cooked lamb loin with ramps and artichokes. With that, we sip one of Ravenswood's 1993 Sonoma Valley zinfandels, from Bel-loni Vineyards. One of my guests, John Kunkel, the CEO of 50 Eggs in Miami, is blown away by the flavors. And I must admit, I love the wine pairings. In our last course, Tom's team pairs a rioja blanco—a 2001 semisweet Spanish re-serve from Bodegas Riojanas—with lemon-thyme glazed doughnuts. Doughnuts!

Here, as in so many of the places we've eaten today, the chefs are conveying a message about the triumph of qual-ity ingredients, a farm-to-table approach, and thoughtful beverages. In fact, I would argue that Tom's craft revolutionized the American restaurant industry, showing chefs around the nation that they could turn out spectacular meals if they had the courage—as he says in his book *Think Like a Chef*—to let great ingredients shine.

Portions are a big part of the story too. Recently, after Tom realized that he and his wife eat only four or five appetizers and rarely order large dishes when they dine out, he moved to smaller portions in his own main dining room. Dining this way, they realized, is the quickest way to get a sense of a chef's creativity. It's the way most foodies I know eat. Because they don't see food merely as sustenance for their bodies, they're constantly looking to experience new dishes they've never had before. That insight transformed Tom's thinking.

If I don't eat huge meals anymore, Tom thought, *why do I expect my guests to?*

Considering the amount of food we've consumed today, he's preaching to the choir.

WEDNESDAY, 10:40 P.M.

We travel to the other side of town for another round of dessert and drinks. Pearl & Ash sits on the upper end of Bowery, the long stretch of the city that was once famous for flophouses, and which has since transformed itself into a mecca for the young, hip, and hungry. One of those old flophouses has been turned into a stylish hostel, the Bowery House. The restaurant is tucked into the ground floor. Their sister restaurant, Rebelle, is right next door.

A blue, ethereal glow emanates from the bar at Pearl &

Ash, and the walls twinkle with lights tucked into the little wooden boxes of bric-a-brac decorating the walls. Pearl & Ash is a mecca for '80s music, and as I walk in they're playing A-ha's "Take On Me." The one thing you won't get a clue to when you walk in is what lies in the restaurant's cellar— Pearl & Ash's six thousand bottles of wine.

I scan the crowd. Branden McRill, the founder, is here, as is Alessandro Zampedri, the Italian race car–driver-turned-investor who saved the building from obscurity and is a Pearl & Ash partner. I spot Patrick Cappiello, Branden's business partner and sommelier. Patrick is clad in his signature uniform—black T-shirt, black horn-rimmed glasses, black jeans, Chuck Taylor sneaks, and a wide grin. He grew up in a middle-class family in Rochester, New York, an ordinary kid with an interest in comic books, skateboarding, punk rock, and tattoos.

Patrick, a genial guy now in his forties, has worked in the cellars of New York restaurants for more than a quarter of a century. He's been hailed as Wine Person of the Year by *Imbibe* magazine and Sommelier of the Year by *Food & Wine* magazine.

As chef Richard Kuo sends out plates of cheese to our table, Patrick opens a magnum of a Savigny-les-Beaune Premier Cru burgundy by Domaine Tollot-Beaut et fils. I encourage him to tell my guests about his approach to wine.

I should confess that I'm something of an oenophile. Everywhere I eat, I can spend a good chunk of my time studying the wine list. And lately, everywhere I go, when the general manager asks me what I think of their wine list, I tell them the same thing: *Lower your prices and you'll sell more!*

They hem and haw, chuckle, pat me on the back, and bring me the wine I order. But I still hold out hope for a New Guard mentality about wine—one that is currently practiced at Pearl & Ash, but also at other restaurants such as Marta, Estela, Charlie Bird, Pasquale Jones, Casa Mono, and Wildair. The standard practice is to mark up a bottle of wine at twice its retail cost or more. I venture to say that most guests' gut feeling about restaurant wine is that it's a ripoff—but what choice do they have? Either bite the bullet and order a bottle, sucking up the perceived injustice, or make do with a single glass. Overpriced and unthoughtful wine in these restaurants often languishes in cellars, peaking out.

Patrick arrived in New York City during the heyday of great wine restaurants and lavish spending. But working at restaurants like Tribeca Grill and Gilt and Veritas, where he curated his biggest list, he saw something shift in the New York wine scene in 2008, the year of the great financial crash. The incomes and wallets of guests shrank, and restaurateurs had to alter their ambitions to cater to this new reality. New restaurants arose that emphasized small, casual, and affordable. Patrick was approached by Branden and Richard with the idea of assembling a wine list for a casual restaurant aimed at young urban millennials who didn't want to blow their rent on a single night out.

Patrick empathized with his guests. He lived in the same neighborhood. He ate out constantly. And he didn't have a lot of money to spend. He also knew that a lot of the millennials who came into their new restaurant would not hesitate to do what *he* did on a night out—use a smartphone to research a wine right at the table. They'd know the retail price instantly. They'd also know if they were being gouged. "You don't want to be known as the place that rips off your guests," he says to our tour as he pours our wine.

So he searched for wines in up-and-coming regions of the world that didn't typically get a lot of play. Wines that were interesting, quirky, and not costly. He searched for values in major wine regions as well. He began pricing them all for his list, in many cases adding only a 50 percent markup and hoping that guests would get excited about the great deal they were getting. In fact, Patrick's resulting wine list—all ninety-two pages of it—was driven by that single thought: *What would I, as a consumer, be excited about paying for this wine?*

As Pearl & Ash analyzed its data, a couple of fascinating facts emerged. Their sales of beverages, when calculated as a percentage of their total sales, were higher than at many other restaurants. And their average checks were higher too. "It's really not rocket science," he tells my tour guests. "If you price wine reasonably, eventually word gets around that there are some really great values to be had. It builds loyalty with wine lovers. People know they can come here and not be constantly checking their phone. They trust us. And we actually sell *more* wine per table now, not less."

When the restaurant opened, the partners didn't have a lot of money to invest in high-end vintages. So Patrick called upon his wine collector friends to see if they'd allow him to cellar and sell their wine on consignment. Believe it or not, many wine collectors are stuck with wine that they want to get rid of. Either their tastes have changed, or they can't drink what they own fast enough, or because selling to a restaurant and earning some money on their invest-ment is just plain fun. Armed with statistics about what his guests buy, Patrick can take on consignment bottles he is fairly certain will sell.

In 2015, Pearl & Ash was one of only eight restaurants in the world to win *Wine Spectator*'s Grand Award for its wine list. But Pearl & Ash can't be summed up solely for its wine list or its analysis of data. Branden and Patrick are also fun-loving guys who know that guests love spectacle, as our tour group is about to find out.

"I'm glad you guys came by tonight," Patrick says. "I have nice champagne I wanted you to try." (By the time he says this, we've already polished off the Burgundy, and a late-harvest Marcobrunn Spätlese Riesling by Schloss Schönborn.) Now he holds up a heavy magnum and pro-duces a giant black-handled sword from behind his back.

Everyone gasps.

What the hell is he going to do with that? everyone is thinking.

Patrick leaps up onto the bar, taking up the bottle and sword from one of the bartenders. He announces to the cheering crowd that he's about to open a bottle of Fleury Blanc de Noirs.

The entire restaurant is watching now, eyes rapt. In the background, "Don't Stop Believin'" by Journey plays on Pearl & Ash's speakers. Patrick grips the bottom of the bottle in his left hand and holds the sword aloft in his right. (He bought the sword on eBay because he loved the bas-relief images of skulls on the hilt.) People are gathering around the bar now, smartphone cameras in hand.

The bartenders suggest they take a step back.

In one effortless motion Patrick swings the sword and whacks the top of the bottle. The tip of the bottle flies off behind the bar. Carbon dioxide gas wafts out of the severed neck of the bottle.

The crowd erupts with cheers and applause.

He passes the bottle down to the bartender, who begins to pour.

Sabering champagne is perhaps Pearl & Ash's most famous ritual. Patrick first witnessed this old military tradition, known as sabrage, at one of his previous jobs. A regular at Veritas so enjoyed having his champagne opened in this ceremonial manner that he actually kept a saber at the restaurant. Patrick used a chef's knife to saber a bottle of champage at a party for Gilt staffers, and was astonished by the emotional impact the ritual had on the staff. He renewed the tradition at Pearl & Ash, practicing the art until he became an accomplished sabreur in his own right. Fans started posting photos and videos of him opening bottles on social media under the hashtag #sabertownUSA.

After we've sipped a bit of the champagne, I go looking for the severed piece behind the bar. The cork is still inside the opening of the bottle; the piece in my hand and the tip of the bottle being poured are razor sharp. As Patrick explains to our group, a bottle of champagne is under so much pressure that when the saber hits the bottleneck, the glass breaks and the piece with the cork—known as the annulus—is blown clean away. The bottle is reduced to two pieces. There's not a shard of glass to be found anywhere.

As a close to our meal, the servers bring around a whimsical dessert—a Fernet Branca ice-cream sandwich. Fernet Branca is a classic Italian digestif with a thick licorice-clove flavor. Someone in the kitchen has drawn a smiley face on the brown waxed-paper wrapper of our sandwiches.

As we're sipping our champagne and licking the last of our ice-cream sandwiches, Patrick comes over to ask how our tour is going. "What other places have you been?"

I look around the table. My guests are bleary-eyed, exhausted, and full, but they manage to rattle off the names of the places we've been on our first day.

"Where are you going next?"

"This is it, dude," I tell him. "You guys are the last stop tonight."

"Really? That's it? I'm just getting off. We should go out."

"What do you have in mind?"

And so a serendipitous last trip of the night begins. Patrick snags some disposable cups and another magnum of wine from behind the bar. Then he, Branden, and the rest of the gang troop up onto the bus. The driver, shaking his head—it has been a long day—spirits us uptown to Park Avenue. Patrick insists we try this amazing fried chicken place he knows about. On the way to the chicken shack, Patrick pops open the Beaujolais and passes it around the bus. It's not the first time our restaurateur hosts have hopped on the tour bus. One year when the tour visited

DBGB, chef Daniel Boulud's hip French bistro on the Bowery, Daniel himself got on the bus with us, a bottle of wine
in tow. Maybe there's something inherently festive about
life and work down on the Bowery that makes everyone
want to keep the good times rolling

The fried chicken establishment looks promising, but
it's packed to the rafters and can't seat us. The maitre d'
looks askance at a busload of out-of-towners who have
shown up out of the blue on his doorstep. He directs the
bulk of his scorn toward the half-empty magnum in Patrick's hands.

"You can't bring that in here," he snarls.

My guests eye each other nervously. I forget sometimes
that to folks who aren't from New York, the city's casual
social niceties can seem a tad, well, scary.

"Back on the bus!" Patrick commands. "I know another
place!"

Don't ask me how, but before we drop everyone at the
hotel, we end up polishing off several plates of table-grilled
Korean barbecue at New Wanjo in Koreatown, a fitting
close to the day.

"Good night!" I tell my guests. "See you tomorrow morning, bright and early!"

It's well after midnight. All fifteen stomp off the bus,
eyes drooping, stomachs stretched. Patrick and Branden
hang out with me a little while longer, finishing off the
Beaujolais. I'm accustomed to their late-night insanity. But
if you're not, I suggest that you steer clear of fun-loving
sommeliers bearing swords.

· **4** ·

PERFECT CUT

You're sitting in a restaurant called Fogo de Chão in Atlanta, surrounded by a cornucopia of grilled meat. Every few minutes, someone in colorful period attire swings by your table with a steaming skewer of lamb chops, chicken, sausages, or beef.

This, of course, is a *churrascaria*—a Brazilian steakhouse. Every time one of your servers raises a knife to carve off another slice of filet mignon or rib eye, every time you lift your tongs to assist him, you are both participating in a tradition that reaches back several hundred years.

Since the fifteenth century, when the earliest Spanish explorers brought cattle to the New World, ranching has become a way of life throughout the Americas. In the same way that Americans revere the cowboy as an archetypal figure in the American West, South Americans revere their gauchos—the nomadic band of colorful men who still tend cattle on the rolling hills of the South American Pampas.

Historically, the South American gauchos dressed a little like the servers swirling around the tables of the restaurant. They wore flat hats with broad rims, baggy trousers that kept them cool in the heat, and kerchiefs to protect their necks from the sun. When hunger seized them as they traveled from place to place, they slaughtered and butchered one of the herd, and skewered and grilled its meat over an open campfire.

That's the narrative behind these restaurants, and it's as proud and authentic a tradition as American BBQ or shepherd's pie in an Irish pub.

Old food traditions continue to exert a powerful influence on our contemporary lives. When I was boy, I used to live for Fridays, when my father arrived home from work and allowed my sister and me to help him make a homemade pizza, stretching the dough and tossing it in the air. My dad was an HVAC system salesman and a son of downtown Philly, and this particular Italian American tradition was part of his family heritage. Eating pizza on Friday nights still happens in my family, and I still make my own pies on special occasions with my kids. When our family vacations with my parents, Pop-pop Mogavero brings his pizza stone and pizza peel, while Grandmom brings the meatballs, pasta, and tomato sauce for her signature dishes. And so the family tradition continues.

Modern-day Brazilians have a similar food tradition. Rudimar Bonfada, the Atlanta restaurant's general manager, says that he grew up grilling meat every Sunday after church in his parents' home in Brazil. His father prepared the beef, salted and skewered it, and set it out on the fire to cook. (Many Brazilians have working charcoal grills built into their living rooms, the way Americans have decorative fireplaces.) His mother's job was to prepare the small side dishes that are considered essential to the *churrasco* experience: potato salad with flecks of sweet tomatoes, seasoned rice, savory black bean stew with chunks of beef, and a traditional yucca topping called *farofa*.

As you watch Fogo de Chão's modern-day gauchos serving meat to guests at their tableside, it doesn't take much to see how this unforgettable experience can quickly become a logistical nightmare. It's one thing to cook a traditional meal—pizza or *churrasco*—with your family, but another to cook for an entire restaurant of guests. At home, if you make too much food, you can tuck the leftovers into the fridge. Someone will eat it tomorrow, or the next day. If you make too much in a restaurant, that food must be consigned to the trash by the end of the night. In a restaurant setting, leftovers are an expensive waste of money and food.

Restaurants like Fogo de Chão—the name literally means "fire of the ground," or campfire—are particularly vulnerable to this problem. The *churrascaria* experience makes two explicit promises to customers when they walk in the door: a) for one set price, you can "eat all you can enjoy," and b) you'll have access to a *continuous* stream of perfectly cooked meat at the drop of a colorful chip.

Off to your right, a party of six people in their twenties enters the restaurant and sits at a table. They order a round of caipirinhas, the traditional Brazilian cocktail, and flip over the small green chip on their table, signaling to the bevy of gauchos that they're ready to begin their meal. Every guest in the restaurant has one of these round cardboard chips. Green means, "Bring on the meat!" The red side means, "Whoa, cowboy, slow down. I'm taking a break!"

Lo and behold, the gauchos start swarming, one offering chunks of pork ribs, another displaying parmesan-encrusted pork loins, a third carrying baby lamb chops, and still more filet mignon. But not every guest at the table is biting. They tend to accept a few slices of the first few items that come by, whetting their appetite, but then they become more selective.

"No thanks," they tell the gaucho who comes by offering links of *linguiça,* plump pork sausages. "We had those already. Do you have any sirloin?"

"I had some of the bottom sirloin," one of the young women says. "It was really good. Can I get more of that?"

"Sure," the gaucho says. "How do you like it?"

"Medium."

"I'll take some, too," someone else says. "Medium rare."

"I still haven't tried the rib eye," another guest says. "Can I get that?"

"Of course. Coming right up."

And off the gaucho goes.

For the rest of the night, you never see a moment when a patron's request for a particular cut, at a particular doneness or temperature, isn't fulfilled in a matter of minutes, if not seconds.

This kind of on-the-fly ordering is tricky to manage. I call it the Perfect Meat Dilemma. It's like being an air traffic controller, only instead of shepherding 747s you're juggling about sixteen different cuts of beef, pork, lamb, or chicken, cooked to a variety of different temperatures and levels of doneness. It's not like these guests are ordering Cokes and Pepsis that can be easily dispensed from a machine. In general, meat, seafood, and poultry are the highest-cost food items a restaurant carries.

By design, Fogo can't wait for you to order. If they want to provide a continuous stream of meat perfectly cooked, they need to start cooking the right cuts of meat, in the right amounts, to the right temperatures, at the right time, before they know you're going to ask for it. In short, they have to be mind readers.

But since psychics are in as short supply in Brazil as they are in the United States, Fogo de Chão has come to rely on a more effective technique for preparing and serving its food. *They use data.* Specifically, they have mastered the art of knowing their restaurant's trends.

All restaurants struggle with trending. How much food to order? How much staff to bring on? How many busboys? How many chefs? Those kinds of questions are tough enough for small, mom-and-pop restaurants to grapple with. They are insanely difficult for chain restaurants, because huge operations are historically less nimble than small indie restaurants. Fogo de Chão is a publicly traded firm whose reach is spread across two continents. They have thirty-two locations in the United States, one in Mexico, ten locations in Brazil, and an army of third-party stock analysts and investors looking over their shoulders.

Fogo started in 1979 as a Brazilian company, in the city of Porto Alegre, in the state of Rio Grande do Sul, in the heart of gaucho country. Early in the 1980s, two sets of Brazilian brothers who grew up on farms and were themselves gauchos—the Ongarattos and the Cosers—acquired the company, nurtured it, brought it to other cities in Brazil, and exported the concept to the United States. There, the brothers teamed up with Larry Johnson, an American attorney whose background had prepared him in a rather unusual way to become Fogo's eventual steward. In 2007, Larry joined the company as CEO, determined to broaden the company's reach across the United States and the world. Larry is both an excellent businessman and a fearless dreamer. Thanks to his efforts, Fogo is today the premier Brazilian steakhouse in both Brazil and the United States, the largest and most upscale chain. The Portuguese language and Brazilian culture are still the heart of the company.

The chain leads the pack in its class. The company believes it delivers an experience that's less expensive but on par with approachable fine dining chains such as Del Frisco's or Ruth's Chris Steak House.

Before I show you how they got it right, I want to show you how another chain got it wrong. Let's see how a poor grasp of one's trends can doom a poorly run casual chain restaurant.

By the time the plane hit the tarmac it was well past seven p.m. My colleague Paul and I hadn't eaten all day.

We'd flown out to this city in the midwestern United States to meet the CEO of a legendary chain of casual restaurants. Our meeting was tomorrow, Monday morning. One of the company's restaurants wasn't far from our hotel. Why not stop in for a bite?

We dumped our bags at the Sheraton and barreled down a state highway that glowed with the lights of fast-food places and various sit-down chains. Our client's restaurant had a down-home look, with a clapboard house exterior and signage that harked back to the style of the 1950s. They served burgers and steaks and salads, all of them huge and comforting. Servers in white dresses and aprons whisked out heaping sundaes to patrons who packed the Formica and Naugahyde booths inside.

When we walked in the entrance at eight p.m. on a Sunday night, there was no hostess to greet us, only a sign reading PLEASE WAIT TO BE SEATED.

Just past the entrance we could see the place was hopping. Tables were jammed with families. But many four- and two-top tables sat empty, piled high with dirty plates and messy remains in a way that only a combination of children and melted ice cream could make them. Paul and I waited, shifting from foot to foot, inhaling the smell of fries and onions, watching as toppings-laden sundaes shot past, tempting but painfully out of reach.

One of the frantic servers, a young man, finally caught my eye. He'd probably heard my stomach growl. He waved as he rushed past us, as if to say *I see you, but I can't get to you now.*

"Can we get a seat?" I asked another.

"Uh," he said, his arms brimming with plates of hot food. "Can you wait a sec?"

In a short while, another man appeared from the back, dressed in the remnants of a uniform, his black bow tie missing, sweating profusely. "What can I do you for?" he asked.

"Well, we would like to eat."

"So sit," he said, trying to sound generous. "Take any seat that's empty. I'll send someone over with a menu."

As it turns out, we didn't need menus. The table we found near the counter already had two finger-streaked menus on the table, along with the remains of someone's dinner. Paul and I scanned our options, trying to skirt the puddles of ketchup and milkshake splatters that littered the tabletop.

After some time, a harried but exceptionally friendly server appeared to take our order. I went with the turkey burger, along with a milkshake. Paul got a cheeseburger and a small sundae. I think we both would have preferred ordering our main meal first, and *then* dessert, but in light of how short-handed the place looked, we figured we were smart to get our full orders in early.

The server stepped away, then turned back. I could read her thoughts. *I should probably clean up some of this stuff.* She grabbed an empty plate off the table and disappeared.

I looked at Paul.

"This place is a zoo."

He nodded over to the entrance. A line now stretched out the door. Not a maitre d' or hostess in sight.

While we waited, I gazed out at the décor, colorful ads

for '50s automobiles and smiling carhops. They projected the old-fashioned notion that dining out should be a clean, fun experience. But every table was beginning to look cluttered with the remains of meals.

Our server returned to snag more plates and deliver some bad news. "We can't do the turkey burger. We don't have enough ripe avocados."

"I don't need the avocado."

"Oh, but we can't serve the turkey burger without it. It's our signature combination."

I decided to switch to a cheeseburger as well.

"Oh—and the sundae," she said to Paul. "We're out of walnuts. I can do slivered almonds. We usually charge extra for them, but we'll just add 'em for free."

Paul said fine.

"Busy night," I said, glancing around.

"Oh yeah. We're totally slammed."

"Where are the busboys?"

"They sent them home early when it was dead."

"And the hostess?"

"She gets off at five."

"Is there a manager?"

"He doesn't work at night."

What a nightmare. The person who had put together the schedule was home watching *Duck Dynasty* reruns. He or she had checked out and consigned the place to hell.

Not surprisingly, the food took forever to arrive. My hunger aside, I almost didn't mind—I was mesmerized by the sad spectacle of what had happened to this nostalgic restaurant from my childhood. From the family in the next booth I gleaned that a nearby amusement park had sponsored a regularly scheduled fireworks show that night. As soon as the fireworks had ended, hordes of families hit the highway in search of a late-night meal or snack. Hence the larger-than-normal Sunday night crowd.

When our cheeseburgers came, they were just okay. But the ice cream and milkshakes were top-notch.

The next morning, I sat in the company cafeteria with a gentleman I'll call Edward, the chain's CEO. I found Ed to be a pleasant guy, dressed casually in khakis and a polo shirt with the chain's logo over his right breast. In New York, we would say he was *on brand*.

In the course of our meeting, he asked if we'd ever eaten at one of his restaurants.

"We ate at one last night," I replied.

"Oh, did you? How was it?"

So I broke it down for him, piece by piece. The short staffing, the messy tables, the long waits. I praised the desserts, but I couldn't overlook that they had inadvertently charged Paul for the slivered almonds.

The CEO exhaled dramatically. "Wow," he said, chuckling awkwardly. "I'm *so* sorry you had to see us that way."

The stores in their chain were corporately owned. There were no franchisees to lay the blame on, he knew.

Unfortunately, the dysfunction we experienced is typical of Old Guard casual chains. In the parlance of the restaurant industry, casual dining is defined by food served to you at a table where you give your order to a server. The food is higher priced than fast food but still modestly priced, relatively speaking. Menus are fixed by region, and meals are brought out fairly quickly. The ambience is family friendly and casual. Depending on the chain, the atmosphere can be sedate and tasteful, down-home rural, businessy, or themed. It can be a sports bar chain with numerous flat-screen TVs tuned to sporting events, or it can be one of countless venues with Irish-sounding names and a variety of antiques and signage tacked to the walls as display. Historically, casual dining restaurants have been the backbone of the dining industry, and they were once regarded as bulletproof.

Chain restaurants have several vulnerabilities that leave them open to competition. The biggest is that their size often prevents them from being nimble. They can't easily adapt to changing customer tastes and demand. Unless ordered to do so by corporate fiat, they're locked into serving the food they have always served. Depending on the chain, the quality of the meals they serve will range from a cut above fast food to pretty good. For decades, if the executives who operate these chains ever found themselves questioning the quality of their food, they rationalized to themselves that the consumer probably didn't know the difference.

But customers today are far more sophisticated. Foodies unhesitatingly make distinctions between a chain and indie restaurants. They can detect when food is truly special—or not. Where once the big casual dining and upscale chains were a welcome respite from fast food, they are increasingly under pressure internally and from a host of new competitors on the dining landscape. If given a choice between paying more—the cost of the food plus the gratuity—for average food and service, or stopping by Chipotle to build a healthy and satisfying burrito, foodies will choose Chipotle. Why go to the expense and hassle of a sit-down meal? That's why the fast casual dining sector is growing, and why so many smart chefs and restaurateurs are adding fast casual dining establishments to their portfolios.

I believe that the casual dining sector will continue to lose market share. Yes, there will always be a demand for the kind of convenient experience they provide. In some cases, these restaurants have a lock on superb locations where they're among the only options for dining. But the minute people have a choice, they'll go elsewhere, even if they have to pay more to get the quality they want.

What made me so frustrated is that the smart use of data and technology could have eliminated what Paul and I experienced. On a fundamental level, this venue was not being staffed in the right manner. The fireworks show was a regularly scheduled event; it was *predictable*. If the general manager had been given some software that integrated with local events calendars, he or she could have saved and uploaded all upcoming events relevant to his area—parades, sporting events, fireworks shows, everything. When the time came, he or she would have been in a great position to do stellar business. The GM wouldn't have sent busboys and hostesses home to save money. They wouldn't have run out of avocados and walnuts.

Ed listened to me intently, but said little. I could tell he felt terrible and deeply embarrassed. But his hands were tied. A while back, his company had been acquired by a private equity firm. This is a common enough scenario in the industry. Ed's investors could have chosen to set themselves up as stewards of a fine tradition, innovating their brand for the next generation and empowering their managers to make nimble decisions. Instead, they seemed determined to squeeze every penny of profit out of the chain. Unhappy with the small margins that characterize the restaurant business, shortsighted investors often pressure chains to cut corners. Inevitably, the companies cut corners on food and labor. That's the new reality that is threatening many historically great brands. It pains me to think that some of the fun, nostalgic brands I knew as a kid and young adult are losing relevance because they are not innovating for the new foodie generation.

Unfortunately, I knew what Ed's answer would be before he did.

"I'm really sorry we couldn't have had a better welcome for you," he said. "But what you're talking about, well, we can't make those kinds of moves right now. We just don't have the capital. And the use of data you're talking about? Our operators are just too slammed to be able to adapt to something new."

When he was a boy growing up in Milwaukee in the 1960s, Larry Johnson would often dip into a set of the *Encyclopaedia Britannica*. Again and again he'd return to the same volume to page through the entry on the nation of Brazil.

Young Larry became fascinated by that culture, the Amazon River, and the cowboy lifestyle of the gauchos. The thought of visiting such a fascinating place took hold in his mind. One day, he would go. He didn't know exactly when—but he would.

He was in his late twenties when he realized his dream. By then, he had studied both Spanish and Portuguese in college and had graduated law school, hoping to make his mark in international law. His first employer out of college, the international law firm Baker & McKenzie, sent him to Rio de Janeiro to develop their practice because he was one of the few Americans who spoke Portuguese. He lived there for two years, drinking in the culture. His time there ended when he left to be the cofounder of Baker & McKenzie's first office in Dallas.

In 1986, two of the founders of Fogo de Chão appeared in his Dallas office. The pair poured out their story. Some years ago, US president George H. W. Bush had eaten at one of their restaurants in São Paulo. He enjoyed himself so much that he told the brothers they should bring their concept to the US. The Coser and Ongaratto brothers could not have asked for a better invitation. The American president himself had beckoned them to Texas! They had struggled to find a restaurant location in Houston, but their lack of English no doubt contributed to their difficulties. A friend in São Paulo had tipped them off about an American attorney in Dallas who spoke flawless Portuguese.

Larry found their story about President Bush charming, and he was well aware of their brand. He had enjoyed dining at Fogo de Chão during his Brazilian sojourn. The brothers confessed that they foresaw opening only one or two restaurants in the United States. Larry admired their modest aspirations but pushed them to dream bigger. "Americans love meat," he told them. "Fogo could be huge!" He explained that they would want to demonstrate the concept's viability, eventually opening restaurants not only in Texas, but throughout the southeast, and possibly the west coast.

Larry had little idea then how much work he was getting himself into. He'd never had restaurateurs as clients. Fogo faced certain challenges going forward. At the time, it was not easy for foreign businesspeople to get liquor licenses in Texas. And if the founders wanted to hire authentic gauchos from Southern Brazil, Larry would need to bone up on immigration law to understand which visas their workforce would need.

But they were lucky in another sense. Dallas was quickly becoming the casual dining capital of the United States. Operational costs were lower in Dallas than in many other major cities. And because the cost of living was lower, customers had a higher disposable income to spend on dining out. Dallas was and still is a perfect place to launch a restaurant concept.

The team dug in and went to work. Along the way, Larry the attorney turned into Fogo's unofficial culinary adviser as well. It was his job to gently break it to the brothers that Americans didn't like their meat as salty as it was served back home in Brazil. And it would sometimes fall to him to explain to American meat purveyors how to butcher various cuts of meat to Brazilian specifications if they wished to win Fogo's business.

Over the next fifteen years, Fogo grew to be a major

dining phenomenon. Patrons and media were fascinated with the story of the gauchos. The company started with one restaurant outside Dallas, in Addison, Texas, and then opened others in four other major American cities: Houston, Atlanta, Chicago, and Beverly Hills. Change came as Fogo entered the twenty-first century. In 2005, the Cosers bought out the Ongarattos, and a year later, a private equity firm bought a stake in the company. It was time for Fogo to have a CEO, and it would be good if that person had business experience, understood the company, and spoke Portuguese. The Cosers and the private equity guys came to Larry. "Would you do it?"

Larry thought it over carefully. He was making a good living as an attorney. But how many times in your life do you get to build a company like this? How many times in your life do you get to share the culture of your dreams with the world?

"I could have said no," Larry says today. "I didn't understand the business of restaurants. But we're all on a journey in life. You don't always know where it's going, but you have to be adventurous enough to go down that path."

In 2007, Larry said yes to leading Fogo into its future. In 2011, the remaining founders, the Cosers, retired from the company. In 2012, a Boston private equity firm acquired Fogo and asked Larry to stay on to lead the company. By 2013, Fogo had twenty-seven locations—nineteen restaurants in the United States and eight in Brazil. They were profitable, robust, and enjoyed a great reputation. The restaurants were led by strong managers and got great reviews from customers. But the firm's dreams were bigger still. The new owners had presented Larry with a challenge: grow the company and take it public. Fogo believed that the United States alone could support more than one hundred locations.

Like most companies, Fogo probably could not proceed into the future the way it had in the past. If they wanted to expand, attract shareholders, and still be a leader in their restaurant class, they needed to evolve. But they had to do it in a way that retained the brand's integrity. They could never lose the gaucho way that guests found so irresistible and charming.

In order to move forward, Larry hired some new executives whose job it was to begin looking at the company through the lens of data analytics. As it turned out, one of those execs, a man named Barry McGowan, happened to be a past attendee of our Underground Culinary Tour. Our tour pushed Barry beyond mere numbers to a powerful emotional epiphany.

"I think we were all humbled by what we saw on that tour," Barry says today. "When you walk into the restaurant of a no-name chef and you see what he's doing, you realize, 'Wow, this guy's talented.' And it hits you: If you lose sight of trends, then any new young chef who comes along is going to be able to chip away at your market share."

In particular, on that tour we saw that small indie restaurants didn't have rafts of money like the big chains, but they focused their energies on the two things they *could* control: ingredients and service. The ethos of fresh and local wasn't just nice, it made good financial sense. When New Guard chefs bought produce in season, they realized great savings, and they spun that bumper crop into amazing seasonal dishes or cocktails. Small restaurants knew that little things added up. When Barry saw the finely etched cocktail glasses bartenders placed before him and his colleagues at Maison Premiere, he was taken aback at how special they made him feel. "Beautiful glassware elevates the experience!" he says.

During those early meetings, Barry and other newcomers learned that the company had thrived for nearly thirty-five years. With that kind of history, it was only reasonable to ask some critical questions: What did Fogo want its legacy to be? How did they see the business going forward in the next thirty-five years? How were they going to keep innovating?

What this data-driven approach brought to Fogo was a powerful grasp of operational know-how. The executives, new and old, worked together to dive deeper into the firm's best practices. Yes, Fogo had reams of data, but it was often looking at profit and loss data weeks after the fact. When you're swimming in data, it's often hard to know where to begin optimizing.

With both these fresh eyes and the existing experienced management team, Fogo saw an opportunity to simplify what they were looking at and ask themselves an easier question: "How can we enhance the guest experience?" This in turn led to other questions: What is guest behavior telling us? How can we make sure we're in sync with what guest behavior is telling us?

They knew that, like a lot of companies, Fogo could probably stand to optimize its labor force when guests were most likely to be on the premises. They suspected that even with thirty-five years of success under their belts, the company could also improve its meat and produce procurement. Waste was a perennial problem. Any all-you-wish-to-eat dining experience is going to have challenges estimating how much its guests will consume. Encouraged by Larry's team, Fogo focused on getting a handle on its trends and perfecting its forecasting. How many people were coming in the door? Are there any other metrics that matter to this brand? To answer those questions, Fogo incorporated our software to begin collecting data.

As the weeks went on, Fogo was able to build a solid database of its trends. It could track seasonal variations and anticipate changes due to the weather or sporting events, as well as local events such as conventions. The operators had long known, for instance, that in Brazil, dinner/lunch trends were *reversed*. In the United States, Fogo saw more guests at dinner than lunch. In Brazil, Fogo saw more people at lunch than dinner. The dining trends of the two nations could not be more different. In Brazil, Italy, and Spain, lunch is the most important meal of the day. In the United States, Canada, Britain, and Germany, dinner is the biggest meal of the day. Moreover, a Brazilian lunch was a lengthier affair than an American dinner, which had an impact on food consumption. Fogo already knew this. It's the kind of information that every general manager, depending on his geographical location, internalizes without even thinking about it. But hard data helped them grasp the magnitude. It revealed how a subtle, everyday pattern can impact your bottom line. Granular data provides remarkably nuanced insights. Fogo could, for instance, figure out when and how to improve their preparation for each of these different dining periods. How was Monday lunch different from Wednesday lunch? How were those dining periods impacted by the weather, or by local conventions? And what could they do to improve these specific meal periods?

It now became clear that they had a solid opportunity to improve the way the company ordered meat and produce, both in the United States and in Brazil. And they needed to enhance the way they staffed. Each shift had to become more nimble about preparing for the *next* shift. This may sound obvious, but it didn't always happen because the granularity and timeliness of the data they were using lacked the specificity to be hugely beneficial. Fogo was certainly moving toward better data collection and analytics, but they needed to share their findings with all their managers, in North and South America.

Working at Fogo is a bit like working at the UN. Newcomers probably feel that acutely when they attend their first meetings in Brazil, where some people speak English while Larry or Selma Oliveira, the company's COO, a native speaker, relay their words back to the group in flawless Portuguese. Brazilians had been grilling and serving steak their way for close to five hundred years. They were the originators of the concept. Their culture, their language, their grilling tradition, their brand of hospitality—it was all so much more than just "the way we do things around here." Once, when one of their American colleagues asked a Brazilian-born general manager if he could sum up the Fogo experience in three words, the man responded in English, "I don't need three words. I can do it in two. 'My life!'"

That response alone attested to the brand's charm, strength, and soul. Fogo started projecting its new approach to data on the screens of the company boardrooms. They showed charts that broke down the flow of guests in fifteen-, thirty-, and sixty-minute increments. In most cases, the graph of the flow of diners was a classic bell curve, peaking at certain hours before falling. In some cases, on a long weekend day, for instance, there were two peaks. They drilled down into the data, exploring, for example, how weather, local events, or even just the specific day of the week could impact those trends.

They would point out the peaks and explain their rationale: We know we need the gauchos in the restaurants when the guests are there. Now we believe we know exactly when that is. So let's get granular! Let's grill the meat just ahead of those curves. If we do it this way, we'll deliver amazing guest service!

This evolution in thinking didn't happen overnight, but in many training sessions I heard about, Fogo's managers were always blown away when they saw the data. Their eyes lit up. A flicker of understanding turned into a ripple and then a wave. I have seen that moment many times, and I regard it as one of the most amazing things about my work. You can tell people how data analytics will changed their lives till you are blue in the face. But when they see their own data in front of their eyes, something extraordinary happens. Wow, they think, my own data is telling me what to do in ways I didn't appreciate before. It's a magical, epiphanic moment. *They get it now.*

In a bicultural firm like Fogo, they had always worked

hard to make sure everyone was on the same page. But here were revelations that didn't matter if you spoke English or Portuguese. Data spoke louder than words.

Numbers, they all realized, were an international language.

There are tons of things that go into running a restaurant chain, but very few are visible to the guest. What the guest sees, tastes, sips, or otherwise experiences is the tip of the chain's spear. Those are things that guests will remember when they walk out the door. And those are the first things a leadership team should be concerned with.

In the most basic way, the gauchos are the all-too-human tip of Fogo's spear. The gauchos' attire might give you the impression that they are mere bit players in the daily pageant of meat, but they are far more critical to the operation than most people realize. In other restaurants, servers don't cook the food; they relay orders to the kitchen. But at Fogo, every gaucho acts as butcher, chef, and server, wrapped into one. They go through an extensive, one- to two-year training program to hone their cooking skills. And to retain the authenticity of the brand, Fogo has brought as many as 150 gaucho chefs from Brazil to train others how to cook in the gaucho way.

One innovation Fogo instituted was empowering its managers with technology. With strong tools in hand, the managers soon became, in Larry's words, "data hounds" who enjoyed studying the data and seeing for themselves when they needed to make adjustments to ordering ingredients and scheduling labor. At the end of each week, the locations reviewed how much meat they purchased and reconciled it with how many covers they did in the previous week. Next, they drilled down to explore the nuances I discussed earlier. Weather impacts. Conventions. Unusual shifts in day-of-the-week data. They took the time to schedule their staff more efficiently in light of any changes. In this way, they could prepare for the coming week.

When the restaurant opens in the morning, the kitchen staff prepares the salad bar. By ten thirty a.m., the first wave of gauchos begins arriving to prep for lunch. This early in the day, they have two types of data at their fingertips—historical data from the location's past six weeks, generated from our software, and Fogo's own report of the day's incoming reservations.

Reservations are just one of many indicators of how busy a restaurant will be. They can give you a good handle on how many people you're about to serve—but they can be misleading. Not everyone makes a reservation to eat at a restaurant like this. And people who do reserve sometimes don't show up, even if they've confirmed earlier in the day. Also key is understanding that each day of the week could potentially have different trends. Since the Atlanta location is surrounded by conference hotels, it can be hard to tell when they might get slammed by a large group of convention guests. So the restaurant's own historical statistics are a more accurate barometer for discerning which hours they're most likely to see a spike in guests.

Armed with solid data, the first team of gauchos enters the cooler and begins tackling the day's meat. Fogo buys boxed meats, choice or prime cuts, just the way the butchers at your local supermarket receive them. The first team uses the projected number of guests to butcher meat for lunch *and* the next shift. The meat that's going to be used for lunch is skewered and stacked in the refrigerator, where it can be grabbed at a moment's notice. The meat for the later shift is not skewered, but set aside within easy reach.

So as they get closer to lunchtime and more gauchos arrive, everyone can review the figures and make adjustments to the meat inventory. Some of the gauchos have already fired up the charcoal grill. The kitchen warms up as the embers glow red. The grill runs about twelve feet long, two-tiered, with teeth cut into its steel facade to permit insertion of the skewers. Near the grill, another gaucho is setting up the seasoning station, where sea salt and other spice rubs can be sprinkled on the skewered meat before it's inserted into the grill.

During peak times, the gauchos know that if they're cooking *picanha,* for example, those beautiful semicircular cuts of prime sirloin, they need to load each skewer with three to four pieces. Off-peak, they knock that down to two steaks per skewer. This way they can ensure that the steaks that are circulating through the dining room are as fresh as possible. The steaks will have come off the grill very recently. They'll be hotter, juicier, and ready to be served at the proper temperature. If the restaurant cooked four pieces per skewer during the off-peak time, a lot of that meat would be sitting around getting cold while waiting to be summoned by guests. This way, with proper planning, no matter when a guest arrives, they're getting the freshest cooked meats.

Earlier I mentioned that smaller restaurants can more nimbly purchase bumper crops of produce when in season and on sale, which chefs can turn into any number of specials. If Fogo's buyers are armed with six-week projections, they can do the exact same thing for the entire chain. Fresh seasonal vegetables enhance the salad bar, and fresh fruits are turned into cocktail specials that guests won't find at the bars of other chain restaurants. Accurate projections empower buyers and ensure intelligent procurement. Believe it or not, the national wholesale meat market exhibits strong seasonality as well. So Fogo's buyers can buy pork or strip steaks when they're on sale and in season and reap the benefits across the entire chain. By implementing these kinds of strategies, Fogo's meals were increasingly fresher, and they were still able to significantly lower their inventory costs on both continents. Normally, when a company says that they're cutting costs, lowering inventory, and minimizing waste, those actions negatively impact the guest experience. Here, Fogo's diners are getting a more tailored, more attractive assortment of meat and a greater choice of fruits and vegetables.

Larry and the company took actions that were guided by the infusion of data. But on our culinary tour, which is more of a qualitative, "gut feel" experience, we absorbed lessons *beyond* the numbers. And Barry, the exec who attended our tour, was eager to put some of those into practice as well. If you have the courage to innovate creatively, to be a trendsetter, you'll find the marketplace will often reward you.

Still dreaming of those beautiful bar glasses at Maison Premiere, Barry suggested the company improve the quality of the firm's glassware on select cocktails. There was another big menu change as well. Fogo had long been toying with the notion of adding seafood to their menu. They were aware that many times they were losing parties because a seafood diner would object to visiting a steakhouse. Seafood seemed to be a no-brainer, but how to do it right? Their competitors were adding seafood options to the salad bar and leaving it at that. The team thought Fogo could do better, and set out to find options that were appropriate to their brand.

They ended up adding their first new à la carte dishes to the menu in thirty-five years: a Brazilian-themed shrimp cocktail appetizer and a pan-seared Chilean sea bass. It was a risky move, since so much of the restaurant's identity revolved around its all-you-care-to-enjoy pricing structure. (As I write this, Fogo's lunches are about $32; dinners are $52 in most cities.) But the brand got almost immediate praise on social media for adding seafood options, and those dishes now generate an additional revenue stream.

All of these things—solving the Perfect Meat Dilemma, seasonal ingredients, the seafood dishes, the scheduling, the glassware—were policies Fogo implemented across the continents. When guests leave Fogo dining rooms at the end of the night, they remember the heft of those stylish cocktail glasses, the savory perfection of the beef, and the freshness of the ingredients.

Fogo has been looking for ways to improve the work of the gauchos. They understood that their business model depended on the gauchos being available to guests as much as possible. Even when the gauchos aren't on duty to slice meat, they are taking the temperature of the crowd, seeing how they could be of assistance, or relaying requests for particular cuts or doneness. But sometimes, during high-volume periods, gauchos may find themselves taking food or beverage orders if the non-gaucho servers are busy. These days in the Dallas location, they're experimenting with handheld electronic ordering devices that allow non-gaucho servers to relay drink, appetizer, and dessert orders directly to the bar or kitchen. This way, the servers don't have to leave the floor and they don't have to bother the gauchos. Everyone can do the work they are tasked with doing.

They are also building a database will help Fogo better understand server productivity. Typically, as we've seen, tracking who sold what to which table is an onerous task. At a later date, a general manager should be able to track down that information. But doing so is often so laborious a task that no one bothers taking the time to do it.

Mobile ordering technology tells you exactly who sold what during which shift to which table. That allows you to better train servers, drive sales, and improve the guest experience. This innovation is still in development, but a tiny digital tool has the potential to kick a five-hundred-year-old tradition up to the next level.

"Technology helps us track our peak times and manage everything better," Larry says today. "We're more productive and we manage our labor force in an ideal manner. If we had just done what we've always done, it wouldn't have been good enough today. The climate was changing, and we were ready for it."

Thanks to focusing more intelligently on the data that mattered, Fogo did in fact grow stronger, and it added more than fourteen restaurants to the brand in two years. I was there the day Larry and his entire organization opened their largest restaurant in the United States, a 16,000-square-foot location in midtown Manhattan. And while I was a bit bleary-eyed as a result of the festive celebration, I couldn't help but be impressed by their sense of corporate pride.

What Larry accomplished was really amazing. When Fogo first began in the late 1970s, it was privately held and its every move was a closely kept secret. Today the company has successfully transitioned from being a family company to a publicly traded company, where every move is transparent. The irony is that the key to that change— the successful integration of data—was placed into the hands of those who first trained as gauchos. The fact that Fogo could weather thirty-plus years of change, two sets of private equity investors, and still manage to keep the primacy of the gaucho culture alive is astonishing. Usually, businesses lose the magic as they get bigger. Fogo preserved and enhanced it.

About two years later, in June 2015, when Fogo took the company public, they flew every general manager in the chain—even those in Brazil—to New York City. For most of these people, it was the first time they had ever been to Manhattan, not to mention the first time they'd been outside of South America. Brazilian dancers delighted the crowds in Times Square, while their international team of gauchos had the honor of ringing the opening bell on the NASDAQ exchange.

Watching their exuberant celebration from nearby, I couldn't help feeling that Fogo de Chão was more than a chain; it was a family. The gauchos of previous generations cemented their friendship around a campfire, the original *fogo de chão*. Today, their descendants were building fresh bonds in response to two new tools: data and creative thinking.

· 5 ·

THE CELEBRITY CHEF EVOLVES

Guy Fieri flew to Las Vegas to meet with Tom Jenkin, who was eager to bring a number of hot chefs into the fold at Caesars Entertainment. As you probably know, Guy has an enormous platform. His TV shows, *Guy's Big Bites* and *Diners, Drive-Ins, and Dives,* are some of the top-watched shows on Food Network. Millions of people binge-watch episodes that feature the goateed and tattooed wild man of casual cuisine as he visits greasy spoons all over the country and stuffs his face with reckless abandon. Guy's been working in the restaurant business his whole life; he has written numerous bestselling cookbooks, and launched his restaurant empire with pasta and sushi/BBQ eateries in California. It was only a matter of time before Guy's empire grew beyond California, beyond TV. It was only a matter of time before Guy took on the world.

Tom Jenkin, you'll recall, had been Jeffrey Frederick's old boss at the Rio; the same fellow who'd marched Jeffrey around the casino back in the day, asking his young men-tee, "What do you see? What do you see?"

Tom and his fellow executives had concluded that they had to start incorporating celebrity chef restaurants into their casinos. Who better to draw guests by the busload to new eateries than chefs who were already household names? But if Caesars was going to make this work, they would have to convince some of the world's most visible chefs that they could trust Caesars to safeguard, enhance, and amplify their brand.

That day, Guy and Tom kicked around a few ideas in Tom's office. Then Tom suggested they walk over to look at the site Caesars had in mind for Guy's restaurant. Back in 2005, the company had acquired an old casino, the Impe-rial Palace, which was currently in the process of a massive makeover, and the construction of an adjacent entertain-ment complex. The two men stood on the construction site, squinting at a mountain of dirt and the occasional steel girder.

"You gotta imagine what this will look like someday," Tom told Guy.

From where they stood, looking across South Las Vegas Boulevard, they could see the Caesars Forum Shops and the Mirage Resort and Casino. A steel structure that looked like the bare bones of a carport loomed over their heads. It took a lot to imagine the place that was to come—a natural wood and glazed-brick temple of American comfort food indulgence.

There could be a cool bar over here, they said. *Huge plate glass windows here! An outdoor patio!*

In about twenty minutes, they had a rough concept and

an understanding that Caesars was going to be in the Guy Fieri business.

Meanwhile, in New York City, things were not all peace, love, and taco grease, as Guy likes to say. In September 2012, Guy opened Guy's American Kitchen & Bar, a five-hundred-seat restaurant in New York's Times Square, and a terrible thing happened. A food critic from the *New York Times* visited and had a bad experience.

Depending on your point of view, what emanated from critic Pete Wells's computer was either the most entertaining review in the 163-year history of the newspaper—or the most devastating. Thousands of *Times* readers e-mailed his negative review to their friends. By that afternoon, the article had taken on a life of its own on the Internet. It was tweeted, Facebooked, and amplified.

For Guy Fieri, the fire had to be contained. He and his team went into damage control mode. The review appeared on a Wednesday morning. And by Thursday morning, Guy appeared on the *Today* show to defend himself.

Friends of mine in the restaurant industry feared for Guy. He has an incredible passion for American food, and his cuisine was marked by a certain genius. He created versions of American classics so good that your palate took over, and though your rational mind knew these mouthfuls weren't the healthiest menu items in the world, you just didn't care. Burgers too big to hold with two hands. Mega-cheesed nachos with brash, bold, rip-your-face-off spices. My personal favorite is his mac-and-cheese bacon burger, which packs twenty-two different ingredients and six different cheeses into a huge, garlic-butter-brushed bun.

It's a super-decadent burger, and every nutritionist's worst nightmare.

Tom Jenkin and his team at Caesars had the vision to land Guy for what would eventually become the LINQ Hotel & Casino. But now, naysayers in the restaurant community would pull me aside and wonder aloud: *Will he get a second chance? How could he come back from such a terrible review?* The Las Vegas restaurant was as good as dead.

No, I told them, *it's going to be awesome. You watch.*

And lo, when the Vegas restaurant opened in spring of 2014, the fans showed up in droves, and their reviews were ecstatic. In some cases people who had eaten the very same dishes in New York City proclaimed on Yelp and TripAdvisor—the two largest and most influential social media restaurant review sites online—that the Las Vegas dishes were the same but *better.* The *Las Vegas Review-Journal* pronounced Guy's breadsticks—which are wrapped with pepperoni and served with melted pizza cheese dipping sauce—"addictive." I know those breadsticks well. They're a guilty pleasure that I enjoy sharing with visitors who are new to Las Vegas.

The reviews that came in were incredible. People were bowled over by the flavor at Guy's. They urged their friends, family, and colleagues to go: *Guy Fieri's Vegas Kitchen & Bar is not to be missed.* Even Pete Wells, the *New York Times* food critic, made the astonishing admission in an August 2014 tweet that the Vegas restaurant was "easily twice as good as his restaurant in Times Square."

At the time Guy's restaurant was being planned in

Vegas, Caesars was signing deals with other celebrity chefs, such as Gordon Ramsay and Giada De Laurentiis. As we'll see, the way they went about creating restaurants for those celebrity chefs was nothing short of brilliant.

Some years earlier, Tom Jenkin had tried to convince Giada to open a restaurant in the Paris Hotel and Casino—the resort with a replica of the Eiffel Tower soaring over it—but was unsuccessful. Now Caesars was developing a luxury boutique hotel just across the street from the famous fountains of the Bellagio Hotel and Casino. The Cromwell would be small by Vegas standards—only 188 rooms. If they were going to build a restaurant in this location, it had to feature the cuisine of a chef whose brand was so iconic that it would entice guests from other hotels. To Tom it was clear—it had to be Giada.

Giada is America's sweetheart of California-Italian cuisine. The granddaughter of the Italian film producer Dino De Laurentiis, a graduate of Le Cordon Bleu, the legendary French cooking school, she went from preparing dishes in her family's kitchen to working for Wolfgang Puck at Spago, and then straight to the realm of Food Network cooking shows. At the time she was preparing for her Vegas debut, she had published seven bestselling books, won four Emmy Awards, and presided over four different TV cooking shows. But she didn't have a restaurant of her own—yet.

Tom flew to Los Angeles with some mock-up plans and met Giada in her trailer, not far from where she was filming one of her shows. As he'd done with Guy Fieri, Tom asked Giada to use her imagination. "The building is a parking structure today," he said, "so you're going to have to visualize what I'm showing you. I think it's going to be a very romantic spot. You'll be right on a corner and you can see everything from the Mirage to the north and Aria to the south, with the Bellagio fountains dancing in between. I think it's the greatest view in the world."

As the two of them spoke, they got more and more excited. When he left Giada's trailer, Tom came away with the feeling that she would say yes.

And of course she did.

But as the restaurant's opening day drew near, I would from time to time hear snarky comments from cynics in the restaurant world. Pointing to Giada's experience, skeptics whispered that her restaurant could fail.

Nope, I said. *You watch. It'll be awesome.*

And when the eponymously named GIADA opened in June 2014, they were already knee-deep in reservations; the earliest guests returned high rankings across key online review sites. The *Review-Journal* called Giada's restaurant "a hot commodity," with the second-highest bookings of any Caesars restaurant. It was clear that Giada—and the entire Caesars team that pulled this deal together—had another hit on their hands.

Now, you might well ask why I was so confident that these places would be successful. I knew that Tom Jenkin's team, which included people like David Hoenemeyer, the regional president who oversees Planet Hollywood, the Paris, and Bally's; Gary Selesner, president of Caesars Palace; and Eileen Moore, the regional president who oversees the Flamingo, Cromwell, and the LINQ—not to mention

Jeffrey Frederick—were in charge of building and designing those restaurants. With the input of the celebrity chefs,
they would be shaping everything from the menus to the
décor to selecting and training the staffs. My confidence
boiled down to my understanding of Caesars and Jeffrey's
approach to restaurant creation. I knew that the food in
both of these places would hit its marks, and that the staff
would be exceptionally well trained.

The pacts celebrity chefs make with Vegas resorts are
tricky, to say the least. In the real world, chefs who open
their own restaurants can typically call all the shots, with
input from a small group of partners or investors. But
Vegas celebrity restaurants are a corporate endeavor. Since
the resort owns the restaurants and foots the bills, it can
theoretically do as it likes. But Caesars knew that the celebrity chef is the reason people walk in the door. They had
to work hard to nail down the chef's identity and radiate
that style throughout every inch of the restaurant. Guests
understand that celebrity chefs are not working daily in
their signature restaurants. They can't be everywhere at
once. Many have more than one restaurant. They are far
too busy with their TV shows and book tours to be working in the back of the house, or wherever their far-flung
restaurants are situated around the globe. But what those
chefs and their teams do is spell out a certain standard,
enumerate a certain style of food, and leave it to the resort
that has licensed their brand to refine the concept. And the
chefs check in from time to time to monitor the progress.

Around the time the *New York Times* review broke, Jeffrey was in talks with Guy Fieri and Fieri's group chef to

discuss ways they could enhance menu items at the new restaurant. Noticing that the *Times* review complained about the New York restaurant's blending of lasagna noodles with tortilla chips in the nachos dish, and closed with a dig at the Vegas fries, Jeffrey told Guy, "I think we can invent something better than those nachos. And I *know* we can make a more amazing dish of fries."

Guy threw down the gauntlet. "Go for it."

To begin the process of menu development, Jeffrey typically picks a Caesars kitchen to head up the new project, then visits to give the chef and his team their marching orders. "We have five months to put together a menu for Guy Fieri," he might say. He'd spell out the dishes Guy was interested in and leave them to go to work. He'd visit frequently to see what they'd come up with. The young chefs would eye him nervously as he went down the line, using knife and fork to slice into, say, a selection of hamburgers, tasting them to see which seasonings best approximated the flavor a guest expected from a Guy Fieri burger. Then he would whip out his phone and photograph everything. During restaurant ramp-ups, Jeffrey's wife Jenn has been known to joke that he has more pictures of food on his iPhone than pictures of their kids. Whenever Jeffrey does a recipe check, his chefs stand at attention, waiting for the big man to weigh in on their efforts. He deconstructs the food, edits ingredients on the fly, suggests new approaches, and then leaves his chefs to get to work. For the last step, Guy would fly in to taste the flavors himself.

One time, Jeffrey wanted to create a brown butter ice cream to accompany the sticky toffee pudding dessert in

Gordon Ramsay's new steak house. Ramsay, of course, is the British star of such popular cooking shows as *Hell's Kitchen* and *Kitchen Nightmares*. Famously pugnacious and colorfully foul-mouthed, the former footballer nevertheless has managed to rack up no fewer than sixteen Michelin stars in his remarkable career. His food is renowned for its quality. But as Jeffrey tasted the ice cream his chefs had developed, he knew that it was not good enough to be included in Chef Ramsay's upcoming menu. Every version was somehow lacking in flavor. He finally figured out that his chefs were browning the butter, then adding both the milk solids *and* the butterfat to their ice cream mix. "Guys," he said, "the strongest favor is in the solids, not the oil!" The next time he came around to do a taste test, the ice cream was perfect, just the right balance of creaminess and buttery flavor. So he ramped up the challenge: "When it comes to the table, it has to look like a stick of butter."

"Won't that confuse people?" someone asked.

"Yes, but they'll love it."

Caesars knows that a Vegas restaurant isn't just about the food; it is about treating the guest to a spectacle. *We are trying to wow them, people!* Jeffrey would tell his chef teams. When the burger in Guy Fieri's restaurant came to the table, it had to awe guests. One look, and they had to be impressed by the visuals—the over-the-top collection of toppings. Conversely, at BurGR—the burger place they were creating for Gordon Ramsay—the burger is all about minimalist perfection: the erect, peppy bun speared to a hefty slab of meat that has been lovingly brushed five times with Devonshire butter, and nothing more.

In the end, Jeffrey's team presented Guy and his group

chef with a plate of nachos that drew its flavor from the addition of meaty brisket. And then, for the Vegas fries, they used a "sidewinder" potato cut—thick crescents of potato that have a bit of a twist to them—dusted with dry buffalo seasoning powder and served with hot sauce in a shot glass and a side of creamy blue cheese dressing. Insanely, they *look* like fries, but *taste* like chicken wings. They pulled off a similar flavor conflation with those addictive breadsticks I mentioned earlier. Jeffrey told the team he was interested in creating an appetizer that tasted like pizza but looked nothing like a pizza. The secret was developing a fondue dipping sauce that tasted like the cheesy top of a pizza without the bread. When they presented the dishes to Guy, he was blown away.

When celebrity chefs start talking about a new restaurant, they immediately begin by describing the kind of food they want to serve. That makes sense, right? It's their job to focus on food. To them, food is brand, food is identity. But to succeed in Vegas, a restaurant needs much more. The job of the team is to look at the bigger picture, and to go where chefs don't think to tread. Jeffrey hired Guy Fieri's tattoo artist to design the napkins for Guy's restaurant. He hired one of the Hollywood costumiers of *Glee* and *Mad Men* to design uniforms for the servers. During that process, his iPhone swelled with test photos of models wearing retro British banker uniforms (the prototypes for Gordon Ramsay Steak) and motorcycle vests (the prototypes for Fieri's restaurant).

Jeffrey would take meetings with the architects and designers. And he would say, as he did in the case of Gordon Ramsay Pub & Grill, "I want a floor-to-ceiling wall of beer kegs!" Or in the case of Gordon Ramsay BurGR, "I want a wall of flame." As they were talking about the design of Ramsay's steak place, which would be located in the Caesars Paris-themed casino, Jeffrey said, "I want something to transport us to another world." At the time, the working idea was to remove the three Parisian-themed faux building facades that occupied the site, and replace them with a three-story red glass window. But taking Jeffrey's challenge to heart, the designer in charge came back with something even more appropriate. He proposed building an entrance reminiscent of the Chunnel leading into Gordon's restaurant. When guests enter, it's as if they're leaving the French-themed casino floor, crossing the English Channel, and arriving for dinner in the UK.

In their zeal to protect their reputations, the celebrity chefs sometimes get skittish about the spectacle. But Jeffrey knows that spectacle is at least a third of the guest's experience. When he helped the Scottish-born Ramsay roll out Steak, his carnivore's paradise and one of more than twenty restaurants in the chef's international empire, Jeffrey hit upon the notion of designing a meat trolley. The trolley would feature several arms fitted with plates, upon which would rest various cuts of beef. Mirrors would reflect views of those marbled slabs to the entire dining room. Experience had taught Jeffrey that most guests had no clue what part of the cow they were eating. They would order a filet mignon and be disappointed that it isn't a huge, bone-in slab of meat. Many didn't know a tenderloin from a shank, a broil from a strip, a T-bone from a beef tip. Visuals helped clinch the deal. And perhaps more important, out-of-town guests were not going to get a meat trolley in Minnetonka or Peoria.

But the trolley relied on each server's ability to succinctly describe each of those cuts of meat. As he began training the servers, Jeffrey was appalled to discover that every one of them trotted out the same tired adjectives: "tender" and "juicy."

One night Jeffrey went ballistic. He locked the doors of the restaurant's upstairs dining room and told the servers that no one was leaving until they all agreed on the precise descriptions for those cuts. The staffers who survived that two a.m. intervention will today joke about what happened, but every one of them can distinguish those cuts for you in under a minute.

As each restaurant debuts, the celebrity chefs are required by the terms of their contracts to appear at various kickoff functions. The first time Chef Ramsay saw the trolley at the restaurant's inauguration dinner, he blanched. "I'm not fucking putting that thing in my restaurant."

Chefs obsess about the food; they forget about the spectacle.

Jeffrey touched the arm of the most prickly chef on the planet. "I'll tell you what—let's roll it out for the very first meal service. If guests react poorly, you'll never see it again. But I'm telling you, people will *love* it."

Ramsay assented. The trolleys started rolling. And the result? When servers paraded the cart through the dining room, voices shushed, eyes became transfixed, necks craned. And many reviews of Gordon Ramsay Steak mentioned the trolley. People posted photos of the gleaming, meat-laden conveyance on Instagram, Facebook, Twitter, and Yelp, just as other guests had posted images of the keg wall in Gordon Ramsay Pub & Grill, and the wall of flame in Gordon Ramsay's BurGR.

The Caesars team appeared to hit home runs every time they launched a new restaurant. But with so much at stake, there was bound to be friction. The most heavily publicized story surrounded Giada's restaurant. Giada, as it turned out, was the most gracious and hands-on of all the celebrity chefs Jeffrey worked with. She and her group chef flew frequently to Vegas to taste menu items, review design elements, and consult on staffing. And she approved or nixed every single detail of the restaurant's creation.

The biggest issue came down to the food. Giada's style in the kitchen is pretty distinctive. There's nothing like it. Historically, Italian restaurants in the United States have tended to be red-sauce palaces because that's the style of food prepared in the southern tip of Italy, from which the majority of Italian Americans emigrated to the United States. Giada's grandfather, the film director Dino De Laurentiis, himself hailed from Naples, located in the southern "instep" of Italy's famous boot-shaped peninsula.

But Giada's cooking style is lighter, more citrusy, more Californian than old-school Italian. The chef team Jeffrey had hired—which consisted of an Italian-born executive chef and his sous chef—struggled to modify their style of Italian cuisine to turn out Giada's recipes. They'd nail those recipes when coached, but gradually they returned to what they knew best—dishes that were too red, too rich, too dark to be associated with Giada's.

Giada insisted on changing chefs. Jeffrey resisted. Their opening was fast approaching, and he didn't want to start training yet another new team. Things got heated. As Giada later told the Las Vegas media, Jeffrey's message to her went something like this: "Listen—your standards are too high! You have to understand who you are and where you're at. And you're not Thomas Keller. You're not Alain Ducasse. You're not Guy Savoy. You think you are, but you're not. And so you need to compromise a little bit. You need to find a chef you can mold into what you want."

Tough words. But Giada relented. Six weeks later, she couldn't take it anymore. The dishes were *still* not coming out right. She went back to Jeffrey, laid out her reasoning, and pulled the trigger. "I tried it your way. But he has to go!"

"And you know what?" Jeffrey tells me today, "she was right! It took me a while to understand that this wasn't about the authenticity of Italian cuisine—it's about Giada's palate and what her fans were expecting when they walked in the door." With three weeks left to go, they replaced the executive chef with a longtime resort executive chef who had worked on the development of other Caesars restaurants.

It's no question that things were tense during that time. If Jeffrey hadn't been so close to the story, I think he would have realized that he and Giada were both under the same pressure, for exactly the same reason—they wanted to make a good impression. How could he ask Giada to compromise on quality when he himself *hated* to compromise on quality?

Next, Jeffrey turned his attention to the front of the

house. Customer service was critical. Jeffrey could not let a new chef and a month-old team of servers go out and wing it. He needed guests to be blown away by flavor, service, and ambience to such an extent that when they returned home to Parsippany, they wouldn't be able to stop talking about where they had eaten. Only that kind of word of mouth and loyalty would guarantee a restaurant's success. He would have loved to train servers for three months prior to opening, but he knew that was impossible. In Vegas, unions make everything expensive. He asked his bosses for one and a half months to train; they gave him three weeks. Since Jeffrey didn't have the budget to train the way he wanted to, he was forced to rely on something else to hone his teams, something that gave him an edge nobody else in the industry had. He relied on data, technology—and his own uncompromising attention to detail.

Prior to opening, many restaurants conduct mock servings to train their staff. One group of servers will pretend to be guests. They'll sit at the tables and actually enjoy a meal served by their peers. The next night, they'll switch off. Gradually, the restaurant will move beyond server-on-server training, inviting nonpaying family and friends to dine at the restaurant too. Jeffrey was also accustomed to doing one round where his team waited on nonpaying Caesars casino executives.

Knowing that many of his general managers and hosts had never worked as servers, Jeffrey also stipulated that they too had to do a couple of drills working as servers. Management teams didn't always welcome doing this, but Jeffrey's feeling was that managers had to understand the difficulty inherent in a server's job. In the kitchen, it is understood that a chef must be able to jump on the line at a moment's notice to fill in for a colleague. Jeffrey believed that the front of the house should be able to do the same thing.

During the mock trials, it's often common practice to train servers to hit their marks in a carefully scripted way. Jeffrey calls his script "The Guest Journey," which is everything that guests must experience from the moment they enter.

Step 1. The guests enter and are greeted by the host.
Step 2. The host walks the guests to their table.
Step 3. The host tells the guests the name of their server.
Step 4. The server arrives at the table.
Step 5. The server presents the wine list and menus.
Step 6. The server asks if he or she can bring water—tap or bottled, sparkling or still?

And so on, all the way through to the conclusion of the meal. The Guest Journey ensures that every single party is treated exactly the same way.

Up to this point, Jeffrey's team was being trained pretty much like any other team in the industry. But with our help, he raised the game to a new level. At the conclusion of each meal, every party of mock guests was handed their check presenter, which is the faux-leather folder that holds the check and the guest's form of payment. Embedded in each presenter was an iPod Touch, which prompted guests to take a survey.

How do you rate the food?

What were your favorite and least favorite dishes?

What did you like, what didn't you like?

How was the server's menu knowledge?

How friendly was your server?

Did the food come on time?

Did the manager stop by to visit the table?

Will you return?

In a sense, the iPod Touch program that we created for Jeffrey mimicked the social media apps that we knew real, paying guests would be itching to access as soon as they left the restaurant. We figured that as long as they were going to give people a piece of their minds, why not give it to us first? Using this kind of device to analyze and tweak pre-opening rehearsals was revolutionary, if I do say so myself. Suddenly, Jeffrey was getting real-time data about the restaurant's performance. Every response was collected, crunched, and whisked to Jeffrey's laptop, where he carefully analyzed the data. During the rehearsal dinners, when he saw a pattern emerging in the data, he could announce to the kitchen: "You're killing it on the appetizers and pastas. People are loving them." Or "The desserts are subpar. You need to figure out what's wrong."

Out front, he'd tell the general manager: "There's a time issue cropping up with these particular servers. Guests have been waiting too long for the drinks and appetizers."

In other words, before a single paying guest walked in the door, the kitchen and waitstaff were getting feedback on their performance, so they knew exactly what areas they needed to improve. Jeffrey was completely transparent about the server's scores, posting them in a public place where everyone could see how they were performing relative to their peers. This offered opportunities for coaching low-performing servers.

Jeffrey's feedback didn't stop at constructive coaching. He could trace poor guest experiences back to particular servers, and then double-check to see if those servers showed a consistent pattern of poor performance. Prior to serving the first meal to the public, he has been known to let as many as fifteen charismatic, well-pedigreed employees go before completing the training, including a general manager with a long career at several successful Vegas eateries. It didn't matter if they had glittering resumes; if the data showed that they weren't cutting it at Fieri's, or Giada's, or any of Ramsay's restaurants, they had to go. But while the data led to some firings, he didn't actually have to dismiss as many people as you'd think. Because he'd been so transparent about posting servers' scores, the ones who weren't measuring up typically dropped out of his intensive boot camp of their own accord, and sought employment elsewhere.

During the Giada trials, considering everything that had transpired previously, Jeffrey stood at the door of the kitchen with a digital thermometer, testing and inspecting every dish that went out the door. Pretty soon the staff started calling him the Gates of Hell—they couldn't get past Jeffrey without nailing Giada's recipes!

In fact, on one visit, Giada herself asked Jeffrey, "Does every restaurant do this?"

"No," he replied. "Most don't do it this way. But we do."

I don't know anyone in the industry who does this kind of training. I don't know anyone who insists his managers work as servers, just to see what it's like. And very few restaurants use technology at the guest table to collect preopening data. But it's arguably the wave of the future. Think about it: The point of mock trials isn't just to give your team practice, it's also to see if they're delivering a superb guest experience.

This is how Jeffrey and his team sharpened both the staffs and the menus of these restaurants well before opening day. When the real, paying guests arrived, they too were presented with the iPod Touch surveys, but by then both the front and back of the house were working together as a well-oiled machine. They were ready for anything, including today's on-the-fly social media reviews. And it showed.

At the time I'm writing these words, Jeffrey has designed about sixty restaurants. He's come a long way since the day he walked the floor of the Rio with Tom Jenkin, unsure of what he was seeing.

"Every time we do a restaurant with an iconic chef," Tom tells me today, "the question they have is always the same. 'How are you going to protect my brand?' That's what they care about. They want to know that we're not going to screw it up. They want to know we're going to be good stewards of what they're entrusting us with. Every chef we've worked with knows we will be good stewards because of Jeffrey and our team. They helped build those relationships for us."

Chances are that if you've eaten anywhere new at a Caesars property on the strip, you probably have eaten in a place the team designed. Most of the restaurants they've launched are phenomenal successes. These new restaurants brought in approximately double the revenue of the old restaurants that had been in the same spaces previously. Gordon Ramsay's BurGR has become one of the most popular burger locations in the *world*.

Yes, you might say, *but it's Gordon Ramsay's restaurant; that's why it's popular.* But those who say that are making a common mistake. The celebrity chef's name may lure guests in the door, but if the food isn't great, if the experience doesn't deliver, guests won't return or share their delight with millions of other foodies. In fact, if a guest has a bad experience, the fact that it's Fieri's or Giada's or Ramsay's place makes it all the more certain that the guest is going to gleefully post a negative review online.

That's why Jeffrey has also made a point of scrutinizing postopening social media reviews. It's not well known, but websites such as Yelp allow you to search reviews containing, say, mentions of specific entrées or adjectives such as "greasy," "salty," or "sucked." Jeffrey uses those searches to see if people are praising or damning the same menu items. Many in the industry prefer to ignore social media reviews entirely, citing their unreliability. And that's true. In general, social media data has serious shortcomings. Reviewers are not professionals. They often have no background to be judging a particular cuisine. They may even be disgruntled former employees. But they are still an interesting data point to consider. Now, with the help of technology, if a GM knows the date and time of a guest's poor experience, he or she can trace the problem right back to the check and the server who worked that shift and table. But there's no way to track a bad social media review to a particular table, server, or shift.

So if a restaurant's new and only has a few dozen spotty reviews, it's probably wise to ignore them. But once a restaurant starts collecting hundreds or thousands of reviews, the law of averages starts to kick in, and those reviews become valuable indicators of how its food and service are being received. If you do a search on Yelp and lots of people keep saying the coffee tastes like crap, or the steak is overcooked, you have a problem. Fix it.

Attention to details and data has made all the difference. You don't need to be a mathematician to use data and trends; in fact, when a creative person uses these tools, good things happen. For many years, Jeffrey had an edge in a highly competitive city where fickle guests have endless options. It's to the credit of the senior executives at Caesars—people like Tom, David, Eileen, and Gary—that they were willing to allow their food and beverage professionals the room to pursue such a progressive program of data collection. The surveys we created together are still in use in some of their Vegas and Atlantic City restaurants, so don't be surprised if you're handed one the next time you dine at a Caesars property.

Often, when restaurateurs get hold of serious data, they

fall into the trap of taking an increasingly lopsided view of the numbers. They obsess about how to "drive"—that is, increase—the size of the average restaurant check. To them, the perfect check is the most expensive one possible. But Jeffrey was coming to see it differently. The perfect check was the one that was profitable *and* inspired thoroughly delighted guests to tell the world about their dining experience.

He was also beginning to become tempted by the world of restaurants beyond Caesars. Could he make an impact elsewhere? The desire to test himself beyond the world of Caesars would simmer in the background for years, unwittingly setting the stage for a dramatic change in Jeffrey's career.

· 6 ·

NUMBERS IN NIGHTLIFE

The night the cab lets me off in front of the MGM Grand Las Vegas Hotel & Casino, the facade of the largest single hotel in the United States is bathed in the glow of green lights. Just before I hop out, I take in the massive banners draped across the front of the building touting upcoming nightclub appearances by two world-renowned DJs— Calvin Harris on one, Tiësto on the other.

As I cut through the lobby and the floor of the casino, I can see that the gaming floor is busy, but it feels as if everyone I see has another destination in mind. Every guy I see is sharply dressed. Every woman seems to be attired in a tight black dress.

It's club night in Vegas, and people are getting ready to make some noise.

We all converge in a second lobby area toward the back, not far from the entrance to Hakkasan, one of the hottest nightclubs in the city. I send a quick text to my contact, Carlos, the club's general manager. While I wait, I mill around trying to wrap my head around the size of Hakkasan's operation. There's a line of women waiting to enter the club. Another much shorter line for guests with prepaid tickets. A longer line for guests who are buying their tickets last minute. And another line for the high rollers of the evening, guests who have booked VIP tables somewhere in the club. All in all, it's a remarkably efficient way of managing all these different types of clientele.

Everywhere I look, there are security personnel outfitted with ear mics and hosts who are there to welcome the VIPs for whom they have arranged a truly special night of partying and entertainment. Everyone working the lines is dressed immaculately in perfectly tailored gray or black suits.

Carlos appears out of nowhere, a well-dressed gentleman who treats me like an old friend, though we've never met. Later, once we've been enveloped by the darkness and thumping of the club, he gets me a drink, leads me on a tour of the place, and confesses to being something of a data geek.

Turns out, Carlos first used my software as a manager of China Grill, one of my early clients and a trendy upscale Asian restaurant with locations in New York, Mexico City, and Dubai. And he uses it today at the club, against a backdrop of gyrating bodies, cutting-edge music, and colored lasers.

Hakkasan is the first club unveiled in Las Vegas by Hakkasan Group, which has more than forty restaurants

and fifteen club venues around the world, as well as a relatively new concept on the block: dayclubs.

The club we are in now has five levels, and eighty
thousand square feet. Far below us, on the dance floor, DJ
Ruckus is enthralling a crowd of a few thousand people.
Every time I come to Vegas I try to visit a variety of clubs to
see my clients, drink in the spectacle, and get my eardrums
and mind blown. When you are on the dance floor at Hakkasan, with every sense you possess being bombarded by
music, colored lights, blasts of air-conditioned cold air, un-
dulating dancing men and women, and waves of confetti
dropping from the ceiling, it's hard to imagine anyone
dreaming up a more high-energy setting.

But the Hakkasan Group—the bosses and administra-
tive staff, the hosts, the security guards, the cocktail servers
bringing guests their magnums of Grey Goose—would not
be able to do their jobs without the weekly, daily, hourly
crunching of data. What they do is different from running
a restaurant, but not by much, which I'll get to in a moment. It's a little hard to think with all this music.

The next night, I have dinner with one of the executives of this hip young firm. Afterward he drives us over to
the company's newest nightclub, OMNIA, housed at Caesars Palace. The scene is much the same, only bigger, more
lavish, with even more people. And of course it would be—
tonight's DJ is a legend.

As I follow the exec on a quick tour of the 75,000-
square-foot OMNIA, I'm astonished by the finishes. Every
wall harbors a secret life as a flat-screen television, projecting abstract images suggestive of objects in the natural

world—water, bubbles, strobes, waves, light beams. As he ascends a staircase to the rooftop garden, every step on the stair treads pulses with light at the touch of his feet. The designers of the rooftop terrace were inspired by Shakespeare's *A Midsummer Night's Dream*. The terrace is decorated with trees and offers views of the Vegas Strip that outshine the lights of Times Square.

Back inside, we head for a spot just behind the DJ's booth. From here I can see beautiful young women dancing on tables below us while revelers hoist their drinks. The eleven-ton chandelier, constructed of eight oval rings, moves in sync with the music. One moment it looks like a funnel, the next like a spaceship out of a Steven Spielberg theatrical release. On a level below us, someone has ordered a case of Dom Pérignon—effectively, a $12,000 drink order. Six cocktail servers dressed in skintight army fatigues carry the dozen bottles aloft over the heads of the crowd while two drummers beat on electronic drums that glow neon green with every beat. On other nights, you may see a giant, human-operated dragon flutter down from the mezzanine to deliver a bottle of champagne to a VIP's table. Or a nubile aerialist descend from the ceiling to perform before a table of cheering onlookers.

It's over the top, it's insane: it's Vegas.

Hakkasan Group is neither the first nor the only player on the Vegas club scene. There are several companies in the city that have brilliantly merged clubbing and partying— Wynn Resorts, Tao Group, Drai's, SBE, and Hard Rock. These venues offer an entertainment *spectacle* that you can't find anywhere else. Imagine Cirque du Soleil meets the world-class electronic dance music (or EDM) DJ move-ment, and you might be getting close. The performers are so well known that you've probably heard their music on FM radio, iTunes, Pandora, Spotify, or whatever your streaming platform is. One such performer is DJ Zedd, a Russian-German twentysomething who most often plays at the Wynn's dayclub Encore Beach, or their nightclub XS, and is renowned for his song "Clarity," which has been played 100 million times on Spotify, went double platinum in the United States, and won a Grammy Award for Best Dance Recording.

When a guest buys a ticket to get into one of these clubs, it's not like hitting a club back home, where the DJ may be a local favorite. Vegas is the big time, on a national scale. You'll be feet away from some of the biggest names in the music business.

At one thirty a.m., just as the party on the dance floor reaches its height and the fog machine is sending tendrils across the floor, the door behind us opens. Out march a half dozen bouncers, escorting A-list DJ Calvin Harris, ar-guably the best-known and highest-paid DJ in the world. (In 2016 *Forbes* magazine clocked his annual earnings at $63 million.) The Scottish-born performer became the first solo artist in Britain to reach one billion streams on Spo-tify. For a moment, his hands work magic at the turntable. And OMNIA is suddenly filled with the lyrics of his song "Sweet Nothing."

The crowd goes wild; my eardrums are about to explode.

It's one of those Vegas moments when you think you're consumed by madness. But that, of course, is illusion. The story of modern-day clubbing is actually a story of geekery and data analytics. Hakkasan Group is renowned today for being the most analytical in the nightclub world. In early 2015, their nightclub Hakkasan hit Nightclub & Bar Media's Top 100 list for doing what once seemed impossible—bringing in revenue of $100 million in the previous calendar year. Only one competitor, the Wynn Resorts nightclub XS, had equaled that.

In the United States, the city of Las Vegas is the epicenter for club life. If you assume that these firms achieved their success on gut instincts alone, you would be wrong. If you look at Nightclub & Bar's 2015 Top 100 list of the highest-grossing nightclubs, seven out of the ten Vegas clubs on that list are all within two miles of each other. And they all use my Avero analytical software.

So what I'm witnessing tonight at OMNIA may look unscripted, but it's actually a perfect example of how numbers can give managers the confidence to create—as the firm's US president, Nick McCabe, describes it—"perfectly controlled chaos."

The world of nightclubs might seem like a departure for a book called *The Underground Culinary Tour*. But remember what I said early on: food and beverage venues are extraordinarily diverse. You'll find them everywhere, and most venues—from cruise ships to movie theaters to food trucks—do not conform to the image of a sit-down restaurant. In a sit-down restaurant, what's luring guests in the door are the atmosphere, the chef, the restaurant's reputation, and the food. At a nightclub or dayclub, that paradigm shifts. The food and beverages are secondary to the real draw, which is the entertainer hired to perform that day or night. And in the day and nightclub setting that entertainer is typically a DJ or duo, as in the Chainsmokers.

Whether they know it or not, all of these businesses—from the clubs to fine restaurants, Broadway shows, movie theaters, circuses, and snack bars—are in the service or hospitality industry, or both.

Not long ago, my friend Danny Meyer turned the industry on its ear when he astutely redefined those terms. Operators of all stripes always like to say that they provide great food and service. Danny's innovation was to observe that that promise doesn't go far enough. As he explains in his bestselling book *Setting the Table,* service is what is done *to* a guest, while hospitality is what is done *for* guests. "Service is the technical delivery of a product," he says. In the example of a music venue, you buy a ticket, they give you a seat in return, and they are happy to sell you food and drinks whenever you want them. The service present in your transaction with a movie theater or stadium is pretty impersonal. "Hospitality is how the delivery of a product makes its recipient *feel*," Danny says, adding, "Hospitality exists when you believe the other person is on your side . . . Those two simple prepositions—*for* and *to*—express it all."

Hospitality is truly a higher-order experience. Very few places deliver it well, or necessarily even understand the difference. But Danny's enlightened definition is at the core of Hakkasan's value proposition. Yes, you will pay quite a bit for a day or night out at one of their clubs, but their staff is listening to your needs the entire time, trying to execute on whatever it takes to make this the best bachelorette party, the best anniversary, the best corporate party you've ever experienced.

There are countless music venues in the world, but in general, if you want to hear and see a major star, the venue has to be able to pay that star, pay the venue staff, and make a profit. Huge stadiums like Madison Square Garden are the perfect laboratory for making those economics work for everyone. The more you pay, the better the seat. Ticket prices vary per engagement, sometimes fluctuating like securities on the stock market. There are always inexpensive seats, though most of us would agree that they're rarely a bargain. Because there's always a trade-off. Buy a low-end stadium ticket for $150, say, and you spend the night in the nosebleed seats at the top of an arena full of eighteen thousand cheering fans, watching your idol as if through the reverse end of a telescope. Another option is a massive venue like Coachella, the annual music and arts festival in Indio, California. You have your pick of hundreds of artists, but the $399 general admission or the $899 VIP ticket buys you a three-day pass to be one in a potential crowd of ninety-nine thousand screaming fans.

In an era when Broadway shows cost $150 to $250 a seat, or a Las Vegas Mixed Martial Arts bout ticket up in the top rows runs $200 or more, a night of Las Vegas clubbing comes off as relatively inexpensive. For a comparable price, patrons get access to a relatively smaller venue that holds about 3,800 people, tops, where they can dance in much closer proximity to the DJ who played the Garden or Coachella. I attended Coachella one year. It's an amazing festival, a musical nirvana and transformative cultural experience on the order of Woodstock. But I spent the whole time in a sea of thousands of fans. When you're dancing at Coachella, you are one with the music and the throng. You have to dance a certain way, always with the crowd, and always within the one square foot you can claim for yourself.

In Vegas, it's a totally different experience. For one, it's much more intimate in a nightclub or dayclub, where you're hanging out around a pool. In both settings, proximity is a key part of the experience. And so is comfort and luxury—at least for VIPs. Whether you're on the dance floor or you're sitting at a high-priced table, you still feel like you're close to the artist.

Hakkasan Group is striving to give guests a night that they simply can't get anywhere else. But the company doesn't have the luxury of spreading the entire cost of the evening across 80,000 to 90,000 people, or even among a stadium crowd of 18,000. So to be able to hire the high-end performers they want, and make their revenue-expense-profit matrix come together, they offer a VIP table option that gives high-end guests—the high rollers—unprecedented proximity to the star DJ at a significantly higher price. To their credit, firms have been recently challenging themselves to tinker with this formula. In 2016, both Wynn Resorts and Hakkasan Group debuted two new "boutique" nightclubs—Intrigue and JEWEL, respectively—that are smaller still, with a maximum capacity of between 1,900 and 2,000. The value proposition in these clubs promises even more intimacy for high rollers, who can enjoy the performances and insanity from secluded booths or suites.

The business model is still the same. The whales pay more, so the walk-ins pay less. In a sense, the presence of the whales makes the experience possible for the rest of us who don't have thousands to drop on a pool party. Ironically, the trade-off becomes relatively democratizing.

Nailing the venue size/value/profit matrix is what elevates the enterprise to both an art and science. And software is critical to nailing down the economics.

In 2012, Hakkasan Group's Las Vegas corporate office was mired in the grip of the Old Guard mind-set. Every Tuesday Nick McCabe and the rest of his team would gather around the conference table in a room with windows that gave them a bird's-eye view not of the Vegas Strip, but of a more pedestrian vantage point. Their corporate offices on Rainbow Boulevard were separated from the city's prime tourist destination by about six miles of flat, quasi-suburban desert landscape festooned with parking lots, office parks, and strip malls. They'd look across to the promised land of the Strip and ask each other: Guys, how did we *not* crush it this weekend?

And they needed to crush it—too much was riding on it. If Hakkasan could not make it in Vegas, then the company would have to fold up and walk away, conceding the

Vegas club scene to some other firm. And that they could not let happen.

In theory, they had everything in their favor. Vegas had undergone a seismic shift after the worldwide housing bubble burst. The resulting financial crisis had forced the hospitality industry to rethink itself (once again). By one estimate, Vegas had nearly a hundred thousand hotel rooms. That was fine before the meltdown, but the people who were coming to Vegas now were having trouble paying their mortgages back home. Those who came out to the desert on a vacation were still going to spend their savings on gambling, food, and drinks, but they were probably going to seek cheaper accommodations. The resorts needed to make up that lost revenue somehow. They needed something bigger, grander. They needed high-energy venues that would drive people, especially the as-yet-untapped market of young people, to come and have the time of their lives.

The biggest mistake those creating new venues in Las Vegas make is assuming Las Vegas is an easy market. That if they build it, customers will come. But in fact the market in Vegas is very sophisticated. When people visit New York City, they want to return home and tell their friends about incredible hole-in-the-wall joints that no one else knows about: the dive bar with great cocktails; the cabaret with the long-forgotten chanteuse; the phenomenal locavore pizza you can only get in Brooklyn.

People coming to Vegas, on the other hand, are not looking for subtle or overlooked. No one comes to Vegas for the familiar, or the heartwarming.

Hakkasan Group learned this the hard way. One of

their first venues was a small lounge in the Luxor—the casino built to resemble a pyramid—that specialized in high-end craft cocktails. The place grooved on a speakeasy vibe. But the lounge tanked. People don't come to Vegas for subdued, quiet drinks in classy, upscale lounges. If Hakkasan Group was going to crack Vegas, they had to build something *epic.* They had to build places tourists would come to and leave with an over-the-top story for their friends back home. So Hakkasan the company built Hakkasan the club, an $80 million, 80,000-square-foot nightclub.

At the same time, resorts all over Vegas were exploring new ways to entice young people. If the city could successfully give them nightlife, why couldn't it also give them *day*life? The concept seemed feasible. After all, Nevada's daytime temperatures hit an average of 100 degrees in the summer—perfect weather for what could be the world's greatest DJ-guided pool/dance party. One of my favorite dayclubs is Wynn's Encore Beach, which features a massive screen over the DJ's booth. Recently I watched as a guest ordered a cake to celebrate a birthday. The cake was escorted to the table by six bikini-clad women on a trolley manned by two musclebound bouncers. They've also recently rolled out a small, Ferris wheel–like contraption also featuring bikini-clad women. Utterly insane, but impossible to forget.

Hakkasan Group's contribution to the dayclub market was Wet Republic, an outdoor venue featuring 6,000 square feet of pool areas alone. Imagine an *epic pool party,* throw in endless rounds of $2,200 magnum bottles of Dom Pérignon and about a thousand beefcake guys and women in bikinis, and you'll get the picture.

Dayclubs are probably the most brilliant innovation to come out of resort casinos in recent years. Before this, the outdoor pool at most casinos was an underutilized space. Now, because club operators leveraged their DJ relationships, they transformed those dead spaces into another revenue stream and drive club-goers to their nighttime venues as well.

What these resorts have done with daylife is absolutely inspiring, and they don't get enough credit from the business community. Those outdoor pools were just sitting there all along, an afterthought in Vegas's traditional stream of diversions. But through sheer creativity, these clever operators transformed an ordinary pool into a must-do/must-see. They did it by surveying their operation and saying, "Okay, we have these assets and these resources—how can we maximize what we have?" There's a lesson in there for every single entrepreneur on the planet, whether you serve food to paying guests or not. Every day you should be asking yourself, "How can I use what I already have to deliver a whole new experience for my customers or guests?" Every business on the planet should be so lucky as to find their inner daylife.

Historically, the club scene worldwide was run like any Old Guard operation, by savvy operators who knew a few key performance indicators and little else. A seasoned club manager could tell you that on a fight night in Vegas, with a top DJ, the front-row tables in the house commanded a premium of $15,000. The customer booking such a table was, in effect, promising to run up a tab of *at least* that much in the course of the night.

Who has money to spend like this? Wealthy business-people booking corporate events. A whale throwing an unforgettable party for his far-flung friends. Bachelor and bachelorette parties. Well-off executives or professionals throwing themselves a fortieth birthday party. The biggest challenge these venues face is putting on such a show, such a spectacle, with such flawless service that guests leave at the end of the night feeling that they've gotten their money's worth.

Yet, despite the high average check, at the Tuesday morning meetings Hakkasan Group's management team couldn't get a handle on why their revenues were not matching their projections. If they were going to make it in Las Vegas, they knew, they needed their clubs to be wildly successful. Competition in a city like Vegas is fierce. And Hakkasan's costs—labor, talent, overhead, their prime casino location on the Strip—were through the roof. If they couldn't stand out from the pack, they wouldn't attract younger visitors. And if they couldn't attract the younger set, they'd fail to hit it big.

"We'd come in and do nothing but argue," Nick, the president, told me about their Tuesday meetings.

"Lots of finger pointing," admits Derek Silberstein, the company's vice president of operations.

Nick, a bespectacled gentleman with a British accent, first trained as a graphic designer. Upon graduation, he developed a happenings website that focused on Miami's club scene. To him, it was a perfect way to meet people and get free tickets to shows and clubs. But his long tutelage in the industry over the years had taught him to be wary of operators who had a poor grasp of their financials. "You'd ask them how much revenue they would make this year," he says, "and their answer was to take how much they earned in a week and then multiply it by fifty-two. Ridiculous."

Previously in New York, Derek had worked restaurants and catering venues where the proprietors had used no analytics whatsoever. "They'd look selectively at check averages and then multiply by how many people they *thought* were coming in the door. Or if they knew how many people they'd served, they'd just divide their total revenue by that number to get a check average. It was bullshit. There was no accuracy. How can you tell anything if you don't break it all down in decent categories? How else can you figure out, say, how the well drinks compare to the top-shelf items?"

They were determined not to be those guys who based their entire operation on two numbers. Nick started generating his own spreadsheets to see if he could tease out the most minuscule insights. One day he met Jason Aranas, a financial analyst who had worked in institutional investing, the student loan industry, and mortgages before being lured to the Strip. At the time the two of them met, Jason was helping the resort he worked for inject rigor into its produce-, beef-, and alcohol-buying programs. Nick asked him if he could help Hakkasan Group's Vegas office run its clubs—night and day—with acumen.

I can't do it alone, Jason told Nick. *You'll want an analysis group. Six or so people to collect data and start breaking it down.*

Done, Nick said, sounding both excited and a little relieved.

Looking back, Jason thought it refreshing and maybe even a little bit odd that this ultra-hip company was so hungry for numbers and analysis. When he started coming to the Tuesday meetings, occasionally whispering in Nick's ear, he realized that he was not the only geek in the room among a sea of impossibly cool clubbers. He was among fellow geeks, among friends.

What the hell, he thought. *Nightclubs have got to be sexier than produce and beef.*

When Jason's analysts looked at the data, they quickly confirmed what management and on-site club operators had suspected: clubs exhibit strong hourly, nightly, weekly, and seasonal trends.

The biggest *duhs?* Fridays and Saturdays are the biggest nights in terms of attendance and sales. But, depending on which DJ they book—what club managers call the "content"—the club can manage to wrench another great night out of the week. The more Hakkasan Group's brain trust crunched the numbers, the more they realized that orchestrating one big weeknight would have a huge impact on their bottom line. Their nightclub OMNIA, for example, programs shows five nights a week in-season, but the hottest shows are on Friday, Saturday, and *Tuesday.*

And that data in turn *directed* their corporate decisions. Since they know Thursday and Sundays nights tend to be slow, they can decide not to open all the rooms and all the levels of their clubs on those nights, which saves money in staffing and overhead. Hakkasan Group is also focused on preserving the health and sanity of its staff. Nightclubs are physically demanding places to work; bouncers, servers, and other staffers have to be on alert and high energy from ten p.m. to four a.m.—and often beyond. There's no point burning out your staff unnecessarily if you can help it. Data helps them to focus and conserve their staff's resources and prevent burnout.

Las Vegas's revenues are strongly influenced by the weather. March to September are the big months in the desert. The biggest single month is May, when college lets out and the weather is still relatively cool and pleasant. Not surprisingly, the strip starts to slow down after Labor Day as students head back to school and vacationers head back to work. As in Montauk, the season starts in spring, around the time of spring break and Easter vacations, and crashes after Labor Day. The summer months are steadily solid, and December's a dead month, with only one hot night— New Year's Eve. Then tourist visits drop off a cliff until spring.

How does knowing all this help a club's management? Remember the absurdist math of the Old Guard managers Nick and Derek complained about earlier—guys who did some third-grade math and believed it told them everything they needed to know about their business?

The Hakkasan Group managers have raised the ante to an entirely new level. With a deeper understanding of their trends, they now walk into negotiations with DJs and their managers or agents empowered by the facts. They don't like to talk about what they pay DJs, so I'm going to stick with what's been reported in the press. The firm is prepared to pay top dollar—as much as $400,000 a night, according to the *Las Vegas Sun*—to the top DJs, because the data has shown that having the right DJ on the right night in the right season will earn them far more money in the long run.

The world of nightclub DJs is highly volatile. Audiences are brutally fickle. Who's hot right now might not be who's hot six months in the future. Moreover, a hot performer might draw huge crowds in Europe or in Chicago or at similar Hakkasan Group venues worldwide, but tank in the fishbowl that is Vegas. But Hakkasan Group, thanks to Nick, Derek, and Jason, has eliminated much of that guesswork. To them, choosing an entertainer is a little like using modern-day baseball statistics to assemble an amazing ball club. Since they know exactly how many people a DJ has drawn in the past, they can predict the income they'll earn when they book that star.

They can, for instance, draw up a list of all their current DJs according to their relative draw power, ranking them from A-list to E-list, and use that scale to determine how much they'll pay people at each level. They can also plot each DJ's popularity according to seasonality. That gives them bargaining power other companies don't have when they go into negotiations.

Yes, they can tell the agent of an A-list DJ, your client does a phenomenal job for us in-season, but we can't justify paying him that much in November. There just aren't enough bodies in Vegas to make him worth it to us at that time of year. But we can pay him an off-season rate that we feel is commensurate.

There are always surprises. Moments when the data reveals something you would never have realized if you ran your business on gut alone. They noticed that in certain cases, the right DJ could actually alter seasonal trends. In other words, the venue might actually attract a larger than expected crowd in the off-season because they booked a D-list DJ instead of the E-lister they first considered. A good but inexpensive DJ might actually raise the level of a dead night in November. In those cases, booking him suddenly looks like a genius move—you're getting an incredible deal on an undervalued player.

With the right data, picking the right DJ can be elevated to an art form. Yes, they know that they may be overpaying to get the A-lister who will draw huge crowds and keep their top reputation, but they balance those costs out over time by reaping the rewards that come when they book an undervalued DJ in the right day and time.

The change that data had made in their organization didn't hit the entire management team at Hakkasan Group until a 2014 briefing with the London office. Nick McCabe casually announced that his team projected that OMNIA, their new club, would earn $100 million in the first year.

At the time, it was almost unheard of to hit a figure like that in the club world.

Executives in the London office immediately shot back: *Are you sure you want to go with these numbers? It's a new club . . .*

Nick, Derek, and Jason responded, *Yes, let's go with it. It's based on what we're seeing in the club. Let's run with those figures—we won't be off.*

And that's the thing. Strong data builds confidence; the more you collect and analyze, the better able you are to predict your success. In the wake of the London meeting, the Old Guard at Hakkasan Group had become unabashedly New Guard. Gone were the days when they couldn't figure out why they'd had a lackluster night. Now they had all the figures at their fingertips; they trained their managers and staff to respect them and use them to take action.

Globally, they knew, for instance, that 65 percent of their nightclub income was derived from VIP tables, which ran anywhere from $1,000 to $10,000 a night and were typically booked months in advance. The remaining 35 percent of their income came from the remaining guests, people who didn't have the means or desire to book a $10,000 table, or even a $1,000 table, but who nevertheless helped drive sales of admission tickets and drinks, filled the club, and spread the word that this was the place to be. Such guests would line up in the casino lobbies an hour or more in advance, willing to spend anywhere from $50 to $150 just to get into the door. Once inside, they'd drop $12 to $18 per drink, and they and their friends or dates would party for hours. A nightclub like OMNIA would see about 6,000 people in the course of the night, with as many as 1,800 people departing the club when they were partied out, replaced by a new crowd desperate to get in.

The key to the firm's success was depth of the analysis. It was more than knowing how many people would come out on a particular night, but which *hours* they would come, how much they would spend *per table,* or how much they would spend *at the bar.* Club managers know, for instance, that spending declines when the head-liner DJ arrives, because people shift from drinking and socializing to dancing and enjoying the music. Knowing the crowd's patterns helps them plan how fast to let people in—typically in fifteen-minute increments—and find the right balance in the club's overall energy. (A packed club is far more exciting to guests than a club whose crowd has dropped by even 10 percent.) Having such data points al-lows the firm to work more efficiently, opening and closing rooms and floors or levels of the club as necessary. One key concept that my company's software added was *table analysis,* which allowed Hakkasan to see the top-selling and bottom-selling tables at a glance, by the season, by the event, and per DJ.

Over time, Hakkasan Group subtly started encouraging repeat guests to order their tickets online so they could get into the club faster. Guests loved the convenience of that, as much as Hakkasan loved the idea of capturing the advance sales, and their guests' e-mails to add to their growing list. Having that e-mail list, and running their own online box office, allowed the firm to make increasingly nimble online ad buys and stage more effective marketing campaigns. In-creasingly, they could e-mail past guests about deals and special events.

Each guest's bar tab averages about $30 in the night-clubs; in the dayclubs it averages $50. That data makes sense when you think about it. In high season, dayclubs operate for seven hours in the punishing Vegas sunlight.

People have more time to eat, and drink, out of necessity. By contrast, the nightclubs operate for only five hours. The checks from the VIP tables average about the same, day or night. The sort of people who book a table in either venue tend to hit their minimum, regardless of how many hours they and their guests stay.

When Nick, Derek, and Jason stacked up that kind of intel, correcting for the season, they could arrive at a very robust revenue projection. Jason's analysis team has gotten so good that they can project with uncanny accuracy how much on a particular date an individual nightclub will earn months in advance, and their forecasts will only get more refined as that date draws near. For example, six months out, they'll know if a date will be a $300,000 night or a $400,000 night. Thirty days out, they'll know if it's a $350,000 or a $400,000 night. A week out, they'll know if it will be a $375,000 night or a $400,000 night. And twenty-four hours before the guests start lining up at the casinos, twenty-four hours before cabs start discharging droves of beautiful women in tight black dresses at Caesars Palace or MGM Grand, twenty-four hours before anyone on the dance floor realizes that he or she is thirsty, Hakkasan Group knows whether that night will be a $390,000 night or a $400,000 night. Their data simply gets more precise, more granular, as the night approaches.

It's more than just knowing how much money is coming in. Data makes it easier to calculate more accurate projections and fine-tune how the clubs are run. That results in better planning, better staff scheduling, and, ultimately, better service.

Once the numbers showed Nick, Derek, and Jason how

to be profitable, they could more thoughtfully plan ways to enhance the guest experience. When you get to this level, it goes back to being all about people. And just as we saw in the story of the bottle-shy server, the data reveals the invisible.

Derek had one such insight a while back as he was reviewing one of several reports Jason's team sent to his inbox. Derek and his on-site club managers had been using our software to spot high and low performers and train their staff in response to the results they saw. Moreover, the company rewarded and offered career paths in management to those staffers who excelled in the club setting, to move them up before they burned out from the pace of the club floor.

The result? Hakkasan Group staffers are impeccably trained. This is probably one of the only companies I've worked with that prefers new hires who have no club experience before they come to work for them. Management wants to be able to train staffers from the ground up, and they don't have the patience to train new hires to shed bad habits acquired at other clubs. They conduct training sessions before a venue opens for the first time; after that, every staff member is required to undertake continuing education and preshift training every night. One night I was backstage before OMNIA opened its doors, and I caught a glimpse of a dance recovery room in the back. I also watched as the general manager summoned all the cocktail servers—as many as sixty-five work on any given night— for a "nail check." The women lined up and presented their fingernails for inspection. Management inspected their nails for cleanliness, and to ensure they didn't have *artifi-*

cial nails that could pop off and fall into someone's drink. That's how focused they are on even the smallest detail.

The typical cocktail server undergoes three months of training to learn how to serve drinks and interact with demanding VIP clients. If you are a VIP guest, you never have to wonder where your server is at these venues. The server sticks to you like glue the entire day or night. You never have to reach for a bottle. The servers do it all. They also watch out for how you look in front of your guests. They're highly articulate, knowing just when to quietly suggest that you probably ought to order another bottle. They summon runners to whisk away empty glasses and bottles, and mop up spills. They know just how to make you feel like you are the king or queen of your own personal fiefdom. It's a grueling job for the servers, but the payoff is high. It's not unusual for them to earn a six-figure income. The hosts—the young people responsible for finding VIPs and booking them into the high-end tables—can earn a similar income.

But as Derek reviewed the numbers, he knew that success on the club floor—night or day—was all about generating a perfect storm. If you put the best cocktail server in the right booth with the highest spender, magic happened.

We need to have our aces in places, he thought.

It became a mantra throughout the company: *Get our aces in places!*

That said, Derek knew that if you simply assign last month's top server to a wealthy client who has promised to run up a $15,000 tab, you're going to miss chances to increase sales and blow guests away. What sets Hakkasan Group apart is that they do what so many Old Guarders insist is impossible: they work hard to crunch their data as the scene is unfolding at the pool or on the floor, even if they have to do it manually.

Nick, Derek, and Jason realized that they would miss opportunities if they waited for the monthly P&L (profit and loss) statements. Jason started generating weekly reports of key performance indicators, which were shared with the club managers and the entire staff. And they trained the club operators to use software on a daily basis. The level of transparency was incredible, but they trusted their staff to grasp the critical equation: if we hit our targets, we'll all have the chance to do more for our guests. So let's get in, let's pay the bills, and then let's make sure they never forget the night they just had.

Let's say you assign a fairly new server to a $1,000 table for the night, and within an hour the GM calculates that she has served that party more than $5,000 worth of drinks. That server's value to the organization just skyrocketed.

Unless they're looking at server milestones, most Old Guard general managers would never understand that equation. Instead they would overpraise the cocktail server who worked the $10,000 table and likely overlook the person who *quintupled* the house's best expectations. If they only look at the absolute numbers, they will value the $10,000 server over the $1,000 server. And the $10,000 server will continue to get the best tables because the manager assumes that she's the best server they have. If you run a club or restaurant this way, eventually such decisions become a self-fulfilling prophecy. The overpraised make the best tips, and the undervalued look for a better job elsewhere.

But if the firm uses software to analyze server ability, it can easily spot servers who consistently surpass table minimums over time versus a single night. A GM who is monitoring tables as the night progresses can quickly intercede and offer some options. "Okay," the manager can say to a server, "this VIP has earned the right to a better table as soon as one opens up. If one doesn't open up, I'm authorizing you to comp them *xxx*. And by the way, congratulations. Great work." If that server consistently goes over the table minimums, he or she will be permanently assigned to higher-ticket tables.

Derek, Jason, and Nick have a deep understanding of how many people make a dayclub or nightclub look lively and hopping. Ideally, you want about 3,800 people on the dance floor at the nightclub, 2,800 in or around the pool. Luckily, there's always a long line of people waiting to get in at both venues, so as the day or night progresses, you can cycle more people in as guests leave. Shuffling tables is a trick that helps everyone. The house is happy because they can move loyal, high-paying customers to the busier areas of the club and start breaking down the vacant areas. And the VIP party is stoked to hear that management is moving them to a better table, closer to the action.

Does it work? Again and again. An Arab sheikh appeared one night, ran up a tab of $650,000 for his guests, and lavished his cocktail servers with a tip in excess of 53 percent: $350,000. Nick still has the receipt. "He told the servers to go ahead and add that tip to his check. He had a great time, he said, so why *not* drop a million dollars in one night?"

· 7 ·

THE UNDERGROUND CULINARY TOUR
(PART 2)

THURSDAY, 8:30 A.M.

The next morning of the Tour, after what amounts to a short nap, we're back on the road. First stop is barista training at the Counter Culture coffee lab in SoHo. In 1995, this Durham, North Carolina, firm started sourcing and roasting great, sustainably grown coffee. Besides wholesaling, their emphasis has been on educating baristas at coffee shops and restaurants about the principles of fine coffee making. The company has ten training facilities in the United States devoted to sharing its "counter intelligence."

My guests are bleary-eyed and exhausted from yesterday's whirlwind tour, and today's schedule is no less ambitious. When we arrive at Counter Culture, they graciously serve us coffee, made to order. Cappuccinos, espressos, pour-overs, and my favorite, the cortado—nothing is too complicated for these pros. We sit on bleachers listening to Katie Carguilo, a 2012 National Barista Champion, and Jesse Kahn, one of the company's wholesale sales managers, hold forth on such topics as water temperature, milk steaming methodology, Ethiopian coffee (my favorite), the virtues of "cupping" (smelling and analyzing the aromas and tastes of newly arrived coffee batches), and latte art. In a little while, I find myself thinking, *I could really use a second cup of coffee right about now.*

Luckily, my wish comes true. There's just one catch: we have to make it ourselves. What starts with excitement and good intentions quickly descends into farce. Our plucky restaurant executives manage to create their own cappuccinos on La Marzocco espresso machines—those gleaming, handmade Florentine coffee devices that have become the high-end standard for the industry—but then fail spectacularly at latte art, those exquisite designs in the steamed milk on the tops of their coffees. When we attempt to do what baristas do day in and day out with practiced ease, the truth hits home.

In the world of food and beverage, nothing is as easy as it looks.

THURSDAY, 9:30 A.M.

By the time we reach Maialino uptown, everyone is a little peckish. But Danny Meyer, his managing partner Terry Coughlin, and the staff of his scrumptious Italian restaurant are ready with their Roman-style breakfast.

As we sit, sunlight streams in the windows, filtered by the trees in nearby Gramercy Park. The walls of the restaurant are covered with black-and-white photos of modern-day Rome, as well as countless etchings, maps, woodcuts, and charming Italian advertisements. Italian cuisine is much beloved, even revered, by Americans, but most Italian places in the United States broadcast an ambience that is sadly outdated—a little too old-world. By contrast, Danny's place looks like a thoroughly modern trattoria, the sort of place where well-dressed, busy Roman businesspeople dine today.

After my first meeting with Danny back in 2000, set up by Tom Colicchio, Danny became one of our company's earliest champions and clients. I don't know anyone who doesn't marvel at his success. In 1985, when he was barely out of his twenties, with little hands-on experience, he opened a restaurant that became the epicenter for the modern hospitality movement, Union Square Cafe. In the same way that test pilots yearn to emulate the legendary Chuck Yeager, or cocktail experts style themselves after Sasha Petraske, restaurateurs the world over have learned how they should treat their guests from the example set by Danny Meyer.

Danny has invited our tour group to one of his restaurants every year since the tour's inception in 2007. In many ways his restaurant empire has grown up alongside our tour. Every year he has something new to share with us, and his chefs never disappoint.

Italians favor simple breakfasts consisting of coffee and a light roll. But Danny's team has cleverly imagined what Italians would eat if they *did* do a fuller breakfast. First, they bring us some of their excellent coffee. (Maialino has one of the best coffee programs around.) Next, the table in front of us quickly fills with ricotta pancakes, Pecorino-and-pepper scrambled eggs, and egg-white frittatas, with black pepper pancetta filling in as our morning bacon. The eggs are a play on *cacio e pepe*—a classic Roman cheese-and-pepper pasta dish. The frittata is hearty yet light, studded with mushrooms and sautéed onions. The scrambled eggs are so creamy, so redolent with cheese, that you can practically spread them on the crisp crackers that perch on the sides of our plates. The big winner—the dish everyone at our table passes around with alacrity as the absolute must-try—is the ricotta pancakes. To this day I still don't know how they make them. You can taste the ricotta in every mouthful. They're seemingly weightless, not unlike a forkful of good cheesecake, but not as sweet. But in defiance of physics, they're fluffy as a cloud. The *opposite* of dense.

In addition to the great coffee and food, there's another reason I want to share the Maialino—Italian for "piglet"—concept with my guests. Maialino is open continuously from seven thirty a.m. to midnight weekdays. That means it offers the greatest possible number of meal opportunities to its guests. It's a perfect place to discuss another trend I'll explore in Chapter 10—how restaurants can serve more meals and capture more repeat business with their guests. The restaurant is not a special-occasion restaurant—it's an all-occasion restaurant.

THURSDAY, 10:30 A.M.

The area around the Jacob Javits Center—New York City's massive convention center near the Hudson River—used to be a culinary no-man's-land. If conventioneers didn't feel tempted by the hot dogs sold in the exhibition lobby, they had to hop a cab or walk blocks to find a decent restaurant. But that all ended in 2014, when some clever real estate developers launched a food hall in their new rental high-rise as a way of luring renters to a neighborhood many New Yorkers still think is barren, blighted, and uncool. In malls in the United States, developers routinely lock in movie theaters and department stores as their "anchors"— destination businesses that drive foot traffic. Here, the New Guard landlords have wisely chosen food as their anchor.

And what amazing food it is. As our group wanders a 15,000-square-foot glass temple to cuisine, it's clear that we're looking at the next-generation food court and food market of the future. Most shopping malls serve up the typical second- or third-rate fast food. The Gotham West Market couldn't be more different. Imagine ten one-of-a-kind eateries under one roof. A sushi restaurant. A taco truck. A charcuterie. A meat and beer palace. A kitchen store. Guests can find Spanish tapas, hand-pulled ramen, a burger and chicken stand, cookies, ice cream, coffee. There's also a bike shop on the premises, on the off chance any of us decides to burn off calories with a ride back to the hotel.

Our first stop is the Cannibal, which is sort of like what would happen if a longtime butcher decided to become a

Belgian monk and start brewing beer on the side. The eatery's stock in trade is fresh, succulent meat, most of it locally raised and butchered, and prepared in-house. At their main location on Twenty-Ninth Street, they cure their own meats for their charcuterie and dry their own beef jerky. They couple that with a remarkable number of interesting beers.

Partner Cory Lane greets us and starts pouring goblets of St. Feuillien, a white, fruity Belgian tripel out of a green three-liter jeroboam. Behind the bar, the chef is whipping up a small sampling of their offerings. Out comes one of their signature appetizers—steak tartare, a delicious dollop of diced meat, minced with fresh herbs, that sits on a doughy golden crumpet dripping with a spoonful of creamy béarnaise and sprinkled with crispy shallots. Having learned to moderate our consumption by this point, the group knows it would be wise to take only one bite of the tartare. But once we've put a dent in it, we find ourselves helpless, and quickly succumb to our palates and gobble down the rest.

Next, the chef sets out the Cannibal's homemade kielbasa, sliced into steamy discs reclining in a bed of fresh mustard graced with a sprig of dill. A moment later, he's back serving up their version of the classic Cuban sandwich, delicious pressed sandwiches typically made with a slab of pork married to a slice of ham, cheese, and pickles. The Cannibal does theirs with a slab of pig's head terrine, which is an innovative way to use that part of the animal. Their ham hails from Vermont, the cheese they use is Gruyère, and the pickles are locally made.

Before anyone can protest, I lead the tour group a few steps further into the market, to the long marble bar to the left of the Cannibal's booth. We've just entered Spain, by way of New York's Eleventh Avenue. Our next restaurant is El Colmado, or "the grocer," in Spanish. It's styled after the picturesque gourmet shops you'll find in southern Europe, the sorts of places where you can shop for dinner, buy some wine or olives, and grab a bite to tide you over while you're at it. I love this little eatery; it brings authentic Spanish flavors to busy New Yorkers who don't have time to luxuriate in a long, siesta-style meal.

Like the Cannibal, El Colmado is a satellite of a larger restaurant space elsewhere in the city. El Colmado, and its sister eatery, Tertulia, are the brainchildren of chef Seamus Mullen, a Vermont-raised chef who worked for years in Spanish restaurants and arrived in New York City determined to share those old-world flavors with modern New Yorkers. I love the busy-ness of El Colmado. Behind the glass is a woman shucking oysters; a man is slicing velvety-thin slices of jamón off a whole pig's leg, while another simmers the paella of the day.

Before we have managed to sit at the bar and reach for our glasses of rioja, they're setting out baskets of hot *albóndigas*—Spanish-style meatballs—skewered with toothpicks and *dátiles con bacón,* sweet dates stuffed with almonds and Valdeon cheese and wrapped in bacon.

It's a beautiful space, with the sunlight streaming in through the windows, bouncing off the white subway tiles and the blue glass bottles of seltzer water. One can't help but dream of Madrid.

The whole point of bringing my tour guests to Gotham West Market is to show them how even a food-court-size setting can serve great food with amazing ingredients and manage to transport you to another time and place. The Cannibal and El Colmado do it beautifully, in spaces smaller than a New York studio apartment.

As seductive as the bacon-wrapped dates and wine are, we have to keep moving. Next door is the last stop of our Gotham West crawl—the retro-American fare served by chef Rick Robinson at Genuine Roadside.

This place cracks me up. A giant boom box is built into the wall, surrounded by stacks of cassette tapes. Cheesy wood-paneled walls are decorated with pictures of automobiles, motorcycles, Farrah Fawcett, and Evel Knievel. On a shelf near the ceiling are hundreds of old beer cans—many of long-extinct brands, reminiscent of perhaps your great-uncle's embarrassing basement beer can collection. Whether you realize it or not, you've just stepped back into the 1970s, a time when Archie Bunker, *Mannix,* and the Fonz ruled.

Chef Rick carries over a massive plate of his trademark double burgers with cheese and house sauce. Mindful of the fact that we've been eating nonstop for two days straight, with only a short respite in between, he has sliced every burger in half. Frankly, I intend to skip the burger, but those patties, pink, hot, cheesy, and delicious, practically beg to be devoured. Helpless, I pick one up; the burger almost melts in my mouth. As Rick leaves, one of his kitchen staffers arrives with a tray of buttermilk-battered chicken sandwiches.

Someone swears under their breath. We erupt into laughter.

No effing way. I am not eating another bite!

The chicken sandwiches too are halved, and the cross-sections reveal juicy white meat layered with sambal mayo and an apple-celeriac slaw.

One by one, our hands reach for them.

THURSDAY, 12:01 P.M.

In an old 1820s townhouse on Hudson Street in Greenwich Village, we are huddled around a blondwood table, studying the most astonishing work of edible art we've yet seen on our tour. In the hands of another chef, the food on our plate would be just what it is—four shrimp dumplings and a slice of fried sweet potato.

But we're not sitting in *any* Chinese restaurant. Red-Farm is arguably the most creative Chinese-inspired restaurant in the city, the brainchild of Ed Schoenfeld and chef Joe Ng. They have brought the farm-to-table aesthetic to Chinese food, visiting local green markets to get the freshest produce from purveyors who ring the city. This is another trend we'll see later—farm-to-table has gone global. To reinforce the primacy of farm-fresh food, the interior of their restaurant looks a little like a spotless barn loft, with white painted brick walls and thick oak beams. Most guests share their meals at a large communal table like one you'd find in a comfortable farmhouse.

But RedFarm is not all décor and farm-fed ingredients. The menu has style, panache, and more than a touch of humor—all of which is apparent when the food hits the plate.

Take the Pac-Man Shrimp Dumplings, for instance. The sweet potato slice is cut into the shape of the video game character Pac-Man, famous for chomping his way through his starry arcade universe. Arrayed in front of him are the red, yellow, blue, and orange "ghosts" that bedevil him in the legendary game. Chef Ng's team has cunningly shaped dumpling wrappers to resemble those pudgy ghosts, down to their sesame seed eyes. They're almost too adorable to eat. Everyone at the table whips out his or her smartphone to snap a shot.

"Each has a different mix of shrimp and some other flavor," says our host Ed Schoenfeld, a Chinese food expert and one of New York's legendary restaurateurs. Which might strike you as odd, if you met him. Ed, you see, isn't Chinese at all. He's a tall, white, Jewish American guy with glasses, a snowy white beard, and a raconteur's gift for telling tales, particularly the story of how Chinese food became a misunderstood American staple.

Serious foodies tend be skeptical about Chinese cuisine, even if they love it to death, because they don't want to be disappointed. Often Chinese is synonymous with greasy takeout, embarassingly translated menus, plastic tablecloths, and bad signage.

In the 1960s, when Ed was still a teen and a nascent hippie, he became obsessed with Chinese food, studying with Shanghai-born chef Grace Chu, best known for sharing the secrets of her art in the pages of two seminal cookbooks, *The Pleasures of Chinese Cooking* (published in 1962) and *Madame Chu's Chinese Cooking School* (1975). Several years later, Ed landed a job as the maitre d' at Uncle Tai's Hunan Yuan, a *New York Times*–rated, four-star Chinese restaurant on the Upper East Side. Every night he'd stand in a tacky blue polyester tuxedo and greet celebrities as they entered: Jackie Kennedy, Andy Warhol, Spiro Agnew, Tennessee Williams, Lillian Hellman, Gore Vidal, and Warren Beatty. Since Ed was the only non-Asian English speaker, they'd ask him, "What's good here? What do you recommend?"

They had good reason to ask. As the first Hunan-style restaurant outside of China, Uncle Tai's menu was radically different than those guests had encountered before. China's vast geography encompasses myriad culinary traditions, but historically that diversity has been lost on Americans. The first wave of Chinese immigrants to America worked on the railroads in the 1840s. They cooked Cantonese-style food, and Americans assumed that this one style spoke for all of China. By 1949, the communist revolution was transforming China. Chefs who worked for wealthy people fled to other nations, bringing that knowledge with them. And so in time guests all over the world came to experience Mandarin, Hunan, and Sichuan cooking. But since master chefs could no longer train apprentices the way they did in China, when chefs of the communist diaspora died off, their knowledge and experience died with them. Chinese cooking left the world of fine dining and became a kind of watered-down version of its former self, relegated to takeout meals that hungry customers picked up on the way home so they didn't have to cook. Growing concerns

about high fat, sugar, and sodium in Chinese dishes further eroded the cuisine's reputation.

As we sit here dazzled by the appetizers, it's clear that
Chef Ng has created dishes that are inspired by Chinese
food. His spring rolls come to the table standing vertically,
at attention, their attenuated tops trimmed, shaped, and
fried into the shapes of elegant flowers. One bite takes us
inside a moist, juicy heart of spiced mushroom and vegetables. The Kumamoto oysters come one to a glass, sitting
atop a bed of sweet flavored ice made with Meyer lemons
and Yuzu citrus fruit. Next, we are served small black
bowls containing fat, steaming dumplings. Ed Schoenfeld
hovers over us as they come to the table.

"Do you guys know how to eat this? Damian?"

By now I do. In fact, one of my favorites is RedFarm's
very indulgent, seasonal black truffle and chicken dumpling. But Ed needs to instruct the rest of our group.

"Okay, everyone," he snaps with a martial tone. "Lift up
your dumpling and put it on your spoon."

Off we go, lifting the puffy dough balls onto our white
ceramic ladles. Someone down the table yells, "Damn!" I
look down the row, and broth has splashed everywhere.

"You gotta watch out," Ed says. "These dumplings are
filled with soup. Don't break them. Okay, when you're
ready, bite off a little piece of the edge."

We bite and nibble, and inhale the fragrant broth inside
the dumpling.

"Now you have a hole. Get in there and suck all the soup
out. Go ahead."

Those of us who haven't torn our dumplings and sent

soup flying in all directions follow Ed's instructions and take in the delicious soup broth. Down the table, the guest who broke his dumpling sheepishly tries to drink whatever has splashed into his bowl.

At long last, the soup is gone.

"If you're done with the soup—are you done, Damian?— go ahead and eat what's left."

The empty center of my dumpling remains. I lift the spoon to my mouth and chew the dumpling shell, greeted with the mingled flavors of pork and crab.

Ed rounds the table. "How is that, huh? Did you enjoy that?"

Most of us cannot answer. Our mouths are still filled with dumpling and broth. We nod and give him a thumbs-up, hoping he understands how ineffable we find the dish.

I'm sure he does.

THURSDAY, 1:00 P.M.

Later in the afternoon, we're back in the Williamsburg section of Brooklyn, this time to hear the city's reigning brewmaster, Garrett Oliver, march us through a tasting of sushi, paired with various beers from Brooklyn Brewery. He's teamed up with the chefs and sommelier Sam Ehrlich at Blue Ribbon Sushi in the city to make this all happen.

Garrett is an inspiring speaker, with a profound knowledge not only of beer but of food. In the 1980s, fresh out of college, he traveled to England hoping to land a job with an HBO satellite office. The second he stepped off the train from the airport, he walked into a pub to order a beer. What he got was a pint of cask-conditioned ale. He had never tasted anything quite like it: warm, unfiltered, highly flavored. He loved the tiny bubbles of carbonation streaming from the bottom of the glass. This was nothing like the beer he'd had back home. He knew he had to learn more. Eventually he became a home brewer and spent much of his time tasting, experimenting, and thinking hard about how the United States could return to its beer roots.

When he returned to New York City, he fell in with a crowd of craft beer enthusiasts. This was the 1980s, when the thought of microbrews were a mad gleam in the eyes of a handful of innovative brewers. The top six beer companies dominated 92 percent of the beer production in the United States. By 1993, Garrett had a decent job working at a bank, but he quit his day job to brew beer full-time for a small startup microbrewery, Manhattan Brewing Company. By 1994, he had switched to Brooklyn Brewery, brewing a black chocolate stout that launched his career. Twenty-odd years later, Garrett has authored three books on beer, including *The Oxford Companion to Beer,* a thousand-page encyclopedic masterpiece that is unlike any other book on the subject. In 2014, he won a James Beard Award—the Oscars of the food world—for the category of Outstanding Wine, Beer or Spirits Professional.

I love bringing our tour to Garrett's turf, where the restaurant industry CEOs and managers can gaze at countless wooden barrels filled with aged beers. As he works his way through our menu, pairing Big Eye Toro with an Italian-style golden ale, or Arctic char with my personal favorite, Brooklyn's Sorachi Ace saison, or smoked yellowtail with a high-gravity wheat beer, we begin to wonder why anyone would settle for a boring beer with their sushi.

And that's the point: beer has come so far since the 1980s, when the only choices available to American consumers were a sudsy, ho-hum quaff from an industrial brewer. Garrett and brewers like him have rescued beer from boredom and shown us all that knowledge in the beverage world doesn't have to be confined to coffee, wine, and cocktails. It is a lesson I had to learn myself. I'm more of a wine drinker, so the revolution in craft beer took me by surprise—something I admit to audiences all the time. I don't want them to make the same mistake.

Next, Garrett breaks out a special black brew aged in bourbon casks. The flavor profile falls somewhere between chocolate, coffee, vanilla, and paradise.

"Ladies and gentlemen, I thank you," Garrett says as we conclude our tasting.

We leave Brooklyn, our minds permanently altered.

THURSDAY, 2:00 P.M.

We're hunkered down in a small brick-lined restaurant in Tribeca, the neighborhood in Lower Manhattan just north of the financial district. Our last stop on this year's tour is a snug wine bar named Terroir, presided over by perhaps the most opinionated sommelier on the planet, Paul Grieco.

We've gone from beer to wine, from one James Beard Award winner to another. Paul, who has a kind of friendly rivalry with Garrett, grew up in Toronto in a proud Italian Canadian family that ran a classic Italian restaurant. Even when his parents and grandparents weren't working, they talked about the business. Hospitality runs in Paul's veins. That, and a good Riesling. One day, rather than stick around to help manage the family eatery, Paul hightailed it for New York City, eventually landing a job working for Danny Meyer's Gramercy Tavern. There, under Danny's tutelage, Paul began a torrid love affair with food and wine that shapes the way he runs his own wine bars today.

To understand Paul, you pretty much have to accept that the guy is beautifully, intellectually insane when it comes to wine. As his team sets out wineglasses for my guests, Paul starts pacing in front of our table like Captain Ahab stalking the deck of the *Pequod*. His long sideburns, his whisper-thin mustache, and the tuft of facial chair at his chin make him look like a half-mad Yankee whaler.

"How many of you serve Riesling in your restaurants?" he barks.

A couple of hands go up.

Oh boy, I worry—*here it comes.* For years now Paul has been the nation's Lord High Apostle of Riesling. He's on a mission to correct every wine drinker's opinion of this versatile German varietal. One summer he decided that he would serve no other white wine but Riesling in his wine bar. And that's what guests got when they opened his wine list. He called it the Summer of Riesling. Other wine bars across the country joined in; they singlehandedly taught a nation that Riesling was not to be feared, but revered.

To this day, his wine lists are hefty binders full of Grieco-isms.

Sherry is the most underrated beverage on the planet earth.

And it is our mission to increase sherry knowledge and consumption tenfold over the next 19 months.

So, say yes to sherry. Say yes to the world's greatest beverage!

We drink Madeira because it is America's wine.

Loved by Jefferson, enjoyed by Washington, it fueled the creation/signing of the Declaration of Independence and celebrated the Louisiana Purchase!

New York is the Big Apple.

And in the Big Apple, one must drink cider, dammit!

Beaujolais . . .

And not that crazy Duboeuf shite.

Pinot Noir

Philip the Bold loved this grape above all others.

Cabernet Sauvignon

What Kool Herc is to rap, Cabernet is to grape juice.

Syrah

Holy smogolies, how does a grape actually smell so damn feral?

When Paul gets an idea into his head, he works his butt off trying to convert everyone else to his point of view. But,

I have to admit, he's got a lot of disciples. When it comes to wine, we can all stand to learn more, we can all try to stretch our minds and our palates.

Restaurateurs are no different. Most of them choose very familiar wines for their lists in the misguided belief that guests won't buy something they don't recognize. That's why you see the same old producers again and again, from the same wine regions, everywhere you go. The chardonnay, it seems, is always from California, as is the Pinot Noir. Yes, they're some of the most popular wines on the planet, but at a certain point, don't a restaurant's choices become a self-fulfilling prophecy? Guests only order what they see. If you put something in front of them that they haven't seen before, they just might try it—and like it. Sometimes, it's in a restaurateur's best interest to educate guests about an unusual or interesting wine. Less popular wines are often great values.

But more to the point of a wine establishment named Terroir, wine is about exploring wine regions around the world and a sense of place that makes a wine wholly unique. It's the job of a good sommelier, and a restaurant, to help guests discover that a chardonnay from Burgundy will be different from a California chardonnay from Napa Valley. *Wine is terroir,* as Paul's website proclaims to the world. And how cool is it to learn that you can explore the world with wine?

But before that can happen, these restaurateurs—my guests and Paul's nervous guinea pigs—have to go out on a limb and try something new for themselves.

Paul starts pouring, narrating as he goes.

"What do you guys think of Riesling?" he says.

Most of my guests love it. It's one of the wines they reach for when they're buying and drinking wine at home for themselves.

"What do your guests think of it?" Paul says next.

And the executives on the tour group start.

It's got a bad rap, one exec admits.

They say it's too sweet.

Guests don't like it.

Paul's shaking his head. "First of all, not all Rieslings are sweet, and there's nothing wrong with a little sweetness as long as it's balanced with acidity. If you're eating a great meal, you want that acidity. Why? Because that acidity is like a Zamboni machine on your tongue. It comes out after you've finished a mouthful of food and paves the 'ice' clean." He pours out a golden wine into everyone's glass. "Try this," he insists.

We sip. We nod. We smile. It's perfectly refreshing, easy on the tongue. In this case, the acidity we've all come to expect from a Riesling is balanced by the fruit. Now comes the moment of truth.

"I want to challenge you," Paul says, "to pair this wine with something on the menu at your restaurants back home. In fact, I've already done some of the work for you."

Apparently, over the last week Paul has researched the menus of a number of casual chain restaurants. My guests are stunned by this unexpected diligence. With all he has to do in his day running his wine bars, I'm amazed that he would take the time to pair wine with items on other people's menus.

He begins. "You, sir," he says, pointing to one of the

executives. "You work for a Mexican food chain, is that right?"

"Yep."

"On your menu I found something called the 'Original Queso.' Is that correct? What is that about, exactly? Are you saying you guys *invented* cheese?"

The executive, Steve Clark, is beet-red with laughter, ready to fall out of his chair.

Paul is like a comedian, delivering barbs with humor. Over the next hour, the Apostle of Riesling provokes us into some fascinating pairings, explaining *why* he'd make those choices. First up is a 2010 Kabinett Riesling by the estate of Reinhard & Beate Knebel, whose Rottgen vineyard in the Mosel region of Germany is built on terraced slate slopes so steep that the workers must use a monorail to reach them. It's a cool, fresh wine that is relatively inexpensive. Paul suggests pairing it with Houlihan's crispy fried jumbo shrimp and fries. Next up is a 2009 old-vine chardonnay from Domaine Jean-Francois Ganevat's Les Chalasses vineyard in the Jura region of France. Sitting between Burgundy and Switzerland, the Jura region is known for wines of great value. The soil in Ganevat's vineyard consists of gray marlstone, a kind of muddy limestone. Paul thinks this quirky, delicious chardonnay would be great for the BBQ chicken–stuffed Chicago pizza served by the Patxi's Pizza chain, run by our guest, Bill. It's nothing like the American chardonnays we've come to expect; its oakiness is practically hidden.

Then there's the 2007 Riesling Smaragd produced by Johann Donabaum in Wachau, Germany. The *terroir* in Donabaum's Spitzer Offenberg vineyard is fairly rocky, but the wine has the surprising fruitiness of citrus and peach. Paul tosses off a suggestion that Dave Pace, the president of Carrabba's, might consider pairing this wine with his restaurant's chicken trio. Chris Doody, the founder and CEO of Piada Italian Street Food, a predominantly midwestern chain, is urged to consider for his chicken and pasta dish the 2010 Les Vieux Clos Savennieres from Nicolas Joly in the Loire Valley of France. Joly's wine is grown in fields of schist, quartz, and sand, and though the wine is 100 percent chenin blanc, its dry, full-bodied flavor and wet wool-and-honey notes would stand up nicely to a hearty Italian main dish. Paul has no recommendations for Kevin Boehm, from Boka Restaurant Group, and Kevin probably counts himself lucky to have escaped our host's intellectual wine humor. There's also no recommendations for John Schlegel, CEO of Snooze Eatery, possibly because Paul can't come up with a wine to pair with the pancakes on John's menu.

What are we learning?

We are traveling the world in the hands of a competent sommelier. The more Paul talks, the more we push ourselves beyond the usual suspects to a place where beauty and surprising flavor arrives in a glass. A great sommelier opens your eyes.

Our visit to Terroir runs way too late. But that's how it always goes on the tours. The last stop is always the longest. As shadows lengthen across the sidewalk outside, we drink, laugh, argue, and drink again, this time to each other.

The members of this year's tour arrived as strangers. But they part as friends.

Food and wine, as it always has, pulls us together.

So that's how the most recent Underground Culinary Tour ends. Two great days of tasting, eating, drinking, and an exploding universe of here-and-now trends. The tour may strike some as an exercise in gastronomic debauchery. After all, one could argue, it's extraordinarily New York–centric. You can't really expect chefs in the American heartland to cook like Tom Colicchio, can you? It's unrealistic.

Here's how I answer these objections. First, the location doesn't matter. If I were based in any other city—Los Angeles, Philadelphia, Austin, Atlanta, Minneapolis, New Orleans—I'd be able to take my guests on a similarly eye-opening tour. In fact, I once assembled and conducted an amazing tour of Underground Culinary Tour alumni in Dallas, which blew us all away.

That's what makes food trends worthy of analysis. If they're catching on and easily observable in one big city, chances are they're happening elsewhere. You just have to know how to look for them. That's what separates the New Guard from the Old Guard. Cutting-edge chefs, drink mavens, and restaurant operators know they must constantly evolve. They are forever analyzing the places they discover when they travel to other cities and shores. And they adapt what they learn to their own concepts.

But then there are the rare restaurant execs who seem forever married to their Old Guard practices. They view their trip to the Big Apple as just a fun, foodie vacation, but they resist change, insisting that what they've seen doesn't apply to their chain.

One year the Avero-Elliot Underground Culinary Tour sampled the food at Danny Meyer's Shake Shack in Madison Square Park in New York City. At the time, there was only one Shake Shack in existence—this was the original location. It had first started as a hot dog stand before morphing into something bigger. Alice and I thought that they were doing something special, so we included them as a stop on our tour.

As we manhandled our delicious burgers and vacuumed down our shakes, I noticed one guest eyeing the long line of customers waiting to place orders. People have been known to wait here as long as an hour. In fact, Danny's group had even installed a "Shake Shack cam" over the location so people can gauge the length of the line on their home or office computers before they walk over.

This particular executive worked for a huge national casual dining chain. Believe me, you've eaten in his company's restaurants at least once in your life. They're ubiquitous. As he watched all these Shake Shack customers, he was shaking his head.

"I don't get what all the fuss is about," he said. "The burgers are good, but they're too small. My guests wouldn't go for it."

He was assuming that his guests would equate portion size with quality, ignoring all the other points in Shake Shack's value proposition to the consumer. The burger is 100 percent Angus beef, hormone- and antibiotic-free. The hot dog and burger buns are non-GMO. The shakes are made by hand. The iced tea's organic. And you won't find a drop of corn syrup in the entire place. In short, it's all about the purity of the ingredients. It's also established itself as a unique brand among foodies.

I gestured at the line of people. "I'm telling you, this is the future. If these customers can't find what they want at *your* place, they'll come to places like Shake Shack. *This* is your competition."

At the end of the tour, the exec returned home. A few years later, his restaurant chain was struggling badly.

As for Shake Shack, today they're one of the fastest-growing fast casual chains on the planet. There are sixty-six locations all over the world, as far away as Russia, Japan, Turkey, and the Middle East. Apparently *somebody* likes those burgers. So much so, you might even call it a trend.

· 8 ·

UNDER THE TABLE

A woman I'll call Janice[*] comes from a large foodie family. Her uncles ran their own restaurants; her mother operated a small catering business. Janice got her start working as the general manager of a retro-themed diner in Atlanta. She attracted the notice of the owners, who were interested in going nationwide and wanted to move beyond eateries constrained by theme.

You know when you've walked into a themed restaurant: places like Hard Rock Café or Rainforest Café. There's a shtick about such places that makes them popular with tourists who can't find these unusual chains back home. But themed restaurants can sometimes leave locals cold.

Janice's genius was in flipping the themed dynamic on

---

[*] Janice's restaurant group is a composite of two real-life hospitality companies.

its head. With the concepts she developed for her employers, the food took center stage. The décor was still incredible, but it was not nearly as important. When she built a casual Italian restaurant, it ended up being as beautiful and authentic seeming than anything you saw in Italy. Her Irish pubs conveyed a heightened sense of *Irishness,* but still seemed completely accessible to the average guest.

I assure you that you have been in many of the places Janice has dreamed up. But you'll never say to your friends, "Hey, let's go to that Italian place," or that Asian place, or the barbecue place. You will always say the name of the restaurant. Janice's restaurants are so attractive that they come off as indie restaurants, not part of a larger group.

In North America, that gets people in the door. When you're traveling on a business trip to another city, you'll pass up the obvious chains and choose one of Janice's upscale casual places instead.

Her employer's company now holds in its portfolio dozens of restaurants. And Janice is the service-obsessed executive who makes the magic happen.

As she rose to the top of the organization, Janice never forgot that, for her, restaurants had a strong connection to family. Her new employers had a similar approach to the business. They enjoyed promoting from within and fostering a culture where employees were empowered to make decisions on their own to enhance the guest experience. Though they knew the group was growing, they didn't want to lose touch with the people who ensured the company's success. More than twenty years and countless collective weddings, babies, and even lost loved ones later, many of Janice's original hires continue to serve her customers. She feels proud of the home she has built for herself and her team.

Not long ago I happened to look at the statistics emanating from one of Janice's restaurants. Unfortunately, I found some activities that I knew Janice would be unhappy to discover. About a month later she and I agreed to meet for lunch at one of Janice's eateries. I asked the maitre d' for a table in the center of the room, and even picked the server who would serve us.

We quickly scanned our menus. A crab cake sandwich for me. A seared tuna sandwich for Janice. A Diet Pepsi for her, an iced tea for me. Water for the table.

The gregarious, chatty server nodded at our order and dashed off.

We talked shop for the next hour, shared a few laughs, and had some great food. I marched through a review of her operation, omitting the unsavory stuff for the moment. When the check came, Janice offered to comp the meal, but I snatched the bill and said, "No, I insist." It was a bill I knew only I could pay.

Janice threw her hands up in mock surrender.

I dropped some cash in the check presenter and asked Janice to show me around. We did a quick tour of the restaurant: the kitchen, the wine cellar, their back offices, the freezer. As we were heading back out, I said, "Hey, do you mind if we check how the server rang up the tab?"

Her brow furrowed. "Why?"

"Humor me," I said, somewhat mysteriously.

We went over to the POS device, and I watched as Janice entered her password to access the system and navigated over to our server's recent tabs, finally pulling our order up on the screen.

"What do you notice?" I said.

Janice ticked off each of the items on the list. Both our sandwiches were there. But one of our drinks—the Diet Pepsi—had gone missing. On top of that, at the very end of the tab, the server had applied a 4 percent discount to the entire meal.

"That's weird," Janice said. "Where did he get the code for that discount?"

"I'm guessing it's an old promotion you did months ago," I said. "It's probably still in the system."

"But why—"

I nodded. "I left him cash, remember? So the house has no real record of what I paid. He pocketed the tip, *plus* the cost of the Pepsi, *plus* the 4 percent discount. All told, it only adds up to about six bucks. But if he does it every third time a diner pays in cash, he's probably putting another five thousand dollars a year in his pocket."

The color drained out of Janice's face.

You see, our loss prevention program had flagged this particular server as a potential scammer. That's why, on my visit to Janice's restaurant today, I had specifically asked for him. I wanted a chance to look him in the eye, and then set a trap for him. I must say that he was an excellent server. But that doesn't make him honest. People often forget that a person can be at once a competent professional *and* a thief.

Theft is believed to cost the restaurant industry $3 billion to $6 billion worldwide every year, possibly much,

much more. The reason for this imprecision should be painfully obvious to you, if you've absorbed the central message of this book. *The restaurant industry doesn't keep good statistics on theft.*

One rule of thumb in the business is that a restaurant's food costs should stay between 28 and 35 percent of its food sales. If these food costs go much higher, it's generally acknowledged that the restaurant has a problem in one or more six key areas—ordering, training practices, food waste, portion sizes, meal prices, or theft.

In other words, theft is already built into the cost of a restaurant, right up there with kitchen waste. Restaurant operators don't condone theft, but they expect it. A National Restaurant Association study suggested that theft might well account for 4 percent of a restaurant's total food costs. That seems like a paltry amount, until you recall that a restaurant might only earn 4 to 5 percent profit each year. If the restaurant is particularly bad at rooting out inefficiencies, the easiest way to make up the gaps is to pass the losses on to staff and customers. Employees lose out on benefits, bonuses, and raises. And customers like us end up paying more for meals and drinks. A choice like that ends up costing the restaurateur more in the long run. Good employees get sick of working at a place with no future and leave for greener pastures. Customers get sick of higher prices and eat elsewhere.

To most of us, restaurant theft conjures up visions of a place being robbed, *Goodfellas* style—someone walking off with the contents of a cash register or a case of vodka or a box of steaks in the dead of night. That certainly happens; it's believed that employee theft is responsible for 75 percent of inventory shortages. And there are always stories reported in the media of restaurant partners, bookkeepers, or accountants who embezzle thousands in one transaction or several. Those are the kinds of stories that make headlines when they're uncovered.

But the day-to-day reality is more subtle and insidious. It happens in broad daylight, under the noses of owners and guests, every single day of the week . . . nearly invisible transactions. Employees intent on stealing are too smart to void out a $100 cash transaction. They know it's a game of pennies. So they stuff a few bucks in their aprons that should have gone into the till. They take food or drink without permission or payment. They comp friends and family without a manager's approval. They overpour drinks for their buddies, and then short-pour *you* to make up the difference. They pour well drinks when you ask for the premium stuff, overcharge you, and pocket the difference, betting that you'll never taste the drop in quality. If an employee is audacious enough, he or she will have no problem colluding with an outside scammer to steal and sell the data gleaned off guest credit cards.

It's deflating, nasty stuff. Theft impacts restaurants, honest employees, and guests. The only way a restaurant operator can stop people like this is to constantly monitor the restaurant's transactions and nail shady employees with the evidence—which is easier said than done. I'm not a forensic accountant, but I have to admit that some of the methods employed by scammers are diabolically clever. I don't know why it is, but maybe the brain of someone who spends his or her life working for tips gradually becomes hardwired to think in terms of trivial amounts of money that add up over time, while the big-picture brains of owner-restaurateurs don't.

Waitstaff are intimately familiar with the POS device at their workplace. They know all its ins and outs, its passwords, its discount codes, all the ways it can be compromised, because they're constantly interacting with it. They are adept at taking advantage of doors left unlocked in the POS system. This allows servers to skim small increments of money, which over time can add up to a lot of cash.

At Avero, we call this *transactional fraud.* And like so much of the under-the-radar data I've talked about in the book, such activity would be completely invisible without computers. In a busy restaurant, the manager or owner just doesn't have the time or the bandwidth to focus on every individual transaction. I've met many Old Guard restaurateurs who outright assume that people are stealing from them. But since they have no way to prove it, they make *everyone's* life a living hell. They go around every day being suspicious of their staff. New Guard restaurant owners and managers have a more intelligent approach to theft. They put tools in place to ferret out the one or two who abuse the system so they can focus on and reward the honest, loyal, dedicated employees.

When an Old Guard restaurant has one or two scammers in the place, its owners will find them hard to catch, for two reasons. First, micro-theft is practically invisible unless you're crunching the numbers on a minute-by-minute, day-to-day basis. Second, scammers are constantly evolving, perfecting one technique and then nimbly switching to another strategy when the opportunity arises or they sense increased scrutiny.

In my lunch with Janice, the server used the POS device to *reduce* the amount of the original check so he would be able to keep more of the cash I paid him—the difference between the reported bill and the bill I actually paid. But there are other ways that he could have ripped off the restaurant and raised your food bill. Over time, my team and I have identified at least seven classic scams, which we made public on Avero's blog, beginning in fall 2013. I'll explain them briefly. As you read, think about the times you may have unwittingly played the role of the unsuspecting guest.

THE CHECK REUSE SCAM

A hotel guest chooses to serve herself from the breakfast buffet one morning. At the end of the meal, the server drops the check, and the guest pays with cash. The server pockets the cash and presents the *exact same check* to the next table. This effectively renders the second transaction nonexistent. Since the server hasn't rung it up at the POS, there's no record of that patron's meal. And since virtually every diner typically chooses the breakfast buffet, the server can continue to present the exact same printout of the check until a guest pays with a credit card or other noncash payment. This scam works in any setting where guests typically order the same item: buffets, hotel continental breakfasts, coffee shops, or bars serving a beer, wine, or cocktail that is hugely popular. To work, it's critical that the server or bartender doesn't need to generate a ticket from the POS to request the food or drink from another staffer. Buffets are self-serve, so the kitchen doesn't need an order from the POS system to cook the dish. If the scammer is the bartender, he or she already has access to every beverage—and doesn't need a ticket to request the drinks from the bar. This is a classic scam that has caused the restaurant industry indigestion for years.

THE TRANSFER SCAM

Let's say a guest orders a rib eye steak, a side of creamed spinach, and a beer, and then pays with cash. When the server rings up the sale, he transfers the creamed spinach from that check to a new, fictitious check. He closes out the original check in the correct amount for the steak and beer but pockets both his tip and the cash for the spinach. At the end of his shift, the server asks the manager on duty to authorize a void on the spinach due to a guest complaint. "The spinach was too cold by the time it came out," he tells the manager. If his manager asks why he didn't mention this earlier, the server will claim that the manager was too busy at the time. It's a smart business practice to require managers to authorize voids or promotions. But in this case, the manager has no way of confirming that the guest was actually dissatisfied with the item. Ideally, such requests are made when the guest is still in the restaurant, so the manager can try to make the situation right by offering a dessert or another side. But by transferring the side dish to a fictitious check, the server cleverly complicated the transaction, moving it further afield from the patron. The manager has no way of reconstructing the situation or reaching out to the patron.

THE POS AUTHORIZATION SCAM

In this scam, after a guest pays with cash, the server uses a void or promotion to reduce the amount owed, pocketing the difference. (This is what happened when I dined at Janice's restaurant.) While it's similar to the Transfer Scam, in this case the server doesn't need a manager to authorize or process the void or promotion. Manager approval ought to be required in all cases of check reductions, but as a practical matter, it's often too cumbersome to enforce. Managers are too busy to stand by the cash register authorizing voids and discounts. We've caught servers ringing up discounts for happy hours that didn't exist and using a password they weren't supposed to know to gain access to the discounting system.

THE WAGON WHEEL SCAM

I love this one. It combines elements of all three scams I've already discussed. A guest orders a burger and an iced tea, and pays with cash. The server transfers the iced tea off the check to a new check, closes out the original check with just the burger, and pockets the cash for the iced tea. The next time a table orders an iced tea, the server uses the check with the iced tea item already on it to start the new tab. If this table pays with a credit card, the scam is over. But if this table *also* pays in cash, the server can re-peat the scam all over again: transfer the iced tea to a new check and pocket its cost a second time. Since iced tea and soft drinks are common at lunch, the server is confident that the next table she waits on will have at least one such drink, so she'll feel confident she can reuse the fraudulent check with the drink. Server-controlled items such as non-alcoholic beverages are a common target for this scheme because servers are typically permitted to pour as many as they need over the course of their shift. It's tougher to pull off the wagon wheel scam when you need to ask the kitchen or the bar for a dish or a drink.

THE CASH/COUPON ABUSE SCAM

In this scam, after a guest pays with cash, the server re-deems a coupon he is saving in his apron and pockets the cash for the amount of the coupon. Coupons and promo-tions are a big part of the restaurant industry today, espe-cially with the proliferation of daily deal companies like Groupon and increased attention to loyalty rewards pro-grams. But these deals and coupons are often an oppor-tunity for scammers. If a restaurant runs a promotion in a local paper where the guest simply needs to show his or her ID with a local address to receive 10 percent off a meal, it's the server's responsibility to verify the ID and then de-duct the amount of the coupon from the check. Few checks and balances exist to ensure server integrity. If a paper coupon is actually redeemed, restaurants often staple the coupon to the check and reconcile the paper coupons with cash register redemptions at the end of the night. But there is nothing to keep a wily server from bringing in his or her own copies of coupons, clipped from discarded newspapers or hoarded from other sources, and redeeming them to pocket the cash.

THE VIP COMP ABUSE SCAM

In this scam, two unrelated parties come to the restaurant. The first group is made up of high-profile guests or VIPs whom the manager knows well and whose entire meals he routinely comps. The second group consists of regular paying customers. If the second group pays with cash, the server transfers one or two items from the cash check to the VIP table check, and pockets the cash for those items. The server knows that the manager will comp every item on the VIP table check. Since the meal is complimentary, the VIPs will never see the check, so no one scrutinizes it for items they didn't order.

THE TIP INFLATION SCAM

Here is a scam that doesn't rely on cash. A guest orders a $15 pasta dish and a $5 beer. She pays with a credit card, leaving a $4 tip, for a total of $24. The scammer uses a void or promotion to remove the $5 beer from the check. He adds that $5 to the tip, so that the new check shows a $15 pasta dish and a very generous $9 tip ($4 original tip + $5 from the beer reduction). The guest never notices a thing, since her credit card statement shows the same $24 on her receipt. The restaurant is the only one that loses.

THE AUTO-GRATUITY SCAM

In this scam, a guest at a resort hotel orders, say, an iced tea at the pool bar. Per resort policy, an automatic gratuity is added to her check, which she signs and charges to her hotel room. Later, the bartender adds an additional $1 tip to the check before closing it out. Such scams are rarely caught because resort guests are unlikely to notice a few extra dollars on a single transaction. At checkout, guests are presented with a long list of charges associated with their stay, and they rarely reconcile each charge manually. The longer the person's stay, the more challenging the task. Instead, they accept the charges, pay the bill, and depart. Room service charges are especially vulnerable to this scam, since hotels typically charge an automatic gratuity and a delivery fee for each meal brought up to a room. Guests are easily confused by the various charges and are unlikely to spot an extra dollar or two.

Notice how many of these scams are variants of the ones that came before. It's as if scammers are constantly broadening or refining their competency. Remember the film *Catch Me If You Can*? Leonardo DiCaprio plays a charming, real-life con man who evolves into the greatest perpetrator of check fraud the US banking system has ever seen. Over the course of the film, he becomes more and more bold as he perfects his skills, adapts to new challenges, takes greater risks, and successfully steals greater sums. Restaurant scammers are no different. The more seasoned they become, the more they evolve in terms of the tactics they use.

As my team and I work with restaurants, we see how cleverly such restaurant industry thieves modify the seven classic scams to adapt to the opportunities at their business. For example, as part of her rewards program, Janice had instituted an Employee of the Month system, where her managers would present an employee with a plastic $25 gift card to be used in one of the restaurants in Janice's group. In one case an award-winning dishwasher sold that card for half its value—$12.50—to one of the servers in exchange for cash. The server kept the card tucked into his apron, waiting for the next time a diner paid for a $25-plus tab in cash. When that happened, the server swiped the gift card to pay for the meal—and kept the $25 in cash. It's the classic cash/coupon abuse scam, but with a twist: a backroom employee handoff.

The dishwasher pockets $12.50 in cash.

The server pockets the remaining $12.50 of the card's value, plus his tip.

The guest is none the wiser.

And Janice's employers lose $25 in cash.

You might argue that Janice's company knew she was awarding a $25 value when she started this program, so why do these actions constitute fraud?

First, both the dishwasher and the server subverted the restaurant's intentions by creating a black market in Janice's facility. Second, it takes the team's focus off *your*

dining experience, where it belongs. Third, the employees are putting money in their pockets that rightfully
belongs to the house. Last, the whole point of these programs is to reward employee loyalty by allowing them
to experience the restaurant as a guest—but that's not
happening.

I understand the appeal of gift cards and coupons, but
they have opened an unintended back door to restaurant
fraud that has becoming increasingly difficult to bolt shut.
In one case, our client's restaurant chain offered a 20 percent holiday discount on gift cards. "Buy a $100 gift card and
get $20 in extra value!" So what happened? One employee
bought $3,000 worth of the restaurant's gift cards. Over
the next several months, he played out the cash/coupon
scam, earning 20 percent cash profit on the difference—
or $600.

Other employees went into business with far less overhead. The manager of one restaurant group we work with
nabbed a server in the parking lot with a stack of "20 percent off" restaurant fliers in the trunk of his car. The restaurant had recently published the fliers in the Sunday
circular section of their city's newspaper. The employee
had run around town swiping editions out of newspaper
boxes, amassing a huge collection.

These scams can have a huge impact on the bottom line
of restaurant groups, larger chains, casinos, and hotels, and
ultimately on what it costs you to eat out. Does this mean
restaurants should avoid giving out gift cards and cash?
No. Gift cards are often the best way for customers to discover a new restaurant and to encourage repeat customers.

Restaurateurs appreciate having the extra cash flow to pay vendors and make payroll.

Here's a scam all diners should be alert to: In most restaurants, parties of six or more trigger an automatic 18 percent gratuity. After waiting on such a party, a dishonest server may write THANK YOU! with a huge smiley face. Sounds like a memorable way to express his appreciation, right? But what the server may be doing is defacing the check and obscuring the line that says that the gratuity has already been charged. The server hopes that you don't inspect the tab closely. Distracted patrons, talking with their companions as they head out, will often leave a sizable second tip. This is one scam that takes money directly out of your pocket. It is little better than pickpocketing.

Moreover, if you discovered that this had happened to you, and you shared your experience on Yelp or other social media, would you differentiate between the server who scammed you and the restaurant itself? I doubt it. Which is why restaurants must work harder to protect themselves and their customers against such thieves.

How do restaurants catch them? By the use of data. All the while dishonest employees are going about these activities, an algorithm is busy analyzing everyone's productivity and scoring them. Let me give you an example. Look at the sets of numbers below and see if you can discern a pattern in each of them. Here's the first series, identified by the names of fictitious servers at a restaurant, followed by numbers representing the percentage of cash transactions each handled during a particular shift. Which server appears to stand out from the rest?

Angie 11

Bert 16

Connie 17

Denny 19

Edward 20

It should be pretty easy to pick out Angie. Only 11 percent of her orders involved cash, and she's separated from her peers by a difference of five percentage points. If Angie is reporting considerably fewer cash transactions than everyone else, there's a chance she may be running a check reuse scam, the scam where frequent similar orders aren't rung up and the same printed check is used over and over again, with the cash going into the server's pocket.

Of course, you can't incriminate or fire Angie on the basis of a single statistic. So let's look at how her other performance statistics stack up. We can look at the entire team's *item per cover metric*—that is, the number of menu items each server sells to a guest during his or her shift. Let's say that we find, on average, that Angie reports selling the fewest number of items to guests over several shifts. Next, we can drill down and look specifically at what percentage of the orders our servers are selling to guests on a particular morning include coffee. Does anyone stand out?

Angie 10

Bert 80

Connie 83

Denny 87

Edward 88

Coffee is a server-controlled item. The kitchen doesn't make it; it's all up to the server. It's perfectly possible that some servers will simply forget to ring up drink items, which tend to be the ones patrons ask for the most. But Angie's behavior is well outside the normal range. While her colleagues are selling coffee to 80 to 88 percent of their customers at breakfast, Angie reports selling coffee to only 10 percent of her covers. That point spread is damning. It strongly suggests that her behavior is not accidental, but intentional. It looks as if she's pocketing the price of those coffees, using one scam or another to transfer, void, or discount an item off a check and pocket the undeclared cash. This statistic, combined with her low cash profile, is enough to target Angie for special attention. Next, I can check to see if Angie's orders display a high percentage of coupons, discounts, voids, or transfers, or a high percentage of tips, to see if a pattern emerges.

Granted, I have grossly oversimplified how a program seeks out discrepancies in data patterns. But you get the idea. During the crunch of daily shifts, no manager or owner can keep track of how many coffees are served. But we can design software algorithms that perform complicated computations and spot patterns in data that humans would never see. The computer knows, for instance, that on any given day in a restaurant servers will sometimes ring up an order, then *void* that order. (A burger is poorly cooked, so it's taken off the patron's bill.) There will be a colorful array of *discounts* (gift certificates, Groupon discounts, happy hour discounts, and so on). Managers will *comp* drinks, desserts, or other items to certain VIPs. You may offer to pay for another patron's drink or meal, resulting in items being *transferred* from one bill to another.

Such transactions are an integral part of restaurant life, and servers learn to nimbly accommodate them. Luckily, most servers and other restaurant employees are honest. Each time they punch an order into the POS, they contribute to an ever-growing dossier of their behavior. Their work patterns—what days they work, what hours, whether they worked the bar or the tables, what zone of the restaurant they're working in—can be melded with the transactional record to build a kind of personal work signature.

If one server's pattern of items per cover, cash-to-credit-card ratio, voids, discounts, comped items, and transfers differs strongly from the patterns established by his or her colleagues during the same shift or shifts, the numbers reveal them for what they are—an outlier. We can actually assign a kind of "credit score" to that employee, with 1 being the best score, 100 being the worst. A bad score flags outliers for closer scrutiny.

The same principle is at work when your credit card company detects a deviation from your spending habits and issues a fraud alert on your card. Something about the latest transaction does not conform to your spending signature—so they don't authorize the transaction, or they ask you to phone in, or they cancel the card outright. What is novel is applying this type of data analysis to the world of the New Guard restaurant.

Remarkably, I've encountered some resistance from owners when I raise the issue of theft. In big companies, executives sometimes mask their insecurities. "Significant theft can't possibly be going on in our shop" is their attitude. "If it were, I'd know about it."

Unfortunately, the truth is that in larger chains, a number of employees may be revealed to have imperfect scores. I advise clients to focus on the most egregious ones. When the worst scammers are flagged, I caution managers and owners *not* to call out the perpetrators. The first rule of catching a thief is to let him hang himself with his own data. Let the data accumulate, then monitor him and see if you can force him to replicate his behavior. That's what I did that day in Janice's restaurant. The software flagged a server with a high "credit" score. I asked for that particular server in that section of the restaurant, I indulged his brand of chattiness to throw him off guard, and then dropped cash as payment to see what he would do with it. Once you've singled out a scammer, it's easy to spot-check his or her orders during a shift to see how they've been manipulated. Then you can confront the scammer with the specifics—"You're stealing, Angie, and here's how I know"—and dismiss him or her, or even pursue legal action.

If your business has developed a culture of scams, it's not necessary to bust every single person flagged by the system. All managers need to do is make an example of

224 • THE UNDERGROUND CULINARY TOUR

a few, bundling their dismissals together so the firing is perceived by other employees as a major incident. The rest will fall in line quickly enough, thanks to what is known as "the Sheriff Effect." If you publicize the prosecution of a few people who are stealing, everyone else who is exhibiting borderline behavior will suddenly get the message and straighten out that behavior. I was able to chart this effect in Janice's restaurant to a startling degree. In less than a year, her company was forced to fire more than a dozen offenders nationwide. The employees had stolen an estimated $100,000 via micro-theft transactions. The message was heard loud and clear throughout the company: scams of any kind would not be tolerated. We later observed a *$1 million* annual jump in cash revenues across the entire organization, most likely a result of these dismissals. Any servers who were hoarding gift cards or coupons ditched them. Suddenly, every coffee, iced tea, and soda made it onto the books. That income found its way into the restaurant's bank account instead of its servers' pockets. The Sheriff Effect had a tenfold impact on the company's bottom line.

Of course, the Sheriff Effect doesn't last forever. The organization or company needs to reinforce that message periodically. You need to build a culture of honesty and vigilance. Or as President Reagan used to say, *trust, but verify.*

Understandably, Janice took these revelations personally.

"I thought of these people as my family," Janice complained to me. "I came up with that program to thank them. But they've been stealing from us all along. It wasn't like just learning that my spouse was cheating. It was like finding out that many of my family members had been cheating on me. It stung. And it hurt every guest who visited our restaurants, as we raised prices to try to compensate for our lost revenue."

For a New Guard restaurateur like Janice, such betrayals will no longer be invisible, or be allowed to continue, for long.

· 9 ·

INNOVATING THE FAMILY BUSINESS

Some cities are so closely associated with food that what you eat when you visit is almost preordained. The first time you go to Philadelphia, for example, you must try a cheese-steak sandwich. In Charleston, it is almost de rigueur that you have a bowl of she-crab soup and dig into a serving of shrimp and grits. In Toronto, it's a big messy plate of poutine. In St. Louis, it's BBQ. In New York, if you don't grab at least one hot dog from a street vendor, or a slice of cheesy hot New York pizza, you may find yourself embarrassed to tell your friends that you visited the Big Apple.

And when you head on down to New Orleans, that hallowed city of saints and sinners, you must head over to the seventy-year-old institution Brennan's, on Royal Street in the French Quarter, where teams of servers in salmon-colored ties and black vests or aprons bring you a succession of must-haves: turtle soup, seafood filé gumbo, roasted Gulf oysters, eggs Sardou, and crawfish étouffée or jambalaya. And if you manage to get to the end of a sumptuous repast there with the least bit of room left, you'll finish off the meal with the dish Brennan's brought into the world—bananas Foster. Gazing at Brennan's from the outside—with its pink stucco facade, its tall windows with green shutters and black cast-iron balconies—you would probably conclude that such a place was too old-world, too hopelessly romantic, to be bothered with something as unseemly as data.

But you'd be wrong.

The story of how the Ralph Brennan Restaurant Group came to adopt data and technology is really the story of how my friend Ralph and his team learned to *survive*. When he faced the greatest crisis of his career, the lessons he'd absorbed from data and technology gave him the tools he needed to be a better manager, leader, and neighbor.

Often I encounter restaurateurs who tell me that they don't want to link the magic that happens in their dining rooms and kitchens to a bunch of ones and zeroes. It will distort the reason they got into the business in the first place, they tell me. But there's no way someone can stroll the streets of the French Quarter, sit in the shade of dreamy courtyards to hear the sounds of the fountains, of jazz and blues seeping out of the music halls, and tell me that there isn't magic galore in this city. In New Orleans, the Brennan family is a culinary dynasty. The various branches of this family have been feeding locals and visitors alike since 1946. Ralph owns seven eateries and a catering company in this city alone.

He did not come by his success easily. Since childhood, he's watched his family undergo enormous change—the challenge of new restaurants, family discord, natural and manmade disasters. Somehow, the Brennans survived to become the best-known restaurant family in the city, and one of the best in the world. At first glance, old restaurants might seem like the ultimate dog who can't be taught new tricks. But it just isn't true. If the scion of the leading family of New Orleans dining has embraced data, if *he* has found it to be useful, transformative, and salvational—shouldn't every restaurant that has come of age in the last decade consider stepping in with the New Guard?

Ralph's uncle, Owen Brennan, came from a large working-class Irish Catholic family in New Orleans—six brothers and sisters. Owen married and felt the urge to earn a living that every young man feels when he starts a family. So he bought a bar called the Old Absinthe House on Bourbon Street in the French Quarter (the same bar whose absinthe fountains inspired the replica found in my Underground Culinary Tour destination Maison Premiere in Brooklyn). One day, after a competitor teased him, saying an Irishman could never serve French food, Owen resolved to buy a second restaurant across the street, known as the Vieux Carré, which became the site of his white-tablecloth destination, Brennan's Vieux Carré (French for "old square" and is synonymous with the French Quarter). His parents and siblings all pitched in to run the restaurant's kitchens and serve guests.

In 1955, feeling pressure from his landlord, Owen decided to move the restaurant from its original location on Bourbon Street to 417 Royal Street, where it stands today. Owen had been pushing himself hard to get the new place ready for customers. Tragically, he died in his sleep just before it opened, at the age of forty-five. The bank that had underwritten his lavish renovation of this 1795 building panicked and refused to advance the family the money to complete the renovation. But the family persuaded their contractor to proceed and wait for the money until after the restaurant opened (good luck asking a contractor to do so today). The new Brennan's quickly became famous for excellent food that raised New Orleans's Creole cuisine to the level of fine dining—which, in the 1950s, meant fancy French cuisine.

Ralph, Owen's nephew, grew up being babysat by his aunts Ella and Adelaide. His aunts, unmarried in those days, lived with their parents, Ralph's grandparents. In the mornings, his grandmother cooked breakfast, then the sisters would take Ralph to see a movie, buy him a toy at the Woolworth's on Canal Street, then they would wander over to the restaurant. Ella and Adelaide prepared the restaurant for guests or ran the service, while Ralph played in the stockrooms, behind the bar, or in the wine cellar. He loved feeling the chill of the cellar and peering at the exotic labels that his uncle's wine buyer showed him. Ralph knew that he could always scrounge up a snack or a meal in the kitchen. He'd often just grab a few strawberries and some ice cream, and dive in until the bowl was scraped clean. To this day he's obsessed with ice cream.

When he was a teenager, Aunt Ella hired Ralph to work in the kitchen at Brennan's as a prep cook, where he spent endless, exhausting days peeling shrimp and deboning chickens. Later, he whipped up sauces on the kitchen line. He learned the business side by talking to his Aunt Ella, who ran the place for the family. The two didn't always see eye to eye. Ella was tougher on Ralph than she was on her other employees. But Ella was fond of her nephew and urged him to get a college education. She wanted him to study business. Ella understood that restaurants, first and foremost, were businesses. The family, she felt, would only benefit if all the children were educated.

So Ralph studied accounting and business in college. But he missed the restaurant and the magic of its dining rooms. Once, when school got him down, he announced to his father that he was quitting college. "World War III started!" Ralph recalls. "My father always regretted that he never graduated from college because of his Navy service in WWII."

So he stayed on, got his bachelor's in accounting, and embarked on an MBA. During Ralph's years at Tulane University, a rift tore the Brennan family apart. The Brennan family's disagreements became quite public, recounted with glee by the local media. In 1974, Ella and her siblings were dismissed from their management positions at the helm of the restaurant. Owen's sons took over Brennan's, and the rest of the family went off to another restaurant, Commander's Palace. Aunt Ella emerged as the family matriarch and a New Orleans culinary icon. Blessed with a great palate, an instinct for spotting talent, and a natural flair for hospitality, she presided over Commander's Palace, an upscale dining establishment located in the city's picturesque Garden District, which she and her siblings had acquired in 1968. (As I write this, Ella is ninety and still shaping the cuisine at Commander's.) On Ella's watch, Commander's attracted such extraordinary chefs as Paul Prudhomme and Emeril Lagasse, and played host to every luminary who passed through the Big Easy, from Rosemary Clooney to Truman Capote to Raymond Burr to Robert Mitchum. Many today credit Ella with singlehandedly teaching America what regional cooking is all about.

When he had a moment, Ralph would make an appointment to come talk to Ella in her office at Commander's Palace. He'd talk about what he was learning in school and listen to her views on business. Opportunities walk in the door every day, Ralph, she would tell him. They come in many forms: a customer who falls in love with our food and becomes a lifelong guest, the restaurant critic from out of town who spreads news of our food to the world. You never know what that opportunity is going to be—you just have to be smart and pounce on it. Beyond that, Ella urged Ralph to commit to lifelong excellence. She believed that restaurants—and all businesses—could be plotted along a bell curve. Their excellence rose to a peak, and then, if you weren't watching, that excellence dropped! If you want to succeed, you have to *grow,* she told her nephew; you must always strive to be better a year from now than you are today, or you risk stagnating.

After graduating, Ralph embarked on a career as a certified public accountant, spending six years as a CPA at Price Waterhouse. But the special pleasure of the days he'd spent in the kitchen at Brennan's never left him. In 1980, when he was twenty-nine, his aunt asked him if he would like to come work for her. So he quit Price Waterhouse to chase his true dream in life. He worked at Commander's Palace for two weeks before he was dispatched to be the night manager of Mr. B's Bistro, a trendy casual/fine dining restaurant the family had opened in the French Quarter. In 1985, Ralph, his sister Cindy, and two of their cousins bought Mr. B's from the family. In 1991, Ralph saw an opportunity in the New Orleans market for Creole-Italian food, and a new restaurant, Bacco, was born.

In 1998, Ralph entered into conversations with executives from the Disneyland® Resort about opening a New Orleans–themed restaurant and jazz club on the grounds of the resort in Anaheim, California. The idea seemed like a natural. Each year, tourists from all over the world flock to New Orleans, fascinated by Louisiana's unique cuisine and musical heritage. Tourists at a Disney resort would surely be tempted by the same dishes and music.

The concept—Ralph Brennan's Jazz Kitchen—was an ambitious endeavor for a restaurateur who had spent his entire career in New Orleans. The restaurant would act as the West Coast outpost for Ralph's burgeoning brand. His thinking was that anyone who had a good time at Ralph Brennan's Jazz Kitchen would want to check out the other Ralph Brennan restaurants when they came to New Orleans. The building itself would be enormous—15,000 square feet on three floors, with a 250-person staff and a seating capacity of 450 people. They basically built a replica of a classic New Orleans–style building right in the middle of Downtown Disney® District, complete with iron railings and balconies, tinted stucco, a two-story courtyard with sculptures, a music venue, tin ceilings, and sumptuous upstairs dining rooms with tall windows, fireplaces, ceiling frescoes, and wall murals. Walking through the space, you felt like the king or queen of Mardi Gras.

Ralph was gambling a lot on the venture. The press pegged his investment at $8 million alone. Opening a restaurant in California is not the same as opening a restaurant in New Orleans. Everywhere he turned, Ralph encountered California's costlier ways of doing business. The rent on the Disney property was much higher than rents in New Orleans. Insurance was five times more expensive. *But think of the potential customers!* he said to himself. Disneyland played host to 14 million people a year, with more on the way thanks to Disney's California Adventure™, a new theme park that would open around the same time as Ralph's restaurant. Surely, that kind of amusement park foot traffic was worth the extra cost. When Ralph Brennan's Jazz Kitchen opened on January 1, 2001, Ralph was thrilled to bring New Orleans cuisine and hospitality to a new audience.

The initial months were a struggle financially. Sales were just starting to build when the tragic events of 9/11 occurred, only nine months after the restaurant's opening. The attack on the World Trade Center in New York depressed tourism throughout the nation, impacting theme park visitation especially hard. It took about eighteen months for the travel and hospitality industries to bounce back. But even before 9/11, Jazz Kitchen was challenged. It wasn't that people weren't coming. They *were*. Some days the place was packed, with a line out the door. Yet for some reason, Jazz Kitchen just wasn't hitting its financial targets. Clearly, something was sucking away its profits.

Privately, Ralph began to question the wisdom of opening a restaurant so far from home. The New Orleans restaurant world was a small community, and Ralph had spent his life getting to know all the players. Ordinarily, he ran a very hands-on operation, since he lived in the neighborhood of his other properties. He often felt that he was working at a distinct disadvantage when he tried to figure out the Jazz Kitchen's problems. Fortunately, his restaurants in New Orleans were providing his company with a steady stream of profits that offset the money that Jazz Kitchen was losing. But it was a situation that could not go on for long.

At the time, Ralph was launching yet another restaurant, Ralph's on the Park, housed in an old 1860s building that had once served as the concession stand for New Orleans's lovely City Park. Ralph knew he didn't have the time to get to the bottom of Jazz Kitchen's problems, so he handed the entire conundrum over to one of his staffers, a young marketer named Charlee Williamson. Dropping a sheaf of papers on her desk one day, he announced, "You're going to learn operations!" Ralph has always run an intentionally small operation. Today, though his entire business consists of about seven hundred employees, his central office is run by five people, which includes Ralph himself and Charlee.

Charlee had come to work for Ralph fresh out of college in 1993; she had witnessed the birth of nearly every restaurant in Ralph's portfolio. Over time, she and Ralph had developed a deep appreciation for data and analytics. But back in the 1990s and early 2000s, their office had only a few computers and very little restaurant-dedicated software. In the early days, when Ralph punted the Jazz Kitchen problem to her, Charlee and Ralph would fly out to California to visit the operation, ask questions, and take notes. Back home in New Orleans, Charlee could do little more than work late and phone Jazz Kitchen's general manager to see how the day was going. In the morning, when she came in to work, she would hurry to the fax machine to retrieve reports that the GM had faxed at the close of business, given the two-hour time difference. In the few hours remaining before Jazz Kitchen opened, she studied the data from their old-school POS system, trying to drill down to what was going wrong so she could advise and instruct the team when they came in.

But with traditional POS reporting, it's extremely difficult to extract operational insights. You can't look at a bunch of reports and easily say, "Oh, we're killing it on the beverage program, but we need to figure out why the appetizers are not selling." Or "No one orders three of our entrées on the weekends; maybe we should eliminate them." What you get in the Old Guard accounting world are reams of spreadsheets, which, when a restaurant is in trouble, is like trying to read the fine print on a document while you're sitting in a small boat bobbing furiously in the midst of a hurricane.

They were desperate. In May of 2002, Ralph attended

the annual National Restaurant Association trade show in Chicago, where he happened upon a demonstration of our software. "This could really help us at Jazz Kitchen," he thought. It was the quickest deal our team ever made, and the quickest installation as well. Our software was up and running at Jazz Kitchen within a few weeks. Suddenly, Charlee could more accurately study what was happening in their restaurant two thousand miles away. And with each new discovery, her jaw dropped.

As I suggested earlier, when you come to New Orleans, there are certain things you must do, certain foods you must eat. To many, New Orleans is a party town; to others, it's a bastion of regional cuisine with more than a table-spoon of irreverence. When people took a seat at one of Ralph's restaurants in the Big Easy, they knocked back a cocktail before they ordered. And they ate foods that they couldn't get back home, including shrimp, alligator, turtle, andouille sausage, and okra. They weren't afraid to try New Orleans spicy Creole or Cajun food. They happily devoured their turtle soup or their gumbo (or both), ordered another drink, and readied themselves for the bread pudding or ba-nanas Foster to come. In the endless party that was the Big Easy, children were often an afterthought in term of din-ing. And while many New Orleans pubs and music halls were devoted to casual dining, restaurants like Antoine's, Galatoire's, Arnaud's, and the classic Brennan's emphasized fine dining, where people dressed well for dinner, espe-cially on Sundays and weekdays.

With these kinds of assumptions in mind, Ralph had designed his beautiful California restaurant to replicate the New Orleans dining experience. The upstairs dining rooms were reserved for formal dining. The downstairs focused on casual fare. But as Charlee began analyzing the data, comparing the formal covers and the casual covers, she realized that they'd horribly misjudged their clientele. And that made the work of both the front and back of the house unnecessarily complicated. The data showed that they were serving far more casual meals than formal meals. Remember the long lines out the door? Turns out, those lines dragged because it took too long to educate guests about the different dining opportunities as they came in the door.

Do you prefer a formal dining experience or a casual meal?

Formal dining is upstairs, while casual dining is down here.

The servers and kitchen staff had to develop split personalities to service two different environments. Guided by the data, Charlee began closely questioning the management and staff about the upstairs/downstairs dynamic. She came to the conclusion that most of the guests who ended up upstairs didn't want to be there. And they were confused and upset that they'd been steered into a pricier menu and an environment for which they didn't feel properly dressed. As a result, the upstairs tables were increasingly empty.

The food in Ralph's restaurants is made from scratch. If you looked in their storerooms and refrigerators, you wouldn't find any industrial-size cans or frozen foods. In both New Orleans and Anaheim, Ralph prided himself on getting great seasonal vegetables, fish, and meats from local farms and suppliers and serving a variety of weekly and daily specials. That's the heart of the Brennan's tradition. When you walk in, you never know what's going to be fresh—what fish just came in off the Gulf waters. But you know the restaurant will offer it as an enticing series of specials. As Charlee studied the item-per-cover metrics in California, she saw that on any given night, the three-course specials were ordered by only 8 to 12 percent of the clientele.

"We were going to all this trouble for a small percentage of our guests," she recalls. "And it just wasn't warranted. I had to go to Ralph and say, 'I know this is who we are, but it is too much change for the staff. It's affecting the consistency and executions of our core offerings. We don't have to do this anymore. It's just too complicated.'"

As they studied their list of top entrées, it seemed as if their guests were going out of their way to *avoid* classic New Orleans fare. Guests appeared to pass up unfamiliar dishes or ingredients such as alligator, a Louisiana standard. "We began to see that people outside New Orleans think New Orleans food is spicy," Charlee says. The oysters and redfish that New Orleanians love and that Ralph was going to huge expense to fly out each week were going to waste. His Gulf oysters were perceived as less desirable compared to Pacific oysters. And his California guests had no clue what redfish was. Compounding the issue, it became clear to Charlee that most of the California waitstaff were unfamiliar with Creole and Cajun cuisine, so they had trouble explaining to guests why these ingredients and dishes were special.

Most of the people who came in the restaurant had one drink, tops. Charlee had been astonished to see parties seated at four-, five-, and six-tops where only one or two people in the group ordered an alcoholic drink. How could so many people enter a New Orleans–themed restaurant and not order a Pimm's Cup or a Sazerac—classic New Orleans cocktails?

POS systems are notoriously bad at representing the party size of various tables over the course of a shift or an entire night. But our software can easily pinpoint inefficiencies and anomalies by revenue centers and meal periods. Using our software, Charlee was able to drill down and study the average entrées ordered by those large groups. And she had a sudden epiphany: those large parties *ordered lots of children's meals.* In other words, they weren't groups of adults at all.

They were parents with kids.

In their preopening estimates, the Jazz Kitchen had grossly underestimated how many kids they'd be serving.

I always say that a savvy restaurateur can probably manage one restaurant really well, but your eyes start to deceive you when you operate multiple locations. As Charlee admits to me, "Unless I was going to live in the basement of the building and be there every single day, I would never have seen any of this." As Charlee shared each new revelation, Ralph resolved to make changes to the restaurant, menus, and staff. They would be guided by a single goal: *How can we make our guests happy?*

First, they scrapped the fine dining menu and moved everything to casual. That eliminated the confusion at the door and the schizophrenic bifurcation of their kitchen and waitstaff. Next, they challenged their chefs to design dishes *inspired* by New Orleans cooking that wouldn't drive guests away. *How can we season our dishes with the flavors of New Orleans, and yet make them familiar to our guests without losing our identity?* It took time, but they managed to pull it off, replacing the more exotic fish dishes with more familiar, marketable ones such as mahi mahi, salmon, beef, and chicken. Instead of serving blackened redfish, they blackened a tender chicken breast and served it on a bed of dirty rice, a classic New Orleans dish. Or they added penne pasta, which rarely appears on their menus back home, and served it with pancetta and smoked tomato butter sauce.

They still have great New Orleans meals, like their Louisiana crab cake with citrus fennel slaw, Creole mustard aioli, and blood-orange-infused olive oil. Their top starter is the Gumbo Ya-Ya, which features chicken, andouille sausage, and rice, all in classic dark roux. There's also an awesome chicken étouffée soup with Cajun rice. Overall, though, based on the numbers, their top seller is the pasta jambalaya—Gulf shrimp, andouille sausage, chicken, and Creole seasonings all on a bed of spinach fettuccine. And when you look at their desserts, classic New Orleans beignets are their top seller. So from a distance, this is still a strongly New Orleans restaurant. It's just that certain dishes have been spun to accommodate and appeal to mainstream palates.

When it first opened, the Jazz Kitchen offered only two children's meals—fried shrimp and chicken nuggets. Now, as they came to terms with their younger clientele, they first tried a children-eat-free program as a way to lure more adults to the restaurant. But that served to undermine the brand in their customers' eyes. So instead of giving food away free, they decided to figure out what really worked. They switched to three-course children's meals, thinking parents would encourage their kids to try a variety of different New Orleans–style dishes. But that concept flopped as well. The data showed that kids wanted to eat one thing—something familiar—and servers reported that most kids just ate a few bites and returned to coloring their placemats with crayons provided by the restaurant. In the end, Jazz Kitchen added more choices to their children's menu—mac and cheese, chicken fingers, corkscrew pasta with meatballs, grilled chicken strips, French bread pizza, and a simple cheeseburger, and worked hard to make them special. For instance, the chicken fingers were crusted with corn flakes; the macaroni and cheese was served deep-dish style. To offset their lost drink revenue, they designed an array of kid-friendly, nonalcoholic juice drinks served in collectible novelty cups. They did something similar for adults, creating an array of refreshing "mocktails" that parents on vacation wouldn't feel guilty imbibing in the company of their kids.

A diehard New Orleans foodie might well scoff at Jazz Kitchen's menu. But *the restaurant isn't in New Orleans!* It isn't even in Los Angeles. It's located on the grounds of a huge, family-friendly theme park, and that calls for a different approach. "We thought we were going out west to serve authentic New Orleans cuisine," Charlee says. "Today, a quarter of our entrées are chicken! You'd never see that much chicken on a menu in New Orleans. Chicken is just not a dominant ingredient in our cuisine. We didn't get there overnight. But little by little, the data showed us what made guests happy. The trick is educating guests about the bold flavors in New Orleans cuisine, and then creating straightforward and familiar dishes from which to showcase them."

A good chunk of Ralph's budget was spent on labor costs, which are high in California. Our software helped him analyze how much overtime he was paying, and in which job class, and whether it was in the front or the back of the house. Traditionally, most US states have allowed restaurants to factor tips into the overall hourly wage paid to their employees. This permits restaurateurs to pay servers less money out of the restaurant's budget because it's understood that waitstaff will receive tips from guests. Tips are voluntary, of course, and range from 15 to 25 percent of the bill. But they can be as little as zero if the guest leaves angry for some reason. In Europe, gratuities are automatically added to the diner's bill. But until recently, that has historically not been the case in the United States.

But the state of California, as Ralph and Charlee discovered, does not grant restaurant owners a "tip credit." The state insists that restaurants pay even tip-eligible employees the state-mandated minimum wage. In 2001, the year Ralph Brennan's Jazz Kitchen opened, the minimum wage was $6.75 an hour. It has since risen several times. At the time I'm writing this, Ralph pays his California waitstaff $10 an hour, exclusive of tips. (That number will soon rise to $15 an hour.) His waitstaff back home in New Orleans are paid Louisiana's tipped employee minimum wage of

$2.13 an hour, exclusive of tips. Of course, California has a much higher cost of living than New Orleans. And Louisiana law accepts that waitstaff will make money in generous tips—at a rate that could run as high as $20 to $50 an hour at upscale establishments—while California law assumes they won't and requires that restaurants make up the difference.

Once he better understood the impact the higher overhead was having on his operation, Ralph realized he had to make changes to the restaurant's service. At Navy Beach in Montauk, New York, we saw that the chief challenges were seasons, weather, and time. The resort business, too, exhibits seasonality and weather challenges, but for Ralph, the make-or-break issue was time. "If you come from a culture where labor costs are much lower," Charlee tells me, "and you're [operating] in a new environment where it's $10 an hour, suddenly every hour is critical . . . being wrong costs you five times as much."

So, Ralph and Charlee, along with the Jazz Kitchen's management team, made some critical staffing changes. Ralph had grown up watching patrons of Brennan's being served in a stylish, almost European manner. Each table was waited on by three servers who worked as a team. But that style of service just wasn't sustainable in California. Instead of having one server clearing the table, another taking food orders, and a captain overseeing the meal, all the critical tasks would be performed by a single server, assisted by busboys who cleared tables. In Louisiana, Ralph had grown accustomed to bringing in all his chefs at the same time—about three p.m. each afternoon—to start prepping for the dinner service. When the prep was done, the chefs would hang around the kitchen until five p.m., when orders started coming in. In California, that lag time just wouldn't do. On Charlee and the GM's advice, Ralph decided that only a few staff members would come in at three p.m. to prep for all the chefs. The rest of the team would arrive at five p.m., eliminating much of that waiting-around time.

Ralph found that he could use software to improve the front of the house, too. If you walk into any Ralph Brennan restaurant and ask an employee what his or her chief job is, they'll tell you what Ralph has drilled into them since day one: "Make guests happy and enjoy the thrill of doing so!"

Well, guest happiness correlates strongly to server knowledge and attentiveness. Ralph's business has always stressed five key server attributes:

> *Attitude*: Do they reflect the Ralph Brennan culture of kindness and respect?
>
> *Appearance*: Do they smile and present well to guests?
>
> *Hospitality*: Do they embody Ralph's notion that guests come first?
>
> *Knowledge*: Do they demonstrate a clear understanding of the food and beverages?
>
> *Salesmanship*: Are they effective at selling just the right meal to every party that walks in the door?

Notice that the first three attributes are *qualitative* in nature. They're things you can only get a handle on as you get to know a person. The fourth attribute—knowledge—is both qualitative *and* quantitative. You can get a gut feeling about a server's understanding of the dishes, *and* you can also test that knowledge by asking questions and gauging how accurately and how confidently he or she responds. The last attribute—salesmanship—is solely *quantitative.* But unless you're using data analytics, it's virtually impossible to measure the value someone brings to the organization on the sales side.

The Server Scorecard we created generates a report of each server's sales and their menu categories and shows how servers compare to their peers. Using it, Ralph, Charlee, and their GM could see just who among their waitstaff were the bestselling, most time-efficient servers and get them to share their expertise with other servers. Or if they saw that someone was falling short, they could address that shortcoming with some discreet, customized training.

"We notice that you're not selling many pasta jambalaya dishes." (Or boudin balls. Or étouffée appetizers.) "Do you know what those dishes are, and how they're made? Let's talk about that . . ."

In other words, data changed the way Ralph ran his California business. I summarized it so quickly that you might get the impression that he and Charlee turned it around in a week. In fact, it took months to make changes once each problem had been identified. Intelligent data mining takes time. "I often don't know what I'm looking for until I mull it over in real time," Charlee tells me today. "I need to work the numbers, love them, and have them nudge me a little bit."

When she suspects there is a problem, she starts by asking herself a series of questions to gradually drill down to the real issue. Why are we not profitable? Where is the problem, really? Are the average checks low, or are our guest counts low? Does the shortfall occur on the weekends, or during the weekdays? Do we have a problem one particular day of the week? Is there a seasonal pattern? An hourly trend? And so on.

Each new question sparks another round of data analysis. She doesn't decide overnight what to do with the information she finds. And it takes time to dream up new drinks and dishes, and to train staffers competently and well. But today Jazz Kitchen is alive and well, a robust player in Ralph's portfolio of eateries. If you compare Jazz Kitchen's fiscal 2002 to fiscal year 2005, you'll see a sales increase of 39 percent. Overall, the restaurant is now robustly profitable.

Some might well ask how they could not know children would be a big part of the equation at a Disneyland theme park. How could they not anticipate that casual dining would be paramount? How could they not question how well unfamiliar New Orleans fare would go over with customers who were on vacation with their kids?

In Ralph's defense, over the last fifteen or so years, diners' tastes have changed enormously. It takes time for knowledge of a particular cuisine to permeate the culture. The most visible ambassador of New Orleans food— Emeril Lagasse—didn't get his first TV show until 1994, only seven years before Ralph opened his Anaheim location. The Yelp website, with its legions of guest-penned restaurant reviews and guest-snapped food photos, wasn't founded until 2004. The iPhone—and its attendant apps that allow foodies to share tips and advice about food and beverages—didn't debut until 2007.

Second, all of us have a set of assumptions that comprise our worldview. Restaurateurs are no different. Growing up in New Orleans, Ralph understood how guests behaved when they dined in New Orleans, and he designed a restaurant around that worldview. The moment he relied on data to challenge his worldview, I would argue, was the moment he went from being an Old Guard restaurateur to a New Guard pioneer.

In August of 2005, Charlee was in her mother-in-law's living room in a small town outside Memphis, Tennessee, when her mobile phone beeped with a text prompting her to check her email. She and her husband Richard had evacuated New Orleans to escape what everyone was predicting would be a harrowing storm, Hurricane Katrina. The hurricane slammed into New Orleans only hours after Charlee left town. She and her husband wondered how their home had fared. The images on television and the rising death toll were heartrending. The TV news footage showed a devastated city, where in some neighborhoods only the rooftops rose above the flood waters. It would become the costliest and deadliest hurricane in US history. Charlee looked down at a photo attached to the email in her inbox. One of her neighbors had managed to snap a photo that showed Charlee's home in six feet of water.

Ralph Brennan, his wife, Susan, two of their children, and his ninety-one-year-old mother-in-law had sought refuge at the home of a friend in Mississippi. One daughter was studying abroad and was terrified because she could not contact her family because all phone lines were down. "We were among the more fortunate ones," Ralph says. "Others lost so much, and never recovered." After finding a temporary place to live and a school for his two children, Ralph's thoughts turned to his staff and restaurants. His staff was scattered by the storm, and he knew it would be a challenge to get the restaurants up and running again. But *we have to do it,* he thought.

The news reports indicated that the French Quarter had escaped the storm unscathed. But the information was vague. Until he walked in the doors of Bacco, or Ralph's on the Park, or his casual seafood restaurant, Red Fish Grill, he just wouldn't know for sure how bad the damage was. He and Charlee had texted each other from their cars as they'd fled town. Almost a day into their evacuation, their cell phones ceased to function. Calls to the New Orleans 504 area code didn't go through. So Ralph and Charlee set them aside, bought phones with a different area code, and attempted to contact their staff.

Following calls with the Louisiana Restaurant Association (LRA) and the State Department of Health, Ralph sparked a movement to get the French Quarter restaurants functional as soon as possible. City officials knew that New Orleans had been dealt a crushing blow that would take years to overcome. But in the short term, they realized the need to broadcast to the world that the city's most iconic neighborhood was alive and well and open to tourists. Because of his long history in the business, Ralph was regarded by many in town as a community leader. Ralph and LRA staff, and several fellow restaurateurs, met with health department officials as soon as he could return to the city to develop a plan to reopen French Quarter restaurants.

Because the city had been evacuated on a Saturday prior to the company's Sunday close of payroll, Ralph's employees had left town without their paychecks. In an early conference call with his restaurant GMs, Ralph assured them that everyone would receive their paychecks, a bonus, and continued health coverage. The only question was how to get hold of everyone. The company's comptroller sent wire transfers to employees as the company heard from them. The general managers, with Charlee's assistance, were assigned the task of contacting their staffs. These both became arduous tasks. It's not easy to access your money when you bank in a city that's been devastated. It's equally hard to send money to someone who has been displaced and hasn't had time to establish a new bank account. Charlee found herself running to the local Western Union office to send money to small towns she'd never heard of. Gasoline had been in short supply during the evacuation, so a number of employees were stranded in the towns in which they'd run out of fuel.

Contact with one person led to another person, and another. If employees couldn't reach their GM, they tended to call Charlee instead. Charlee heard more than a few harrowing stories of financial hardship, displacement, suffering. She had foreseen that this was not a simple matter of telling people that they still had jobs and a paycheck. Employees wanted desperately to return home to the normalcy of their neighborhoods and their jobs. But that wasn't possible for many of them. (Charlee later estimated that 70 percent of the homes of their employees had been damaged or destroyed.) Wary of returning to New Orleans, some had begun looking for work in other locales.

Charlee spent two weeks in Tennessee herself before moving to Anaheim to work from the offices of Jazz Kitchen. The Disney company graciously put her up during this time. Back on the ground in New Orleans, Ralph was relieved to see that his own residence was safe and intact. With a skeleton crew of maintenance staff, he visited each of his restaurant properties in turn and discovered that he was indeed luckier than most. Red Fish Grill, situated close to the end of the Quarter near Canal Street, had taken on about three inches of water on its concrete floor, but the damage was limited to a few baseboards. Bacco, farther into the Quarter, was undamaged. New Orleans's City Park had flooded badly, but Ralph's on the Park, located on higher ground on the fringes of the green, had escaped with only minimal damage to the roof. But all three restaurants had lost power during the hurricane, so Ralph was looking at a loss of about $80,000 in food inventory alone. Each eatery had spotty utility service. Red Fish had natural gas service, Bacco didn't. Both lacked city water. But Bacco was outfitted with a massive wood-burning oven. The glimmer of an idea suggested itself to Ralph. *We can cook just about anything in there.*

Ralph and LRA staff met with city health officials to

help rewrite parts of the public health code so that certain restaurants could open without potable water, on a temporary basis only, using a boiled- and bottled-water regimen. Guests would be served off disposable plates, cups, and utensils. Bacco and Red Fish Grill were two of the first three restaurants to open in the Quarter, and they did so within thirty-two days of the storm. The bonuses Ralph sent his out-of-town staffers allowed many to rent U-Hauls and stock them with new possessions. Thirty out of 170 staffers of Red Fish Grill were able to return to work. Twenty-eight of Bacco's seventy-five employees were able to return. Since the traditional lines of advertising were down, the company advertised with yard signs reading RED FISH GRILL—NOW OPEN—HIRING ALL POSITIONS.

Every piece of information—who was working, what food and supplies the restaurants had—got plugged into the digital logbook at Charlee's fingertips; she busied herself analyzing the numbers, using the data to help Ralph, his GMs, and his chefs figure out which entrées they could serve, given the ingredients they could obtain from the few suppliers willing to enter and service the French Quarter. Ralph and his executive chef, Haley Bittermann, worked with the chefs at Bacco and Red Fish Grill to develop a menu that they could serve at both restaurants, using the fewest number of pots and pans possible. In the end, they narrowed the food choices down to four simple items: hickory-grilled redfish, garlic-rubbed roast chicken, wood-grilled rib eye steak, and a hickory-grilled hamburger.

As the first few guests started trickling in, Charlee again used our software to unpack the new information about their new clientele. What menu items were they buying? And she tracked the firm's revenues and costs. Many guests were first responders—FEMA relief workers, cops, medics, and firemen—or journalists covering the recovery efforts. The upscale Ralph's on the Park took longer to open—seventy-three days after the storm. Most of their guests were people from the neighborhood who were working to clean and rehabilitate their homes. They used Ralph's on the Park as their kitchen. Between the neighborhood crowd and the ubiquitous soldiers, Ralph's on the Park was jammed. Customers never knew that all the restaurant's critical operations—reservations, supplier orders, and credit card processing—were being handled via mobile phones.

While the three restaurants were crowded with customers, the data told a different story: Red Fish Grill's revenues were off by 70 percent. On the other hand, sales of alcoholic beverages were way up. New Orleans's party spirit had not dimmed. Charlee suggested to Ralph that they invert their typical three-appetizers-and-a-glass-of-wine special to a three-glasses-of-wine-and-an-appetizer special. Early patrons loved it.

One day that fall Charlee answered the phone to discover that President George W. Bush and the First Lady were coming to New Orleans to meet with a special committee designed to bring business back to New Orleans. They and a party of seventeen wanted to dine at Bacco. The restaurant created a special "Presidential Menu" and faxed it to Air Force One for approval. Ralph and his small crew of chefs and servers met and served the president, his wife, and small group of prominent New Orleanians. After dinner, the president graciously insisted on meeting the people who had pulled together the simple meal. He wanted to hear their Katrina stories. After the president left, the staff headed back to the kitchen to boil water to wash the china the president's party had used.

Ralph was incredibly proud of his staff during this period. Many of them were bunking with friends in homes or apartments, under terrible circumstances, with no potable water, no mail, cable TV, or Internet access. But they showed up for work just the same, looking past their personal circumstances to make a difference in the lives of others. In the spirit of Ralph's guiding maxim, they were making people happy. At a time when supermarkets were not yet functional, people knew that they could always grab a hot meal at one of Ralph's restaurants. Whenever someone thanked him for opening his restaurants, Ralph was reminded of something Charlee had observed about the essential purpose of restaurants: *We nourish people.*

But they were not profitable. Not in the least. All told, Katrina lost Ralph's company nearly a million dollars in direct costs, of which their insurance covered roughly a third, and only after months of haggling. Years before, Ralph and Charlee had crunched the numbers to figure out how they could rescue their floundering restaurant in Disneyland, and the use of data had helped them reengineer Ralph Brennan's Jazz Kitchen to the point of robust profitability. When Jazz Kitchen was in trouble, the cash flow from Ralph's New Orleans restaurants had kept the California restaurant afloat. Now, in the post-Katrina landscape, the situation was reversed. The income stream from Jazz Kitchen kept the New Orleans restaurants afloat. Data and technology had saved one restaurant so it could in turn save all the others.

In June of 2013, New Orleanians woke to a curious news story. The legendary Brennan's restaurant—the original Brennan's founded by Owen Brennan in 1946—had been closed. Owen's sons had run into financial difficulties and were forced into bankruptcy. The local TV news ran images of the shuttered restaurant. The brass letters of its name were later pried off the building. Foodies pondered what life would be like in New Orleans without such a visible culinary touchstone.

What few knew was that after several attempts to help his cousins, Ralph and his business partner Terry White had purchased the building out of bankruptcy and were embarking on a new mission to restore Brennan's to the top of the New Orleans culinary scene. Ralph felt an overwhelming compulsion to act. If he didn't do something fast, the restaurant that had launched his family name, the place where he had spent his childhood, the place in which he'd learned to cook, would be taken out of family hands forever.

He had secretly hoped that this would be a turnkey purchase, that he'd be able to ask the current employees to stay on the job and continue serving guests, with only minor tweaks to the operation and menu. But after inspecting the restaurant, the carriageway, the dining rooms, the kitchen, the courtyard, and the wine cellar, he knew that a complete renovation was needed.

The beautiful old building had stood at 417 Royal Street since 1795. But New Orleans was a different city than it had been back in the 1950s, when his family first rented and began renovating it. The restaurant had numerous dining rooms, but many of them were upstairs, accessible only by a steep staircase. You couldn't ask older guests to take those stairs anymore if you wanted to attract large groups. Elderly and disabled guests would feel unwelcome.

Ralph recalled his Aunt Ella's advice: restaurants had to stay current. They had to innovate. They had to push themselves to be better next year than they were today, or they risked declining.

And so Ralph embarked on what the press reported was a multimillion-dollar renovation project. Every day Ralph donned a white construction helmet, one with a Brennan's rooster on the visor, and visited the premises to oversee the progress of the work.

One day, early on in the process, Charlee got a phone call from one of the workers on the site. "Did you know that there are ten turtles living here in the courtyard fountain?"

"No," she said slowly. "I did not know that. Ten, did you say?"

"Yeah—and they look hungry!"

She got off the phone and asked Haley Bittermann if she knew what turtles ate. The pair lobbed their question at Google, where they learned that shrimp and greens were a chelonian's favorite meals. Soon enough, Chef Haley went home with ten turtles in the backseat of her car. She carefully slipped them into her son's wading pool at the back of their house and tossed them a few vegetables from her garden. And so the turtles began their long wait for a new home. She and her family would tend to their new residents for the next year.

The work took sixteen months. Finally, in November of 2014, a newly designed Brennan's—sporting a new elevator, a new kitchen, furnishings, and artwork—opened to spectacular reviews. Foodies, bloggers, and critics complimented the dishes turned out by the restaurant's new chef, Slade Rushing, who had breathed fresh life into classic Brennan's dishes such as eggs Sardou, eggs Hussarde, seafood gumbo, and, ahem, turtle soup. The restaurant's famous menu items—bananas Foster, the brandy milk punch—were the same as ever, only better. (As I write these words, Chef Slade has been nominated for his second James Beard Award for Best Chef in the South.)

Brennan's, like New Orleans itself, had risen to greet a new day. Elderly women in stylish hats and white gloves sat in the coral-colored dining room whose walls are decorated with fine-china oyster plates and Audubon prints. With straight faces, they told reporters how their husbands had proposed to them in this *very* dining room at this *very* table—although the room and the table had not existed in the restaurant's previous incarnation.

Since Katrina, Ralph closed Bacco but opened four new businesses in quick succession: a stylish café at the New Orleans Museum of Art; two eateries in the New Orleans neighborhood of Metairie; and a catering business that also bakes daily breads and desserts for all of Ralph's restaurants. In the post-Katrina world, the restaurant landscape had changed greatly. So many of the small mom-and-pop eateries that had given the city its flavor had not been able to stay in business. The Museum of Art had lost its previous café; Metairie, a prominent neighborhood, had suffered the loss of many of its small neighborhood haunts. So opening indie restaurants at the museum and in Metairie were good opportunities. But they were also Ralph at his neighborly best. He came to see that his brand was about putting unique restaurants in unique locations and nurturing strong ties to the community.

Over the years, Charlee's role in the firm has blossomed. She now serves as the firm's executive vice president. But I'd argue that she actually has become one of a new breed of executives called marketing technologists. You can't do effective marketing today without solid information, and Charlee knows that information today comes at the intersection of software and technology.

In the new New Orleans restaurant climate, Ralph will need that edge. Before Katrina, the city had about 800 table service restaurants. Today it has more than 1,400, which suggests how many people—locals or outsiders—saw the city as a place of opportunity immediately following the devastation. But a 75 percent increase in restaurants means stiff competition for any eatery that doesn't keep up with the times.

Sixteen years ago, when Ralph first started working on Jazz Kitchen, his firm was tech-shy. Today, his restaurants are run using not just our software, but a dozen or so other software programs that are increasingly important to New Guard establishments, such as BinWise (beverage management system), OpenTable (guest reservation management), Tripleseat (private party planning), and many more. Not to mention nine websites, direct-mail software for e-newsletters, Twitter, Facebook, and Instagram accounts for every restaurant, and a YouTube channel. Keeping up with the social media obligations alone can be exhausting. But those accounts—and the other software programs they use—are critical tools in the arsenal of any modern restaurant.

Analytics have helped Ralph's restaurants succeed and survive where others have failed. I predict analytics will keep the Ralph Brennan brand profitable when many of the newcomers are long gone. "The restaurant business is funny," Ralph says. "It's so busy that people don't always remember what really happened. A chef will tell you the steak is selling great, when it's actually the pork." He adds, "Technology helps us run a tighter ship, an overall better operation. We run everything more efficiently. I suppose a single-unit operator could fly by the seat of their pants, but a multiple-unit operator needs all the help they can get."

But it's not always about the numbers. Days after the reopening, Ralph threw a party for the entire Brennan family. He had the honor of welcoming Aunt Ella to the restaurant she had not set foot in in forty years. She was barely eighteen years old the day she came to work for her brother over at Bourbon Street. Now she was eighty-nine. The inventor of bananas Foster took her seat with the family in the King's Room upstairs and raised a glass to her nephew and the new era he had ushered in.

Some months later, when the courtyard fountain was repaired, the staff of the new, improved Brennan's had the pleasure of returning the restaurant's now-famous turtles to their fountain. This was done in classic New Orleans style—with a parade, of course. Chef Slade, his cooks, the waitstaff, and all their children rolled the turtles in decorated toy wagons down several blocks of the Quarter while bagpipers played. The parade route was lined with people in turtle costumes who had journeyed to New Orleans for the event, bringing their own children and pet turtles in tow. Once in the courtyard, a Roman Catholic monsignor bestowed a blessing on the turtles. And the restaurant's beverage director sabered a bottle of champagne, to the delight of the crowd. I'm told the turtle parade will become an annual event. A Louisiana jurist has already committed to playing her part in the next parade, pardoning the turtles from ever appearing in the restaurant's signature soup.

Some time ago, Ralph received a call from Bill, one of his old CPA buddies, who had news of a fresh opportunity. The Impastatos, an Italian American family of New Orleans restaurateurs, were thinking of retiring. Their restaurant had been in the family for 101 years. Was Ralph interested? The restaurant, the Napoleon House, is a legendary watering hole in the French Quarter. The structure, which has stood at the corner of Chartres and St. Louis streets since 1797, was once intended to be the American home of the disgraced Napoleon Bonaparte, should he ever escape his exile on the island of Saint Helena. (He never did.)

Napoleon House is a special place, its ocher walls flaking in spots, revealing faded brick beneath the plaster. The darkened recesses of the old bar are decorated with glorious old prints of Napoleon, not to mention photos of the Impastato family through the ages. Just beyond the bar is a small but intimate courtyard. If you scale a set of rickety steps to the roof, you are rewarded with three-hundred-and-sixty-degree views of the Quarter from the windows of an octagonal cupola.

Whoever took over the Napoleon House would have to commit to its upkeep, striking the right balance between structural safety and preserving the integrity of its glorious history, interior, and façade. Ideally, the building would be updated—without a hint of those renovations being obvious to guests. Ralph asked himself, *Do I really want to do this again?* In renovating Brennan's, he had rescued his family's legacy and had become a one-man preservation society. Did he really want to preserve the traditions of *another* New Orleans restaurant family? *And fixing the place will cost a fortune,* he thought. But his heart already knew how he would answer.

He pressed the phone close to his ear.

"Bill, let's talk," said Ralph Brennan.

· 10 ·

RESTAURANTS OF TOMORROW

If you were a human being with a pulse during the fall of 2015, you would have found it impossible to avoid ads touting the new Stars Wars movie, *The Force Awakens*. Appearing more than thirty-eight years after the original, the film was the first since director George Lucas passed the reins of his magnificent saga to the Walt Disney Company. Every time they turned on their TVs that fall and winter, viewers spied another spot reminding them that the force was awakening. Not just movie trailers, or ads for McDonald's tie-ins, or ads for children's toys; those would have been too predictable. Instead, Subway, the sandwich company, offered us Star Wars meals and collectible cups. Duracell batteries promoed the film, tying it to their lasts-ten-years-in-storage, longer-lasting "Quantum" batteries. Chrysler rolled out clever, Star Wars–themed ads plugging its Dodge, Ram, Chrysler, Jeep, and Fiat brands. Hewlett-Packard debuted a special Star Wars laptop. CoverGirl makeup promised to make our daughters look like cocktail servers in a remote galaxy cantina. ESPN did a sports TV special on the connection between Japanese swordsmanship and the light saber. Verizon created an old-school cardboard viewer. At the supermarket, shoppers could find Star Wars toys in every box of General Mills cereals, Star Wars pasta in boxes of Kraft Mac & Cheese, and Star Wars Nestlé Coffeemate creamer. There were Star Wars Crocs, Star Wars Adidas sneaks and track jackets, and Star Wars Android Wear watches. At night you could tuck your kids into a Millennium Falcon bed from Pottery Barn. You could download Star Wars "skins" from Google for your computer, and savor the sound of Star Wars voices in the popular GPS app Waze. There were Stars Wars Band-Aids, a Death Star waffle iron, and even—so help me, it's true—Stars Wars BBQ tongs in the shape of a freaking light saber. It was insane. Everyone in the known universe got the message. There was a new Star Wars movie coming out—and we'd better see it.

You know who apparently didn't get the message? The movie theater I picked to see the movie with my wife over the Christmas holiday. We arranged for a babysitter to watch our kids that night. Then we walked to the theater not far from our New York City apartment. I'd bought tickets ahead of time, so we adroitly avoided the blocks-long line outside the theater. Being the chivalrous husband that I am, I let my wife Susie go on ahead to pick out our seats while I stepped up to the queue for drinks and popcorn. I hadn't eaten much all day, so movie theater food would have to do.

I had waited for several minutes before realizing that the line was moving at roughly the speed of the Athabasca glacier. The snack bar had several registers, but only *two* were being used, by a pair of harried young clerks in uniforms. Two overextended, overwhelmed kids consigned by their managers to service an entire theater of hungry moviegoing New Yorkers during one of the busiest movie weeks in recent memory.

Much of this book has focused on restaurants. But as I said at the beginning, there are countless venues that prepare and sell food. Movie theaters are among them, and they're a perfect example of how poor planning can ruin the guest experience. This theater, which is part of a large national chain, clearly did not have a good grasp of its attendance trends. The manager had made the misguided, if not foolhardy, decision to save on weekend labor costs, and his corporate bosses had done nothing in advance to prevent him from making that fateful decision.

Had the chain's bosses provided every theater location with software that collected their own data, and empowered its managers to utilize those insights, all the GMs in the chain would have known to staff up to address the holiday blockbuster's enormous crowds. This film in particular should have been singled out for a highly coordinated, top-down mandate. *The Force Awakens* was a much-awaited, much-publicized sequel to one of the most beloved franchises in cinema history. The film would go on to break box-office records worldwide and become the first film in history to earn $1 billion in its first twelve days of release. Amazing. Impressive. But not really surprising, is it?

The theater chain should have seen this coming.

To make matters worse, it is well known in the movie industry that theaters earn a disproportionate amount of their profits from concessions, not ticket sales. Ideally, theater managers would have brought in more staffers from December 18—the date *The Force Awakens* opened in 4,100 theaters in the United States—until the close of the winter holidays in early January. Each venue would have been able to scale up their workforce as needed. But they didn't. So that poor planning cost the movie theater revenue, and the goodwill of its patrons.

I could have walked away. I'm sure many patrons did. But considering my line of work, I felt compelled to stick around to see just how long it would take to get my food. By the time I reached my seat, I'd missed the first twenty minutes of the movie. I'm told they were awesome.

We are in the midst of a grand foodie revolution. A burgeoning foodie economy in which New Guard restaurateurs are eagerly embracing both data and trends. I'm not a clairvoyant, but I think it's safe to say that the next decade will be filled with interesting surprises as more businesses learn to use data to enhance the dining experience of their guests. I'm convinced the New Guard will be the big winners. The Old Guard, who insist on doing things the traditional way, will be left scratching their heads, wondering why their revenue and patron numbers are falling. In the absence of data, they will blame not themselves but their guests. "Moviegoers just don't eat the way they used to," an Old Guard theater owner might claim. To which I would respond, *no, moviegovers are voting with their feet.* They're getting food before or after the movie, or going to another movie theater entirely, one that serves microbrews and creative meals with fresh, local ingredients—all because they know your venue doesn't serve the items they're looking for and is incapable of selling those items in an expedient manner.

I'd like to peer into a crystal ball and tell you what the future holds, but there are serious impediments to doing that. The industry is shaped by artistic imagination, which is boundless. Restaurant and food trends change on a dime. From the moment you started reading this book, a trend has morphed into something else.

But just because they're changing doesn't mean we shouldn't analyze what's happening right in front of our noses. Every month my firm compiles and publishes what we call the Avero Index, which aggregates $24 billion of food and beverage data and analyzes, among other things, same-store sales growth of restaurants in the United States and in selected markets. We look at cities such as New York, Las Vegas, Chicago, Atlanta, Los Angeles, and San Francisco. Some years ago, as my team and I were reviewing the restaurants in the Index, we noticed wide variation in performance. Some restaurants would be up 20 percent, others down 20 percent, in the same period. We wondered what accounted for that disparity. Asking that question got me to start the Underground Culinary Tour with Alice Elliot. When we take those restaurant executives on a whirlwind tour of New York City restaurants, using New York City as a restaurant laboratory, the whole point is to expose them to as many of those cutting-edge ideas as possible in twenty-four hours. When restaurateurs innovate, they tend to do it in four critical areas: Ingredients, Beverage, Space, and an ineffable something I call X-Factor. Let's look at each of them in turn.

INGREDIENTS

Think back to our adventures on the Underground Culinary Tour. Zona Rosa's kitchen was housed in an Airstream trailer. Fette Sau was serving up BBQ out of an old auto body shop. Foodies will follow good food anywhere. They don't need fancy surroundings. The most important thing is that the food must be awesome.

They believe that there's no reason to ever have a bad meal. As a result, whether they realize it or not, they expect and demand great ingredients in every setting. Restaurants are springing up that are determined to serve the *highest-quality ingredients in the most casual setting* possible, as if broadcasting to the world that great food can be found at almost any location, setting, or price—from food trucks to airports. Casual settings are popular because they're suitable for the greatest number of dining occasions. No one wants to have to dress up for a quick bite out.

This trend cuts both ways. Old Guard fine dining the way it was practiced in our parents' day—with an emphasis on fancy linens and china but not necessarily on delivering great ingredients—will be limited. Modern-day guests have little tolerance for places that snow guests with just ambience. Food trumps all, and people are happy to dine casually if it means great flavors.

In the 1970s, when Chez Panisse began to share the names of its purveyors with its patrons, critics thought they were being precious. Transparency of food sourcing has become so important to the dining experience that today, if your server looks at you blankly when you ask where a restaurant gets their chickens from, you're probably going to think twice about eating there again. One of our former culinary tour hosts and alums, restaurateur Michael Chernow, has started a hip, sustainable seafood concept called Seamore's. One of the restaurant's design features is a large chalkboard depicting various species of fish, and a little information about their flavor. Each day the restaurant indicates the daily catch by hanging a little wooden spoon near whatever's fresh—and they clearly announce on their menu that their fish was provided by, say, Dock to Dish, a fisherman's cooperative out of Montauk, Long Island.

This eagerness to share sourcing with customers has never been so relevant. Serious foodies have a high level of distrust of large agribusiness. They've seen the troubling documentaries, such as *Food, Inc.* They have a good idea what goes on in slaughterhouses. They've lived through countless *E. coli* scares. They're frankly disgusted with the mess we've made of our industrial food production processes. They understand that dining out is a more expensive choice than cooking for themselves, but if they're going to pay top dollar to dine out, they want to choose fresh, local, sustainable, and humane products as much as possible.

At the end of the day, people want to know where their food is coming from. Yet it can be extremely difficult to verify sourcing, so consumers who value local, organic, or wild-caught ingredients must stay vigilant, understand their local seasonal trends, and follow chefs and restaurateurs who are above reproach. Sourcing integrity will become a hot-button issue for restaurants. It may no longer be enough for a restaurant to *say* where it gets its ingredients; they will be pressured to *prove* it on a regular basis.

Going forward, foodies will flock to food they perceive as an accessible luxury. For example, an organic burger made with grass-fed beef is a luxury most of us can afford. More of us will seek out this easily grasped value, pampering ourselves with such simple luxuries on a more regular basis. The farm-to-table movement will spread across all cuisines, regardless of ethnicity. As it continues to do so, foodies will hold Japanese, Indian, Thai, Mexican, Vietnamese, and Chinese (think RedFarm) cooking to the same standard they're used to elsewhere. Old Guard restaurants should expect stiff competition from imaginative restaurants that rely on local ingredients. The Old Guard will not get a pass just because they operate an ethnic restaurant serving "exotic" dishes. The expectation is that farm-to-table has gone global.

We'll see more restaurants dedicated to serving simple food amped up—a single, high-quality menu item, perfectly prepared, with innovative variations. Burgers. Hot dogs. Soup. Fried chicken. BBQ. This is already happening in major cities. Places like these work because all of us are attracted to the foodie version of the simple, nostalgic meals we all grew up with and love.

In Chapter 3, I showed you how chef Marco Canora made a splash with his Brodo concept, selling nourishing bone broth out of a window of his restaurant, Hearth, in the East Village in New York City. Michael Chernow and his business partner Daniel Holzman created one restaurant devoted to meatballs alone. At each of the Meatball Shop's locations, guests start by choosing a meatball—made of beef, pork, chicken, or veggies—and then build exactly the meal they want, adding sauce, sides, salads, veggies, or pasta. The simple menu is eye catching and subtly hints that your meal can be as healthy or as old-school decadent as you'd like it to be.

Vegetable preparation and artistry are flourishing. Restaurants are determined to show patrons that there is life beyond beef, chicken, and seafood. Vegetables will increasingly move from the side of the plate to the center of the plate. Now imagine biting into a burger that is so satisfying, so full of flavor that you can't tell it's not made of meat. The quinoa-and-veggie-based burgers at chef Brooks Headley's Superiority Burger near New York's Tompkins Square Park simulate the charring, texture, and squishy meatiness of a real meat burger. Chef David Chang's restaurant, Nishi, was the first in New York to serve The Impossible Burger, which uses heme, a critical vegetable molecule, to simulate the juiciness of real meat burgers. The burger is the creation of former Stanford University biochemist Patrick Brown. These, and other vegetable-only "meat" dishes, are likely in your future, as more guests are concerned about the environmental impact of meat production. Made from scratch by highly skilled chefs, such entrees are so good that many foodies will incorporate them into their meal rotation as a way of reducing cholesterol and cutting back on their meat intake.

BEVERAGE

You cannot understand the acclaim of venues such as Maison Premiere, Maialino, the Dead Rabbit, or Terroir wine bar—all places we visited on our tour—without understanding that guests are increasingly demanding great beverages when they dine out.

When Old Guard restaurateurs open a new restaurant, they tend to focus exclusively on developing the menu. After all, in their view the menu is king; drinks are an afterthought. A few weeks before their place opens, they'll phone their beverage distributor and instruct them to deliver whatever wines, beers, and coffees are typical for the sort of restaurant they are opening. "I'll have what everyone else is having" is their approach, one that just won't cut it in today's foodie culture.

New Guard restaurateurs know that intelligent beverage programs are integral to a restaurant's success, just as important, I would argue, as the food or the service. To them, *beverage is a differentiator.* The beverage menu is at the forefront, not an afterthought. It sets them apart from other restaurants and enhances or furnishes their identity. They know their clientele expect their drink choices to be as interesting as the meal and to taste better than what they can get at home. In some venues, the beverages are *the* reason guests choose to dine at an establishment in the first place. And we are seeing more thoughtful beverage programs all around—from alcoholic to nonalcoholic drinks, from cocktails, beer, and wine to coffee and craft sodas.

Because beverages are so much more important, the role of beverage professionals is becoming elevated as well. When you eat out in the future, you will begin encountering highly trained mixologists, baristas, and cicerones—certified beer servers—to guide you through your cocktail, coffee, and beer selections. (Filmmakers have recently given us two documentaries on the world of sommeliers—*Somm* and *Somm: Into the Bottle*—and one on baristas—*Barista*.)

As we saw in our culinary tour and at so many other restaurants around the country, smarter restaurants are starting to price wine reasonably. New Guard restaurants such as Marta, Estela, Charlie Bird, Pasquale Jones, Corkbuzz, and others know that if they have a thoughtfully priced wine list, you'll order more wine and have a better time. Social media apps such as Delectable and Vivino will continue to render wine costs transparent, allowing guests to research the average retail price of a bottle at the table as they're perusing the wine list. While restaurateurs regard their wine list as a profit center, they won't want to be perceived as gouging guests. Beverage pricing should be compelling and irresistible. Oenophiles will start seeing wine on restaurant lists that comes directly from wine collectors, who are paid on consignment when the wine is bought. It's a smart, low-cost way to build a restaurant's inventory and reduce overhead. Both of these innovations—reasonable pricing and consignment offerings—encourage guests to explore wines they haven't had before. And I expect we'll see more diverse wine choices coming from a greater array of specialty wine distributors.

While most Americans get a little nervous when approached by a sommelier, many can speak knowledgeably, confidently, unhesitatingly about craft beer. In North America, restaurants risk encountering patrons who know more about craft beer than their servers do—a potentially embarrassing predicament that will lose restaurants revenue unless they commit to carrying craft beer. Before the rise of mass-market beer companies, small independent breweries were a way of life in the United States. According to the Brewers Association, in 1873, the earliest year for which we have reliable figures, the United States was home to more than four thousand independent breweries. But that number tanked during Prohibition, hitting an all-time low of fewer than one hundred breweries by the 1970s. The craft beer movement rescued America's palate. In November 2015, the number of indie breweries in the nation *surpassed* the historical high set back in 1873, and it will surely go higher; 1.5 craft breweries now open each day in the United States. Patrons will begin to look down their noses at restaurants that don't serve at least a few interesting beers beyond the mass-market beers.

Coffee has moved to a new level of prominence—something commonly called the third wave. The first wave was something akin to Folger's or Maxwell House: dull, predictable, but ubiquitous. The second wave was Starbucks, which raised the bar and taught legions that coffee could be an accessible luxury. We're now entering the third wave, represented by small, artisanal roasters such as Counter

Culture, Dogwood, Heart, and Devoción. Counter Culture's emphasis is not only on the quality of the coffee—yes, you can taste the difference—but also on their commitment to proper equipment and barista training, evidenced by its coffee training labs around the nation. If you haven't already, you will start to discover excellent independent third-wave coffee shops, and one day the quality of restaurant coffee will be dramatically improved. As I travel I notice more indie coffee shops popping up in major and secondary cities, all of whom are embracing the third-wave aesthetic and using beans from small, artisanal roasters. Even Starbucks is trying to enter the third wave with the launch of its small-batch Reserve line.

Ultimately, the beverage world will be shaped by authorities on the level of, say, Garrett Oliver, brewmaster at the Brooklyn Brewery. Beverage mavens are sommeliers, cicerones, mixologists, and baristas who have the clout to get a trend noticed and drive consumers to new products. They are truly the next celebrity chefs. Besides their extensive social media presence, such experts write columns and books and make TV and podcast appearances. The result? A rising tide of consumer knowledge about the exciting world of can't-miss beverages.

Today's foodies want to be able to take their favorite beverage anywhere. Camping? A day at the beach? Grandma's house in the country for a long holiday? When you're on the go, glass and paper are not your friend. Why shouldn't you be able to transport your favorite alcoholic beverage in a can, or your cold brew coffee in a rugged Tetra Pak with a spout? We are also seeing the rise of the craft soda movement—delightfully packaged soft drinks made with natural flavors and no high-fructose corn syrup. Overall, soda consumption is down due to concerns about sugar. But when discriminating foodies do spring for a soft drink, they'll choose something beyond Coke and Pepsi.

Regardless of the beverage—coffee, wine, beer, cocktails, and soda—restaurants that don't carry at least a few locally made drinks will be increasingly perceived as out of touch.

SPACE

Whether you know it or not, restaurant spaces are in a radical state of evolution. Special-occasion restaurants—the sort of place guests only go on rare occasions—have their place, but there will be far fewer of them in the future. Dining frequency is where it's at. An extreme example is the Italian marketplace Eataly, which was a stop on our tour in previous years and which has now opened locations in several cities in the United States and around the world. The location in New York City has since become a major tourist destination, and it's easy to see why. It radically alters the way we think about food shopping and dining, raising the experience to the level of food halls, which I'll discuss in a moment.

First, let's look at all the different ways someone can enjoy Eataly. A person can pop in to grab a quick panino for lunch. They can meet a business colleague for a cappuccino, or take it across the street and enjoy it on a bench in Madison Square Park. They can grab groceries and produce on the way home for dinner. Or take the kids for a weekend pizza or gelato. They can sip a beer in the rooftop bar. Take a cooking class. Do an olive oil tasting. Buy a bottle of wine. Stop by the butcher for a special cut. Have vegetables cleaned and prepped for a home meal by Eataly's "vegetable butchers." You can buy a cookbook, a hunk of cheese, or gorgeous Italian designer kitchen utensils—and have them all delivered to your home. This single, big space can be used for many different occasions, simple or special.

On a smaller scale, your neighborhood bistro can be almost as adaptable, if designed properly. A great place for a drink, a quick lunch, a party, a visit with the kids, or even a romantic dinner. Smart restaurants will become tomorrow's repeat visitation engines, serving up food at prices suitable for lots of different crowds and occasions. I call it *experiential packaging*—creating one highly adaptable space to serve multiple demographics, events, and occasions.

On the Underground Culinary Tour, we saw that food is the new real estate anchor, best embodied by the Gotham West Market. This didn't happen overnight. First, farmers' markets gradually infiltrated both urban and suburban landscapes. Food halls—the latest iteration—are venues reminiscent of old-style markets in Europe, where you can buy delicious prepared foods, gourmet items, hard-to-find produce, and a great meal at a small sit-down counter or café. It's as if grocery stores are fusing with high-energy dining under one roof—in such spaces as urban condos, airports, outdoor plazas, hotels, and casinos. It's a massive trend taking place all over the world. Every major city and secondary city in the country will have a food hall in no time, and large cities will have multiple ones. I've been to such locations the world over and know that the setting can vary dramatically. The market can be outdoors and rustic, or housed in a quasi-permanent, climate-controlled indoor space. Ponce City Market in Atlanta is housed in a restored 1920s Sears Roebuck building. I've enjoyed vegan doughnuts at the Pennsy food hall in New York's Penn Station. These settings showcase brand-name eateries and emerging restaurants alike, and the offerings are often in stark contrast to the usual fast-food chains only steps away.

The design of modern food halls varies greatly. In some, guests share communal tables and have access to all the restaurants. In others, each eatery has separate seating. Either way, locals and tourists love them because they're a great way to window-shop, as well as for the whole family to graze on the fly. Shoppers love them because they are high energy and entertaining. And for clever restaurateurs, it's a low-risk way to grow their brand, experiment with new menus, or launch a new line of packaged food.

Don't be surprised if the next time you walk into a tapas place, your favorite tapas dishes are being served in the main dining area, while folks in the bar/lounge area are enjoying delicious grunge pizzas off a different menu. Restaurants know that they can stretch what they do and challenge their patrons' palates by experimenting with different cuisines within the same location. The "restaurant within a restaurant" concept is a great way to innovate, stay relevant, and enliven dead space on slow nights by drawing several different crowds. It's a low-cost way to test a concept using underutilized space. Everyone loves novelty, and the additional crowds will convince newcomers that this is *the* place to be.

The design of some restaurant spaces are determined to blow our minds. At temples of immersive dining such as Ultraviolet in Shanghai, servers set an extravagant strawberry dessert in front of you as the walls of the restaurant project images of a field of strawberries as far as the eye can see. It sounds like something out of Ray Bradbury, but the goal of the design is to transport you to a different place and time, using technology or *not*. It sounds a little kitschy or over the top, but it is not so dissimilar from what other eateries are doing simply with music, decor and furnishings, and server uniforms. Remember the mixologists in period attire who assembled our absinthe beverage at Maison Premiere in Brooklyn during the Underground Culinary Tour? Suddenly we were transported to a 1920s New Orleans speakeasy. At Ralph Lauren's Polo Bar in New York City, you feel as if you've just landed at the Kentucky Derby. One large space has been divided into smaller spaces that are clubby, intimate, and warm, and a paean to the equestrian lifestyle. Visitors to Carbone in New York are zipped back in time to an old '50s-style Italian American red-sauce palace as servers in red tuxedo jackets mix Caesar salads tableside or whisk out rigatoni from the kitchen, while Sinatra croons over the speakers. Music is definitely one strong immersive tool. By contrast, at the Meatball Shop, they focus on curating an '80s to '90s mix of hip-hop music that reminds guests that they're *not* eating at Grandpa's red-sauce joint.

We should expect that fast casual restaurants will continue to be the success story of the twenty-first century. This segment is growing three times faster than the larger restaurant market. The average check at a Chipotle, In-N-

Out Burger, or Panera Bread is only slightly more expensive than fast food, but you get a higher-quality meal. The range of quality—and ambience—in fast casual dining is extraordinarily diverse. Shake Shack specializes in classic comfort foods, but Sweetgreen or Lemonade emphasize healthy, seasonal, local alternatives. Either way, they're luring guests away from fast-food restaurants and casual dining chains. When the food and the ingredients are amazing, people will try any number of surprising venues. In fact, the setting is part of the charm.

Lastly, we are looking at a future of interesting food at hotels as well. In the past, food and beverage outlets were an afterthought at hotel properties. Today, boutique and select hotel chains exhibit a New Guard approach toward food and beverage. They develop their own restaurants or partner with brands they believe will bring foodie excitement and value to their hotel properties, following the trend Las Vegas established with celebrity chef restaurants and brand-name restaurant groups. Companies such as Four Seasons Hotels and Resorts and Fairmont Hotels and Resorts, and boutique hotels such as The NoMad Hotel, Kimpton Hotel and Restaurant Group, sbe Hotels, and Two Roads Hospitality offer unique restaurants that attract attention and buzz, luring patrons who are not necessarily lodging at the property. The message they are sending is clear: imaginative dining options are just as important to us as the lodging we offer. This will become a key guest differentiator in how foodies select their lodging on trips.

THE X-FACTOR

Critical trends that go beyond Ingredients, Beverage, and Space are ones I call X-Factor. Food porn has become ubiquitous. Raise your hand if you've taken a photo of your food at a restaurant before eating it. If you have, chances are you've shared that image with friends, family, or your extended social media following. Never has there been a time when so many people had the ability to tell others what they're eating right now, *and* what they think of it. For guests, it's great fun. For restaurants, it's both a blessing and a curse. *Yay*—in the snap of a photo millions of people around the world are learning about our food! *Ouch*—our food is not ready for its close-up. Social media are increasingly important parts of people's lives. An app like Instagram boasts about 100 million posts devoted to the hashtag #foodporn alone. But the customer practice of posting images of food on social media is increasingly controversial with chefs and restaurants. Guests who snap photos of their meal can distract and annoy their fellow diners, while the quality of their meal suffers as it grows cold or warm while the minutes pass. Unless the services of a professional food photographer and a food stylist are employed, meals are meant to be eaten, not snapped under less than ideal lighting and beamed across the Internet. Some chefs have banned cell-phone use to stem the tide of food photos, but such tactics are likely to rub customers the wrong way.

Overall, we're living in a time of great excitement—and great caveats. There's never been a better time to be eating in the United States, especially in smaller cities. But the new reality means that new restaurants have a short window in which their novelty generates buzz and visitors. Eventually the halo effect wears off. If the restaurant hasn't made a great impression by then, they'll find it hard to survive.

I suspect that big-city restaurants cannibalize each other when a saturation point is reached. There are several reasons for this. Big-city foodies are bombarded with food media. They tend to chase the next new thing. And they live in a metropolitan area with an embarrassment of riches. Which of us wouldn't want to dine out at a new restaurant every week if we could afford it? Young diners especially love the idea of chasing what's hot, highlighted by social media, rarely eating at the same restaurant again. I call this "urban disloyalty." Such a lifestyle is exciting for the guest, but dangerous for restaurants that depend on repeat visitation to drive their numbers. And there's a supply and demand issue as well—the increasing supply of restaurants puts pressure on the incumbents.

What is invisible to most guests is the shrinking pool of culinary talent. Restaurants in big cities are finding it difficult to find and retain young chefs. Why? It's expensive to live in major cities on a kitchen income. As a result, young, talented chefs are fleeing big cities for more affordable smaller cities where they can start a restaurant and raise a family.

The upshot? If you like to dine out, you're in the driver's seat. If you're running a restaurant, you need to tread carefully. Regardless of the market, restaurants today must contend with foodie disloyalty. Competition is stiff, and likely to get stiffer. Even an established restaurant can't rest on its laurels. As New Orleans's Ralph Brennan learned from his Aunt Ella decades ago, good restaurants must innovate or die.

Smart restaurants are beginning to act like software companies. Opening a new restaurant is an inherently risky and daunting task. Leases and construction are expensive; designing menus and training staff are time consuming; and success depends on the fickle, unpredictable appetites of your future clientele. The smartest chef-entrepreneurs are dealing with these uncertainties by mimicking the behavior of tech and software companies. First they're rolling out smaller products—minimum viable products, or MVPs, as Eric Ries, the author of *The Lean Startup,* calls them—to test proof of concept. If a product gets a good reception, they'll roll out the next iteration. Gradually, as their revenues increase, they'll bring on new staff and make fresh commitments. It's a lot like the iterative process behind software creation described in books like *Scrum,* by Jeff Sutherland. Finally, when the time is right, they can sell investors on results gleaned from actual data, not an untested idea or vision.

If they're contemplating expanding to another city, they don't have to commit to a physical presence initially. They can try a pop-up restaurant in the prospective city first, teaming up with another chef to do special, ticketed events where guests can try food from both restaurants while seated in one host restaurant. Or chefs can test a new menu item or concept in a food hall or market to get a quick reaction from foodies without signing an expensive lease. They can trot out a food truck. Or they can integrate vertically: if you have a top menu item in the restaurant, you can serve it at a food market or distribute it to Whole Foods. Or you could open a restaurant with a built-in mini-brewery.

We're going to find that there will be less reason going forward for anyone to rely solely on nearby eateries for their lunch and dinner options. Seamless was the traditional player in this area, but now we are seeing new entrants. Uber Eats, Amazon Fresh, Caviar, and Postmates are all experimenting with food delivery services to satisfy an insatiable consumer demand—the "on-demand generation"—to get what they want as quickly as possible. A local chef-entrepreneur could do something similar, launching a web-based "virtual restaurant" where you could order your food online and chefs would fulfill the order out of a single catering kitchen and have it delivered right to your desk. These new menu offerings need to be able to travel well. If a chef's bánh mì sandwich concept doesn't fly, he or she can scrap the website and launch a BBQ pulled-pork sandwich website. Chef David Chang of Momofuku fame is currently doing something similar to this with food delivery startups called Ando and Maple. These nimble, lower-risk entrepreneurship opportunities can make traditional restaurants seem stodgy by comparison. I predict foodies, soon to be followed by everyone else, will increasingly be availing themselves of this brave new world.

In all, these are exciting, fascinating trends that herald great new experiences for restaurant patrons. But don't get slavishly attached to the trends I've enumerated here. Rather, look no further than the nearest New Guard restaurateurs. They're the ones changing the industry, one clever idea at a time. And they will undoubtedly continue innovating with Ingredients, Beverage, Space, and X-Factor.

Back in the realm of the quantitative, when I talk and consult with people who understand the restaurant and hospitality industry on a deep level, I know that the proper use of data is in good hands. New Guard owners and managers recognize that putting a great meal before guests is as much about artistry and magic as it is about data and accounting.

The irony going forward is that small, independent restaurants—places like Navy Beach, Ralph Brennan's restaurants, Seamore's, and many of the others you've encountered in this book—might just end up embracing the New Guard approach before the multinational, billion-dollar companies. If you wonder why you can't get your popcorn at the movies someday, or you're wondering why the casual chain restaurant on the highway nearest you seems so disorganized, that's why. They are trapped in the trenches of the Old Guard.

That's why I have come to put my faith in smart New Guard restaurateurs.

Which reminds me of my friend Jeffrey Frederick. Sometime in his long tenure at Caesars, he found himself fielding numerous offers to develop restaurants for other firms. So Jeffrey left to start his own company. "Working at Caesars, working with people like Guy Fieri, Gordon Ramsay, and Giada, gave me the skills and confidence to go off on my own," he says. "I'm eternally grateful to them." Today his company, Elite Brand Hospitality, has developed more than three dozen restaurants around the globe—some of them for his former employer, Caesars.

One day in 2009 a couple of his friends invited him to look at a vacant Mexican restaurant that had recently gone belly up in a strip mall near his home. The dining room was open to a large kitchen window and counter. There were snug banquettes spaced around the room. Jeffrey stood in the 2,400-square-foot storefront for a while, peering around without saying much. The housing bubble recession of 2008 had hit Las Vegas hard, and a number of restaurants found it hard to stay profitable.

The Mexican restaurant had been decorated with terracotta pots filled with large, colorful faux flowers. Overhead, forty star-shaped fixtures dangled from the retro, tin-plate ceiling. Some of the stars rotated in their fixtures, conjuring a kind of twirling, starry-night effect.

"What do you think?" one of his friends asked.

Jeffrey knew that he wasn't interested in starting up a Mexican restaurant. But the space had potential. It was small and the rent was reasonable.

Over the next couple of days, between conference calls, he studied the local market and satisfied himself that there were two meals of the day that were always successful with locals: breakfast and dinner. Within those two dining periods, his experience had taught him that two kinds of restaurants always prospered: all-day breakfast places and high-end steakhouses. The items served at those two types of places had little in common, but two of the central ingredients collided in a popular American dish, steak and eggs.

Whenever he had a moment, Jeffrey scoured the menus of breakfast chains online, or in person, as he drove around town, shuttling his kids from one event to another. He rarely saw steak and eggs on the menu in Las Vegas's breakfast haunts. That didn't surprise him. Steak is a high-end item, and most chains avoid committing to that kind of inventory.

But what if a restaurant committed to serving steak and eggs as a specialty? Jeffrey could think of several ways to serve steak. You could chicken-fry it, serve it like a Philly cheesesteak, or do it up with some Mexican salsa, just to name a few. Served with a variety of egg dishes, such entrées would stand out from anything available at the breakfast places in town. From there, he could augment the menu with waffles, pancakes, fresh-squeezed juices, and French press coffee. Yes, he would run higher food costs because of the steak and other high-end ingredients, but profit per item would be higher.

And boom, he had a restaurant concept.

He didn't want to spend a lot to launch it. It was an interesting challenge for a chef who had conceived restaurants that had cost millions to build. This would be a neighborhood place for Vegas suburbanites who wouldn't be caught dead taking their families to breakfast on the Strip.

Frankly, designing a restaurant on a shoestring excited Jeffrey. They wouldn't need much more equipment than what was already in the existing kitchen. The fabric on the existing banquettes was nondescript enough to do double duty for a breakfast place. But his sense of showmanship drew his attention to the light fixtures. The stars were all wrong for a breakfast place. Breakfast in Vegas is the sunniest meal of the day. The décor needed to be bright, colorful, even eye-popping. It's morning, folks: here's your coffee, rise and shine!

One day he spied a woman toting an umbrella imprinted with a single, gigantic flower. He went on the web and discovered that he could buy such umbrellas wholesale for under $20 each. The flowers looked gorgeous—gerbera daisies in a variety of different colors: Pinks. Yellows. Blues. Purples. When they attached these budget umbrellas upside-down to the fixtures, light streamed through the fabric and brightened the entire space. And some of the umbrellas spun just as the stars had, creating an eye-catching, whirling flower effect.

Instead of buying standard-issue diner uniforms for his waitstaff, Jeffrey decided it would be fun if they wore pajamas and slippers. Whimsical, but unique. No server would look alike. Their startup, which they called Rise & Shine: A Steak and Egg Place, cost under $100,000 to launch, and it has since spawned a second location—complete with spinning floral umbrellas and pajama-clad servers. Moreover, it has earned millions in revenue. Jeffrey's team consists of his wife, Jenn, and his son, Tyler, who is fresh out of culinary school. Indeed, by now all of Tyler's younger siblings—Emily, Liam, Gabriel, and Arielle—have worked in some way at the two restaurants.

Jenn and Jeffrey met when they both worked at the Rio. As with many of the best relationships, they seem like opposite sides of the same coin. That comes with some friction. Jeffrey's busy these days running his restaurant development business. On a recent visit, our drive across town was interrupted by a quick debriefing of a young chef who's helping Jeffrey start a client's restaurant overseas. But the Rise & Shine locations are in good hands. For the most part, the Fredericks' kids, and their kids' friends, staff them. And they come in to eat on their days off, which tells you a lot. I try to stop in when I'm in town. The red velvet pancakes are the size of a steering wheel; the chilaquiles are delicious, and the chicken and waffles are everything you could ask for. They found a perfect niche to occupy, and they have nailed it in a way that exploits many of the trends I described earlier.

"Your time is no longer yours when you own a restaurant," Jenn tells me as I'm having a late working breakfast with Jeffrey. "You've got to be one hundred percent dedicated, and aggressive with your marketing, hiring, and scheduling. You're always swimming upstream. You need chutzpah and selflessness."

That morning, Jenn was proud of the fact that she'd saved 30 percent on labor costs because the technology that she used to track sales allowed her to fine-tune her staff's schedule. "Scheduling used to just be letting people go home when it was slow," she tells me. Now, she knows what's coming. She's also been studying each server's productivity to identify which servers need to be better trained to sell their great juice program.

When she excuses herself to get back to work, I get up for a second to watch her and Tyler at the kitchen window. Breakfast in the kitchen of a mom-and-pop restaurant can be as brutal, as hot and fast, as it is in a high-end restaurant in New York City, or New Orleans, or Atlanta, Vegas, or Paris. As I watch the tickets fly in, as I hear the servers call out the substitutions and all the small changes, I am reminded how rewarding this business is—and how demanding.

Having the right information helps. And if data and tech can help in large chains and corporations, if they can help the culinary giants like Wolfgang Puck or Tom Colicchio or Daniel Boulud, they can help here on Main Street, where a mother and her stepson are scrambling eggs and grilling a steak for a regular who comes in every week.

Early on, Jeffrey resolved that he would never critique Jenn's operation unless she specifically asked him for help. But this doesn't mean that he doesn't, from time to time, analyze the restaurant's social media reviews to see where they can improve, or call up our software on his iPhone to study a digital snapshot of his family's investment. When I get back to our table, I catch him in the act. And when he tucks his phone away, he is smiling. A New Guard restaurateur knows it never hurts to check the numbers.

· acknowledgments ·

I have found that the world of restaurants and the world of business have this in common: nothing is accomplished without collaboration and strong relationships. And now I can say that I have found the world of publishing to be much the same. The book you hold in your hands would not have come to life without friendship, mentorship, guidance, and an insatiable appetite for creativity from a great number of people.

I'm eternally grateful to my cowriter, Joseph D'Agnese, whose empathy, curiosity, love for our industry, and patience allowed him to assemble my stories like ingredients in an unforgettable, delicious meal. My literary agent, Yfat Reiss Gendell, has heard me expound on my theories about data and technology in the world of restaurants for so long that she finally pushed me to put those ideas down on paper. She is a terrific friend and listener, and her team at Foundry

Literary + Media deserves the great reputation they enjoy in the industry. Without her careful guidance, this book simply would not have been born. I'm greatly indebted to Roger Scholl, my editor at Crown Business and a longtime foodie, who has touched me with his profound dedication to *story*—and the best possible way to shape it, enhance it, and set it before the world. I have been impressed with the unflagging enthusiasm of his colleagues—Tina Constable, Campbell Wharton, Megan Schumann, Erica Gelbard, Terry Deal, our cover designer Tal Goretsky, and the entire team at Penguin Random House—who offered this book a home and the opportunity to reach a wider audience.

Anyone who visits an Avero office anywhere in the world would have trouble identifying at a glance just what sort of business we're in. Are we a software company or a restaurant business? The truth is, we embrace elements of both. Our offices buzz with dynamic, food-obsessed professionals who want to change the hospitality world. Each day during lunch at our Union Square headquarters, there are debates about the hottest restaurants, restaurant reviews, home brewing, food trends, chefs on the move, and innovative technology. When someone travels on vacation to a new destination, they return with food souvenirs and local or regional favorites for their colleagues to sample. Our corporate kitchen and roundtable have been the site of blind wine tastings, Summer of Riesling tastings, coffee cuppings, and Bagel Thursdays. We have bonded over our themed cooking competitions, including chili cookouts, Thanksgiving potlucks, decadent pie tastings, and the Super Bowl. The wall above our La Marzocca G3 espresso machine and Mazzer grinder are covered with Polaroids of our employees' own latte art. With each fresh infusion of coffee beans, our office blackboard changes with the frequency of a real-life coffee shop.

I am fortunate to share my workplace with a special breed of people. They are foodies, software developers, technologists, businesspeople, and former restaurateurs. They are dedicated to the notion that we can change the industry that we love with special software and superb customer service.

First, my deepest thanks go to my longtime business partner and board member, Doug Hsieh, whose friendship goes back to our Dillon Read days. We have overcome many challenges together and I appreciate his commitment, tireless efforts, and support, which have been instrumental in Avero's transformation from an idea to what it has become today. I am honored to have the trust support of our Avero board members—Oscar Tang, Tracy Tang Limpe, and Jim Osborne. I am blessed to have a fearless and dedicated senior team who also love food, wine, and numbers as much as I do: Bob Barracca, James Broude, Greg Peppel, Peter Storer, and Amanda Moschetti. Together we have built Avero into what it is today.

I am privileged to have had the day-to-day assistance of Julia El Bardai, who with unparalleled wit and ease kept me on track and prepared.

I am indebted to the entire organization, to all my Avero colleagues in New York, Las Vegas, Dallas, and our satellite offices in Chicago, Atlanta, Washington, DC, Denver, and New Delhi, who live and breathe my motto to exceed customer expectations and encourage New Guard thinking. I am forever grateful for your commitment and passion. I greatly appreciate your tireless efforts. The movement to which we are dedicated would not be possible without your innovation.

I thank those who have been with me from the beginning: Mike Portnoy and Oliver Xie. Special thanks are also due to Jillian Weinfeld, Jennifer Sessions O'Neill, and Ally Welsh Burke, who have assisted me in the past and organized previous Underground Culinary Tours, and to all Avero alums who have since gone on to do great things in our industry.

Life is too short to drink bad wine. My dream dinner party would include numerous friends who have shaped my thinking on business, cuisine, and life. They are dear close friends and partners in crime who have gone to the ends of the earth with me to eat and drink well. So thank you, John Higgins, Tim Lynch, Tarek AbuZayyad, Heejae Chae, Elizabeth Collet Funk, Aaron Hsu, Scott Meyer, Raj Kapoor, John Troiano, Paige Daly, Rishabh Mehrotra, Jim Rorer, Alana Lesiger Amaya, Dave Marshall, and, of course, Jeffrey and Jenn Frederick. I'm indebted also to those friends who supported the dreams of a roomful of restaurant data geeks: Shirley Young, David Hsieh, Bill Hsieh, and Rob Stavis. I'm proud and lucky to have the warm, enduring friendship of Scott Atkins, Jeff Kafel, and Kathleen McNichol, all from LaSalle University. And I cannot forget the camaraderie of those late-night pasta parties my roommates and I threw at 9 St. Johns Road for HBS Section H and our other foodie classmates. With Giuliana Berchicci as my sous chef and Stephen Roche, Rob Leone, and Suneet Wadhwa as my cohosts, food, wine, fun, and dreaming were damn near inseparable.

I treasure the mentorship and friendship of Alice Elliot, my longtime co-conspirator of the Underground Culinary Tour; Mike Beck, my most trusted counselor and confidant; and Gary Loveman, Tom Colicchio, and Danny Meyer, my earliest and steadfast champions. I hope this book measures up to all of the invaluable advice and friendship you've given me over the years. A great connection exists between these three influencers and their great food cities, New York and Las Vegas, which were among the first to embrace my ideas and services. Both Avero and I owe gratitude to Tom's Crafted Hospitality and his team, Katie Grieco, Robert Goodman, Kurt Brown, Carmen Salgado, and Cory Sullivan; Danny's Union Square Hospitality Group, including Sabato Sagaria, Ashley Campbell, Terry Coughlin, Sam Lipp, Michael Anthony, Kim DiPalo, Scott Reinhardt, Will Guidara, and Ana Marie Mormando; and Gary's team at Caesars Entertainment, including Tom Jenkin, Eric Hession, Bob Morse, David Hoenemeyer, Gary Selesner, Sean McBurney, Sean DiCicco, Tim Bowen, Cory Johnson, Andrew Economon, Joseph Giunta, and Michael Speagle.

Our first customers are trailblazers and early adopters in ways that go well beyond the world of cuisine. They were New Guard before any of us understood the full meaning of the term, and their influence is felt in restaurants worldwide. I offer a special thank-you to those clients, which include Steven Hanson, Michael Jacobs, Alan Hochhauser, Laura Maniec, Alex Taylor, Jeffrey Lefcourt, Michael White, and Lana Trevisan; Daniel Boulud, Brett Traussi, Marcel Doron,

Ryan Buttner, Michael Lawrence, and Bret Csencsitz; Jeffrey Chodorow, Claude Roussel, Kelley Jones, John Polsenberg, and Franklin Ferguson; Jean-Georges Vongerichten, Daniel Del Vecchio, James Liakakos, and Michael Snyder; Stephen Starr, Josh Levine, and the late Bruce Koch; Richard Melman, Kevin Brown, Jay Stieber, Ethan Samson, and Danny McGowan; Wolfgang Puck, Joe Essa, David Robins, and Matt Dickerson; Scott Gerber, Vincent Mauriello, Dennis Calabro, and Adele Israel; Shimon Bokovza and Martin Cabrera; Steve Weitman, Pauly Freedman, Julia Greenman, and James McGinnis; Michael Mina, Patric Yumul, Raj Parr, and Bill Freeman; Mario Batali, Joe Bastianich, Lidia Bastianich, Mark Coscia, Jason Denton, Nancy Selzer, and Kate Greenberg; Niki Leondakis; Christian Clerc, Gianluca Sparacino, Chrissy Gamble, Chris Hunsberger, Guy Rigby, and Nicolas Kurban; Jeannette Ho, Brett Patterson, Neal Fegan, and Cynthia Paynter; Paul Grieco; Robert Bohr; Marco Canora; Bobby Flay and Laurence Kretchmer; Keith McNally and Roberta Delice; Ken Himmel; John McDonald and Josh Pickard; Tom Dillon; Adam Burke; Elizabeth Blau; Sam Nazarian, John Kolaski, and Matt Erickson; Lou Abin, John Watson; Paul Gordon, Brisa Shoshani; and Geoffrey and Margaret Zakarian.

The hospitality industry is not just about satisfying appetites but also about nourishing souls. It is without a doubt the most generous industry, one that cares about giving back. Every day I am grateful for the model of service bestowed upon the restaurant industry by Billy Shore at Share Our Strength, Richard Grausman and Susan Robbins at Careers Through Culinary Arts (C-CAP); and Melissa Arias at the Epicurean Charitable Foundation. We are all indebted to you for reminding us of what's important.

I have long enjoyed a partnership with the Cornell School of Hotel Administration, which is training future leaders in our industry. So many of Cornell's "hotelies" are part of Avero's culture. I have found every visit to that campus electrifying, and I must thank Michael D. Johnson, former dean, who has given me an invigorating forum to share my ideas with a new generation of deliverers of New Guard hospitality. The young students and professors at Cornell inspire me every time I visit; their program is truly a fount of creativity that I treasure. My thanks as well to Kate Walsh, Giuseppe Pezzotti, Sheryl Kimes, and Lee Pillsbury.

Decades ago, the great food writer M. F. K. Fisher observed, "There is communion of more than our bodies when bread is broken and wine drunk." In that same spirit I am privileged to have grown up with my parents, Gloria and Russ, and my sister, Jeannine. Around that table long ago I learned that love could express itself in great food—and still more love. Mom and Dad, you demonstrated extraordinary patience in dealing with such a picky child eater as myself, ironically resulting in my becoming a foodie. Jeannine—those crabbing trips were about more than the pursuit of those delicacies. Beyond my immediate family, I was privileged to have grown up with a loving extended family that included my Aunt Anna, who took me to some of my earliest dinners out, and Aunt Rita, who made and served the best lasagna I'll ever eat.

When I was just out of business school, I confided in

a young, beautiful woman that I dreamed of starting my own business. That woman became my wife, Susie, whose steadfast love, encouragement, and devotion to my entrepreneurial spirit and my sometimes exhausting curiosity is worth more than all else. Every day I give thanks for our three children, through whom I am again learning the blessings inherent in gathering around a table with those you love. I've taught them to smell everything from the day they were born and I marvel at their tasting notes.

· notes ·

Introduction: Restaurant Metrics

The true story of the bottle-shy server is drawn from Jeffrey Frederick's experience during a pilot study at the Rio All-Suites Resort and Casino in 2003.

Statistics about the restaurant industry in the United States are culled from the National Restaurant Association's 2016 Restaurant Industry Pocket Factbook: restaurant.org/News -Research/Research/Facts-at-a-Glance.

A discussion of restaurant profits, which can range widely from 1 to 7 percent, may be found in the following articles: "U.S. Restaurants Seeing Fatter Margins," by Mary Ellen Biery, June 22, 2014, *Forbes*: forbes.com/sites/sageworks/2014/06/ 22/us-restaurants-margins/#370ee4ec1278; "The Average Profit Margin for a Restaurant," by Aurelio Locsin, *The Houston Chronicle*: smallbusiness.chron.com/average-profit -margin-restaurant-13477.html; "Ten Restaurant Financial Red Flags," by John Nessel, Restaurant Resource Group; "The Average Profit Margin for a Restaurant," by Devra Gar-

tenstein, Azcentral.com: yourbusiness.azcentral.com/average
-profit-margin-restaurant-13113.html.

Regarding tips, I might mention that the current scholar-
ship on restaurant tipping suggests that guests do not tip on
the basis of the server's performance, but on a host of other
factors, such as whether the server smiled. See "Tip Levels and
Service: An Update, Extension and Reconciliation," by Michael
Lynn, School of Hotel Administration, Cornell University, Cornell Hotel and Restaurant Administration Quarterly, December 2003, 44 (5/6), 139–148: scholarship.sha.cornell.edu/cgi/
viewcontent.cgi?article=1109&context=articles.

The failure of restaurants has been greatly mythologized in
the media. The best discussion I've found is "The Restaurant-
Failure Myth," by Kerry Miller, Bloomberg.com, April 16, 2007:
bloomberg.com/bw/stories/2007-04-16/the-restaurant-failure
-mythbusinessweek-business-news-stock-market-and-financial
-advice.

Chapter 1: Maximizing the Montauk Sunshine

The names of large-format bottles are far from clear. The following articles shed light on some of the complexities: "Cheat
Sheet: Large Format Wine Bottle Names and Sizes," by VinePair
Staff, vinepair.com: vinepair.com/wine-blog/cheat-sheet-large
-format-wine-bottle-names-sizes; "Complete Guide to All Large
Format Wine Bottles, Sizes and Shapes," *The Wine Cellar In-
sider*: thewinecellarinsider.com/wine-topics/wine-educational
-questions/size-matters-explanation-large-bottle-formats;
"Meaning of Wine Bottle Sizes," April 16, 2012, WineFolly.com:
winefolly.com/tutorial/wine-bottle-sizes.

The story of how Walmart tracks weather data is discussed in "Hurricane Irene and Walmart's Staff Meteorologist," by Eileen Norcross, "Neighborhood Effects" blog of the
Mercatus Center at George Mason University, August 27, 2011:
neighborhoodeffects.mercatus.org/2011/08/27/hurricane-irene

-and-walmarts-staff-meteorologist/; "How Walmart Beat Feds to New Orleans," by Ben Worthen, *CIO*, November 1, 2005: cio.com/article/2448237/supply-chain-management/how -wal-mart-beat-feds-to-new-orleans.html. The original case studies—"Walmart's Response to Hurricane Katrina: Striving for a Public-Private Partnership" and "Walmart's Response to Hurricane Katrina: Striving for a Public-Private Partnership (Sequel)," by Susan Rosegrant, August 28, 2007—are located behind a paywall at the Kennedy School of Government: case .hks.harvard.edu/wal-mart-s-response-to-hurricane-katrina -striving-for-a-public-private-partnership and case.hks.harvard .edu/wal-marts-response-to-hurricane-katrina-striving-for-a -public-private-partnership-sequel.

The gas station anecdote is one Earl Nightingale told throughout his career. The complete story may be accessed at: nightingale.com/articles/acres-of-diamonds.

The Hamptons rosé wine shortage has played out numerous times in recent memory, always accompanied by tongue-in-cheek articles in the media, such as this one that appeared in *New York* magazine: "There's a Severe Rosé Shortage in the Hamptons," by Maggie Lange, NYMag.com, August 27, 2014: nymag.com/thecut/2014/08/theres-a-severe-ros-shortage-in-the -hamptons.html.

Chapter 2: Startup to Vegas, Baby

Gary Loveman's reign at Caesars was discussed often in the business press. This *Wall Street Journal* article gives a quick summary of his time there: "Caesars CEO Leaves Divided Legacy," by Kate O'Keeffe, *Wall Street Journal,* June 29, 2015: wsj.com/ articles/caesars-loveman-leaves-divided-legacy-1435634297.

The figure cited for the number of US casinos includes commercial casinos, tribal casinos, and all other types. The precise number for 2011 was 1,511 casinos. See "Countries Worldwide Ranked by Number of Casinos in 2011," Statista.com:

statista.com/statistics/221032/counties-with-the-most-casinos. See also "All In: Gambling Options Proliferate Across USA," by Matt Villano, *USA Today,* January 26, 2013: usatoday.com/ story/travel/destinations/2013/01/24/gambling-options-casinos -proliferate-across-usa/1861835.

Chapter 3: The Underground Culinary Tour (Part 1)

The Avero-Elliot Underground Culinary Tour is only open to industry executives and has purposely thrived under the radar until now. Watch a highlight reel of a recent tour here: averoinc.com/blog/more/avero-elliot-underground-culinary -tour-human-capital-technology-industry-tr.

Stories and anecdotes about each of the restaurants and the people behind it are culled from my personal interactions over the years with each of them. You may learn more about each of the restaurants at the following sites: NoMad Hotel (thenomadhotel.com), NoMad (makeitnicenyc.com), Franny's Brooklyn (frannysbrooklyn .com), Zona Rosa (zonarosabrooklyn.com), Maison Premiere (maisonpremiere.com), Fette Sau (fettesaubbq.com), Hearth (restauranthearth.com), The Dead Rabbit (deadrabbitnyc.com), Craft Restaurants (craftrestaurantsinc.com), Pearl & Ash (pearlandash.com).

Details of the World's 50 Best Restaurants list may be accessed at: theworlds50best.com. Eleven Madison Park was ranked third best on the 2016 list.

Some of the highlights of the late Sasha Petraske's career were informed by this *New York Times* report of his death: "Sasha Petraske, 42, Dies; Bar Owner Restored Luster to Cocktail Culture," by Robert Simonson, *New York Times,* August 21, 2015: nytimes.com/2015/08/22/nyregion/sasha-petraske-bar -owner-who-revived-luster-to-cocktail-culture-around-the-world -dies-at-42.html.

Discussion of the history of absinthe was informed by articles such as "France's Green Fairy Flies Again," by Jennie

Cohen, May 4, 2011, History.com: history.com/news/frances
-green-fairy-flies-again.

My understanding of Maison Premiere's oyster program is
based on "Loss Leaders on the Half Shell," by Karen Stabiner,
February 8, 2014, *New York Times*.

Restaurant wine prices range widely, typically between 200
and 300 percent over retail price, with occasional forays into
the 400 percent territory. The fact that restaurants pay wholesale prices for wine tends to complicate the issue when they talk
about markups with laymen. A more comprehensive discussion
of wine pricing may be found in several articles, among them:
"Highs and (Rare) Lows in Restaurant Wine Prices," by Let-
tie Teague, June 21, 2013, *Wall Street Journal*: wsj.com/articles/
SB10001424127887324520904578551532766601460; "Are Restaurant Wine Mark-ups Too Steep?" by Chris Mercer, January
8, 2015, Decanter.com: decanter.com/wine-news/opinion/the
-editors-blog/are-restaurant-wine-mark-ups-too-steep-3545; "How
Are the Markups on Restaurant Wine Lists Determined?" *The Wine
Spectator*: winespectator.com/drvinny/show/id/45306; "Why
Wine Can Cost as Much as Four Times in a Restaurant," by Anna
Bernasek, July 3, 2014, Newsweek.com: newsweek.com/2014/07/
11/why-wine-can-cost-four-times-much-restaurants-257169.html;
"Pricing Your Restaurant's Wine List": musthavemenus.com/
guide/restaurant-management/restaurant-pricing-and-profits/
wine-list-pricing.html; "The Lowdown on Restaurant Markups,"
by Gretchen Roberts, May 7, 2010, WineMag.com: winemag
.com/2010/05/07/the-lowdown-on-restaurant-markups.

Chapter 4: Perfect Cut
Admittedly, the legend of the gauchos of the Pampas has been
mythologized as much as the story of American cowboys. Part
of their story can be found here: "Gaucho: Exploring Their History and Customs," by Lee Carlton, Think Global School, April 3,
2013: thinkglobalschool.org/argentinas-gaucho-exploring-their
-history-and-customs.

Most of the content in this chapter comes from interviews with Larry Johnson, Barry McGowan and Andrew Feldman; personal visits to Fogo de Chão locations in New York, Philadelphia, and Atlanta; and a subsequent interview with Atlanta general manager Rudimar Bonfada.

I have chosen to obscure the name and other geographical details of the poorly run casual food chain for obvious reasons. The events transpired nearly exactly as they are described.

Chapter 5: The Celebrity Chef Evolves

Readers can learn more about the three chefs who figure prominently in this chapter at their websites: Giada De Laurentiis (giadadelaurentiis.com), Guy Fieri (guyfieri.com), and Gordon Ramsay (gordonramsay.com).

For the notorious review of Fieri's New York establishment, see "As Not Seen on TV," by Pete Wells, *New York Times*, November 13, 2012: nytimes.com/2012/11/14/dining/ reviews/restaurant-review-guys-american-kitchen-bar-in-times -square.html.

The comment about addictive breadsticks, as well as the overall Las Vegas reception of Fieri's restaurant, is from "Guy Fieri's Exactly What It Should Be, Where It Should Be," by Heidi Knapp-Rinella, *Las Vegas Review-Journal*, July 30, 2014: reviewjournal.com/columns-blogs/heidi-knapp-rinella/guy -fieri-s-exactly-what-it-should-be-where-it-should-be.

Pete Wells's tweet about Guy Fieri's Las Vegas restaurant was reported in "Pete Wells . . . Has Thoughts on Vegas Dining," by Marcy Franklin, *The Braiser*, August 13, 2014: thebraiser .com/pete-wells-giada-review-vegas.

The reception of Giada's restaurant is described in "Giada's Remains a Hot Commodity on Las Vegas Strip," by Norm Clarke, *Las Vegas Review-Journal*, June 8, 2014: reviewjournal.com/ columns-blogs/norm-clarke/giada-s-remains-hot-commodity -las-vegas-strip.

The conversation between Giada and Jeffrey Frederick was

recounted by Giada during an interview with a Las Vegas reporter. See "The Rising Star of Giada De Laurentiis," by Al Mancini, *Vegas Seven*, June 11, 2014: vegasseven.com/2014/06/11/rising-star-giada-de-laurentiis/.

The iPod Touch survey was still being used at Gordon Ramsay BurGR, located in the Planet Hollywood Resort & Casino, during a November 2015 visit.

Yelp's "Search Reviews" function is typically located about halfway down a selected restaurant's review page, just to the right of the "Recommended Reviews" headline.

Chapter 6: Numbers in Nightlife

The content in this chapter is largely drawn from interviews with Nick McCabe, Derek Silberstein, and Jason Aranas. The descriptions of the clubs are drawn from personal visits over the years, and one fact-finding visit to Hakkasan and OMNIA in November 2015.

More details of Hakkasan Group's operations may be found at hakkasangroup.com.

Calvin Harris's income was reported by *Forbes* magazine in its 2015 Celebrity 100 rankings: forbes.com/profile/calvin-harris.

You may review the list of top nightclubs at Nightclub & Bar's 2015 Top 100 list here: nightclub.com/2015-top-100-list.

Danny Meyer's definitions of hospitality and service are drawn from *Setting the Table* (New York: HarperCollins, 2006), 11, 65 (paperback edition).

Coachella ticket pricing for the 2016 event was accessed via this link: coachella.com/festival-passes.

My discussion of payment for top DJs is informed by several media reports, among them: "Calvin Harris to Get $400K a Night at Hakkasan, Omnia? Pharrell at Hakkasan, Too?" by Robin Leach, *Las Vegas Sun*, January 22, 2015: lasvegassun.com/vegasdeluxe/2015/jan/22/calvin-harris-get-400000-night-work-hakkasan-omnia; "Calvin Harris Reportedly Will Earn

$400,000 Per Gig in New Hakkasan Deal," by Ryan Middleton, *Music Times,* January 24, 2015: musictimes.com/articles/ 25944/20150124/calvin-harris-reportedly-will-earn-400-000-per -gig-new-hakkasan-deal.htm.

Chapter 7: The Underground Culinary Tour (Part 2)

Stories and anecdotes about each of the restaurants and the people behind it are culled from my personal interactions over the years with each of the individuals concerned. You may learn more about each of the restaurants or stops on our tour at the following sites: Counter Culture (counterculturecoffee .com), Maialino (maialinonyc.com), Gotham West Market (gothamwestmarket.com), RedFarm (redfarmnyc.com), Brooklyn Brewery (brooklynbrewery.com), Terroir (wineisterroir .com/tribeca), Shake Shack (shakeshack.com).

Tom Colicchio's decision to cut portion sizes is discussed in "Colicchio Cuts Prices, Portion Sizes at Colicchio & Sons," by Ryan Sutton, *New York Eater,* February 18, 2015: ny.eater .com/2015/2/18/8043181/tom-colicchio-eliminates-entrees-at -namesake-restaurant.

My discussion of the history of Chinese food in the United States is culled from a lengthy interview with Ed Schoenfeld in February 2016.

My knowledge of Grace Chu's contributions to Chinese cuisine is informed by this report of her death: "Grace Zia Chu, 99, Guide to Chinese Cooking," by William Grimes, *New York Times,* April 19, 1999: nytimes.com/1999/04/19/nyregion/grace -zia-chu-99-guide-to-chinese-cooking.html.

Discussion of the craft beer industry was informed by articles such as, "Wasted: How the Craft-Beer Movement Abandoned Jim Koch (and his Beloved Sam Adams)," by Andy Crouch, *Boston Magazine,* January 2015: bostonmagazine.com/ restaurants/article/2015/01/05/jim-koch-sam-adams-beer; and "Will Small Craft Beer Get Too Big?" by Brian Drew, WTOP

News, June 9, 2016: wtop.com/food/2016/06/will-small-craft
-beer-get-too-big-samuel-adams-jim-koch-on-the-future-of-the
-industry/slide/2.

Chapter 8: Under the Table
I have deliberately obscured details of Janice's company for obvious reasons. Her firm is actually a composite of two hospitality companies. All other details—about my sting operation, my
company's review of her company's data, and the subsequent
details of the larger circle of fraud—are, unfortunately, completely accurate.

Statistics about restaurant theft and fraud are culled from a
number of sources, among them LPI Innovations' webinar document, "Restaurant Theft and the Hard Truth about Losses in the
Food Industry": slideshare.net/kobrien613/the-hard-truth-about
-restaurant-theft; "Restaurant Theft—It Happens but It Doesn't
Have to Happen to You," by Cheryl Parsons, Rewards Network,
August 19, 2014: rewardsnetwork.com/blog/restaurant-theft-it
-doesnt-have-to-happen-to-you/; "Using Technology to Stop Restaurant Theft," by Cherryh Candler, FastCasual.com, September 16, 2013: fastcasual.com/articles/using-technology-to-stop
-restaurant-theft/; and Avero's own internal research.

Several of the scams detailed in this chapter have been
described in various forms over the years on Avero's blog
(averoinc.com/blog). As they come to our attention, variations
in the fraud techniques continue to appear in our fraud blog
series. The techniques mentioned in this chapter were first ex-
plored on our website beginning in November 2013 and continuing into January 2014.

Chapter 9: Innovating the Family Business
The content of this chapter is drawn largely from two lengthy
discussions in March 2016: a telephone interview with Charlee
Williamson and a subsequent site visit and interviews with

Charlee Williamson, Ralph Brennan, and members of the Ralph Brennan Restaurant Group.

Readers may learn more about Ralph Brennan's organization by visiting neworleans-food.com.

Discussion of California's minimum wage changes may be found in the article, "California Laws for Tipped Employees," by Lisa Guerin, J.D., Nolo.com: nolo.com/legal-encyclopedia/california-laws-tipped-employees.html.

My understanding of the circumstances surrounding the closure of Brennan's was informed by "Closure of Brennan's in New Orleans Spotlights Family Feuds," Fox News, November 14, 2013: foxnews.com/leisure/2013/11/14/closure-brennan-new-orleans-latest-chapter-in-saga-fine-dining-family-feuds/.

My description of the reopening of Brennan's was informed in part by "Brennan's of New Orleans Reopens with Pomp and Flaming Bananas Foster," by Todd A. Price, *New Orleans Times-Picayune*, November 25, 2014: nola.com/dining/index.ssf/2014/11/brennans_restaurant_french_qua.html.

My knowledge of the contributions of Adelaide and Ella Brennan was informed in part by "The Original New Orleans Diva," by April Siese, Narrative.ly, March 5, 2015 (narrative.ly/the-original-new-orleans-diva) and the upcoming Ella Brennan movie (ellabrennanmovie.com).

My account of the turtle parade is based on talks with Charlee Williams and "Turtles on Parade: The Slowest Second Line at Brennan's," by Kenny Lopez, WGNO, March 12, 2015: wgno.com/2015/03/12/turtles-on-parade-the-slowest-second-line-at-brennans/. Space did not permit me to print the names of all the turtles, but I offer them here for your edification and amusement. Those in the restaurant business will recognize them as the names of "mother" sauces and "New Orleans" sauces: Béchamel, Espagnole, Hollandaise, Tomate, Veloute, Remoulade, Ravigote, Bordelaise, Mignonette, and Cocktail (who is apparently the only male).

My description of Ella Brennan's return to Brennan's was

informed by talks with Ralph Brennan and by "Ella Brennan, for the First Time in 40 Years, Visits Brennan's," by Todd A. Price, *New Orleans Times-Picayune*, November 28, 2014: nola .com/dining/index.ssf/2014/11/ella_brennan_for_the_first _tim.html.

My history of Napoleon House was informed by a site visit conducted in the company of Ralph Brennan and by "NOLA History: Nocholas Girod and the Plot to Rescue Napoleon," by Edward Branley, GO NOLA, May 5, 2014: gonola.com/ 2014/05/05/nola-history-nicholas-girod-and-the-plot-to-rescue -napoleon.html.

Chapter 10: Restaurants of Tomorrow

Marketing tie-ins for *Star Wars: The Force Awakens* were discussed in "These Are the Weirdest Marketing Tie-Ins for 'Star Wars: The Force Awakens,'" by Brad Tuttle, *Money*, December 4, 2015: time.com/money/4136668/star-wars-force -awakens-marketing-brands; "Star Wars Marketing Tie-Ins Have Jumped the Gundark," by Julia Greenberg, *Wired*, November 27, 2015: wired.com/2015/11/star-wars-marketing-integration; and "The Top 10 'The Force Awakens' Commercial Tie-In Videos," by Aldea-Martinez & Co., Medium, December 21, 2015: medium.com/@aldeamartinez/what-are-the-top-10-the-force -awakens-commercial-tie-in-videos-ad58824e664e#.i3nu95qbr.

My predictions and trend observations are culled in part from presentations I've given over the years, personal observations, and the results of the Avero Index survey of restaurants. The latest data from the Avero Index may be accessed at: averoinc.com/media/view/avero-index.

Readers may learn more about the Meatball Shop (themeatballshop.com) and Seamore's (seamores.com) at their respective websites.

Statistics about the history and growth of breweries in the United States are culled from data shared by the Brewers Association: brewersassociation.org/statistics/number-of-breweries.

See also the article, "On Average, 1.5 New Craft Breweries Are Opening Each Day," Sarah Theeboom, FirstWeFeast.com, December 2014: firstwefeast.com/drink/2014/12/on-average-1-5 -new-craft-breweries-are-opening-each-day.

Numerous recent stories discuss the food hall phenomenon. One I might mention is "The 23 Most Anticipated Food Halls in the Country," by Whitney Filloon, *Eater,* March 5, 2015: eater.com/2015/3/5/8105295/23-most-anticipated-food -halls-eataly-market-hall-ponce-city-market.

An extensive exposé by a food critic in 2016 highlighted the fraud potential in restaurant sourcing and claims. It's a riveting read that will appall foodies and remind them to be more vigilant. "Farm to Fable: At Tampa Bay Farm-to-Table Restaurants, You're Being Fed Fiction," by Laura Reiley, *Tampa Bay Tribune,* April 13, 2016: tampabay.com/projects/2016/food/ farm-to-fable/restaurants.

Food porn concerns have been with us since the invention of the smartphone. This article gives a good overview of the issue: "As Restaurants Ban Photos, Some Worry About the End of Food Porn," by Dominique Mosbergen, *Huffington Post,* January 24, 2013: huffingtonpost.com/2013/01/24/restaurant -photo-ban-death-of-food-porn_n_2543306.html.

Readers curious about Jeffrey and Jenn Frederick's latest venture can learn more at Rise & Shine (bestbreakfastvegas.com).

· index ·